stronger than dirt

How One Urban Couple Grew a
Business, a Family, and a New Way
of Life from the Ground Up

———

# stronger than dirt

———

Kimberly Schaye
and Christopher Losee

THREE RIVERS PRESS • NEW YORK

All of the people, places, and events described in this book are real; there was no need to fictionalize anything in this story. In writing the dialogue and describing the events that occurred, our memories were aided by stacks of spiral-bound notebooks that we kept during this period of time, as well as the recollections of many of the people involved. In a few instances, we changed names and/or some personal details in an effort to protect others' privacy.

Copyright © 2003 by Kimberly Schaye and Christopher Losee

Published by Three Rivers Press, New York, New York. Member of the Crown Publishing Group, a division of Random House, Inc.
www.randomhouse.com

THREE RIVERS PRESS and the Tugboat design
are registered trademarks of Random House, Inc.

Printed in the United States of America

DESIGN BY LYNNE AMFT

Library of Congress Cataloging-in-Publication Data
Schaye, Kimberly.
Stronger than dirt : how one urban couple grew a business, a family, and a new way of life from the ground up / Kimberly Schaye and Christopher Losee.
1. Farm life—New York—Columbia County.  2. Family farms—New York—Columbia County.  3. Schaye, Kimberly.  4. Losee, Christopher.
I. Losee, Christopher.  II. Title.
S521.5.N7 S32   2003
630' .9747'33—dc21   2002151555
ISBN 0-609-80975-X

10 9 8 7 6 5 4 3 2 1

First Edition

*For Samantha and Juliana, our two most precious flowers,*
*and in memory of James R. Losee*

# Acknowledgments

We are grateful for the help of our outstanding agent, Regula Noetzli, who expertly guided us not only through the book-writing process but also to a great place for picking wild black-eyed Susans.

Our editor, Carrie Thornton, is as good at her job as she is at ours. Thanks for the excellent editorial advice and for showing up promptly for work at the farm stand.

David Schaye and Julie Abbruscato, the early readers of our manuscript, were very skilled at pointing out where we weren't being as funny or brilliant as we thought.

Our entry into the world of small-scale agriculture would have been an even rockier ride had it not been for the support of Tony Mannetta and his fine staff at Greenmarket. An extra bouquet goes to Tom Strumolo for putting up those paper signs to keep our parking spot clear. So what if no one really believes "towing begins promptly at six"?

For editorial suggestions, flower arrangement, manual labor, and/or help with the kids we thank Linda Loewenthal, Suzanne Goodhart, Nora Krug, Susan Cannell, Rhoda Siwek, Jill Losee, Michael Finnegan, Brenda Jones, Mary Orlandi, Laurena Malarchuk, and Vinny Manzi.

And a truckload of thanks to our parents, who did more things to help us during the writing of this book than we could possibly list on this page.

# Contents

stronger than dirt

The voice of Kimberly Schaye appears in Bernhard Modern.
The voice of Christopher Losee appears in Futura.

❖

# Prologue

KIM: It's a Friday morning in mid-July 2000, and I've been blessed with perfect picking weather. The humidity is mercifully low. Plenty of fluffy white clouds are floating overhead to offer relief from the burning sun.

I have just driven our black Chevy pickup a quarter mile down the steep gravel driveway and across the quiet road that borders our fields. I now stand inside the electric fence that guards our four acres of flowers from ravenous deer. Tomorrow is market day, and I have to decide what to cut first.

Before I begin I look to the right at the neighbor's old red barn. Set against the lush green hills and crayon blue sky, it is a postcard-perfect scene of rural life. This is my favorite view in the area of upstate New York I now call home.

Turning back to our land, I catch my reflection in the truck's rear window. I'm long past being shocked by what I see. The outfit I'm wearing is the usual: a cheesy, broad-brimmed straw hat with a sloppily glued-on pink ribbon that I bought at a discount store to protect my already too-pink skin; a long-sleeved, pink-and-white-striped Ralph Lauren shirt from the Salvation Army with a permanent orange stain on the cuff from a particularly juicy garden slug that got smushed there; heavy olive green canvas pants that are a little too big for me, likewise purchased from the Salvation Army and likewise permanently stained—in this case from kneeling in mud; and formerly decent high-top white leather sneakers covered with dirt, the toe of the right one comically flapping open like a cartoon hobo's. With this ultra-strange, mud-encrusted getup and dirty fingernails, I look like I've just tunneled out of a mental institution. And, in a way, I have.

Only a short time ago I was a tabloid newspaper reporter. I covered politics and state government for the New York *Daily News*. I went to work in skirts and high heels. I wouldn't have thought of leaving the house without lipstick. I spent most of my days chasing the governor around the state capitol in Albany. But if I were to show up there today, I would undoubtedly be escorted from the premises by the state police before I got within quoting distance of the governor's dog walker. I laugh just thinking about what a difference a year and a half can make. Was my former life more glamorous? No doubt. Do I miss it? Not hardly. Well, enough reminiscing. It's time to get to work.

I could start picking in the section closest to me, the annuals. That way I'd have the satisfaction of filling my five-gallon buckets with fuzzy blue ageratum and spiky pink celosia before I hear the blast of the noon air horn at the firehouse in town two miles away. Or I could save the easy stuff for later, when I am really dragging yet still have perhaps a dozen buckets to go. Maybe I should wander a few hundred yards west to the perennials and struggle with the tangle of tissue-thin coreopsis and cheerfully striped gaillardia while I still have some energy. Yes, that seems like the best course of action.

I get back in the truck and slowly ramble up a slight incline through a clump of weeds that we never mow to encourage whatever interesting wildflowers might come up. I park near the perennial beds, take two buckets half filled with water out of the truck, and carry them to the head of a row of flowers the color of raw egg yolks. I take out my clippers and begin cutting. Right now there's nowhere I'd rather be.

Chapter 1

the magical bouquet

KIM: It started with a bouquet I neither bought nor sold but merely found on my dining room table one day after coming home from work. It was like nothing I had ever seen before, and it would change my life.

With silver-green leaves, spiky purple plumes, and translucent lavender and white petals, it had an airy quality, as if a summer breeze were still blowing through it. Standing in the dim light of our third-floor dining room in Brooklyn, New York, I stared at the flowers but couldn't come up with any names for them. I think the only flowers I could identify then, in the summer of 1994, were the daisy, rose, and tulip. I didn't see any of those here.

"Chris," I called to my husband, whom I knew must be within shouting distance because he worked out of our home. "Where did you get these gorgeous flowers?"

"Aren't those great?" Chris said, as he came down the creaky stairs of our narrow brick town house. "Dan and I picked them in Staten Island today. There's actually a working farm out there that's part of a state park."

Dan was a landscape architect for New York State. He often hired Chris's construction company to put fencing around state parks in the New York City area. The two were becoming fast friends, united by a common love of nature.

"I didn't know this, but Dan used to be a sort of weekend farmer," Chris continued. "He and his ex-wife used to grow flowers on Shelter Island and sell them at farmers' markets in the city—until she got the land in the divorce."

"Do you know what these are?" I asked.

"Dan told me the names, but I don't remember them all," he said. "I think one of them is sage—you know, the herb. And the ones with the large, thin petals are cosmos. Dan said he made a decent amount of money selling them."

"I can certainly see why," I remarked as I stroked a silky cosmos petal. Our talk then drifted to the topic of dinner. The Staten Island farm was forgotten. At least by me.

"How about we eat outside tonight?" I asked Chris, who was gently rearranging the bouquet on the table. My hour-long commute underground in the stifling subway system to and from my newspaper job in Manhattan always left me as ravenous for air as it did for food come dinnertime. I wanted to sit out on our small second-floor deck, which faced away from the street, even though the view wasn't much: just a labyrinth of tiny backyards.

"Hello?" I said to Chris, who seemed lost in thought as he fingered the flowers.

"Sure," he said, snapping out of it. "But we don't have anything to grill. We'll need to go buy something."

"Okay, I'll be down in a second," I said, heading upstairs.

I gratefully changed from business attire to shorts, a tank top, and sandals, and we stepped out into the muggy evening air. As we walked up our largely residential but busy avenue of three- and four-story row houses, our feet involuntarily took up the beat of the salsa music issuing from the bodega on the corner. We turned toward the main commercial strip on the avenue to the east of us and stepped into the invigoratingly air-conditioned supermarket in the middle of the block.

"Let's see if they have any fish," Chris said.

We headed to the small seafood department at the back of the store and tried to get the attention of the teenage fish salesman, who was wearing a Walkman.

"Do you have anything that's good for grilling?" Chris asked, when the kid removed his headphones.

"I don't know," he answered with a somewhat apologetic smile. "I don't eat fish."

"You don't?" I asked.

"I don't really like it," said the fish guy, putting his headset back on.

I looked over at my husband.

"Steak?" Chris queried.

"Sure," I said, and we headed toward the meat department.

A few minutes later we were sitting on wooden folding chairs, waiting for the charcoal in the hibachi to fire up. It was already past 8:00, and the sliver of sky we could see through all the houses and one large courtyard tree was darkening.

"How was work today?" I asked Chris, who was smoking a cigarette a respectful distance away from me.

"The usual," he said. "Let's not talk about it."

We waved to a couple of neighbors, who entered the yard directly in front of us. This was no place to have a private conversation anyway. There were people above us, below us, and on all sides of us. There were neighbors living so close to us that sometimes we literally had to beat them off with a stick; or at least Chris thought we had to.

Once a guy in the building next door was playing loud music at about two in the morning, the same side of an album over and over and over again. Chris, who is usually a mild-mannered person, got so fed up he picked up a length of three-by-six-inch board and clobbered the wall. His blow landed like a sonic boom. It left a good-size dent, and the music stopped instantly.

Having grown up in a peaceful suburb, Chris had apparently

never gotten used to the noise of urban living. But, at the time, our urban lifestyle suited me just fine. New York City was where I grew up and where I felt most at home. It was a great place to build a career in my field of journalism. In fact, after having toiled for years in low-level support jobs at several papers, I was finally getting somewhere. I had recently landed a pretty impressive gig, particularly for a thirty-year-old: editorial writer for the New York *Daily News*. At the time I started working there in 1993, just after Chris and I were married, it was one of the city's four major daily papers and, with about 800,000 readers, had the largest circulation of New York's three tabloids.

Because it was widely believed that the city could not ultimately support all of these tabloids in addition to *The New York Times*, the competition among them to attract readers was ferocious. Tabloid front pages became ever more shrill. Staff upheavals were commonplace. And my favorite paper, *New York Newsday*, did eventually fold. That left the weighty and liberal *Times*, the sensationalist and conservative *New York Post*, and the somewhat more moderate *Daily News* to battle it out. But, being on the editorial board, I was far removed from the circulation wars. My daily routine, in fact, was enviable.

I would stroll into the paper's mid-Manhattan offices in the late morning, greet my friendly co-workers, make myself a cup of tea, and read the papers for an hour (editorial writing has to be the only job where you actually get paid for this). I would then attend the daily editorial board meeting, at which my colleagues and I discussed the topics of the day and decided what we wanted to write about. After lunch, I would do my research. This often involved talking to top city officials to whom I had ready access without leaving my chair and who more often than not returned my phone calls. I would then write my editorial, go over it with my editor, proofread the final page, and go home.

Occasionally I attended black-tie events and private lunches with the subjects of my editorials, and it always tickled me when a mayor or governor would greet me by name.

But, truth be told, it wasn't a life with which I was totally satisfied. I was very fond of my colleagues and loved being able to learn so much about issues that greatly affected the city. The problem was that I felt more like a speechwriter than a journalist. As an editorial writer at the *Daily News,* my job was to express the opinion of the paper's management, whether or not I agreed with it. Not that expressing my own opinions in print was exactly what I wanted to do either. I wanted to present more divergent points of view and as many facts as possible so my readers could have the information they needed to make up their own minds. I hoped to become a reporter, even though this would technically be a step backward from where I was now.

But if I wasn't completely at ease with my job as a pseudo-pundit, Chris's work life was far more unpleasant—and vastly different from when the two of us had met, seven summers before, in 1987. I was a twenty-three-year-old editorial assistant, commuting from a Brooklyn apartment I shared with two roommates to my job at a legal publication in Manhattan. Chris was a twenty-seven-year-old photographer who had recently been an art director and photo editor at that same publication but left just a few months before I had gotten there. In one of many coincidences involving the two of us, Chris and I had selected the same person as our best office buddy: a copy editor named Leslie.

"Do you know Chris Losee?" Leslie asked me one day at the office.

I said I didn't, and she explained who he was.

"He's going to be in this big art show Saturday at the Brooklyn Promenade," an outdoor plaza and walkway by the river that separates Brooklyn from Manhattan. "My sister and I are going. Do you want to come? You'd really like his work."

"I'd love to go," I said, being an avid photographer myself.

Leslie later admitted she had intended our meeting as a sub-
tle fix-up, and it worked. I immediately took a liking to this
cheerfully outgoing, slim, blond man wearing a big straw sun hat.
We chatted exuberantly about photography and Brooklyn and
the people we knew in common at my job. I found him delight-
fully easy to talk to about many things. And, yes, I did like his
large, colorful work. But I wasn't looking for someone to date
just then. I had broken up with someone a week before, and that
wound was a little too fresh.

Still, during the next week, I found my thoughts occasionally
turning to Leslie's artist friend. And, when I become curious
about something, I can't let it go until I check it out. So I called
Chris up and arranged to meet him at his house. This couldn't
have been more convenient; it turned out he lived around the
corner from me.

Our first date was rather unusual. First I developed a few rolls
of black-and-white film in his home darkroom as the two of us
chatted about the music we liked. Then I went with him to deliver
one of the prints he had sold at the art show. It was a female nude
who had been posed lying down with her hair streaming behind
her. By rotating the picture ninety degrees, Chris made it look
like she was running. A plume of flamelike colors at her back
made it appear not so much that she was catching fire as that she
was generating it. We drove the picture in Chris's car to an opu-
lent brownstone near Brooklyn's scenic Prospect Park. When the
woman who'd bought the print opened the door and exclaimed
with delight, I felt as proud as if I had made it myself.

Despite my intentions not to begin a new relationship so
quickly, it did not take long for the two of us to become an insep-
arable couple. We met for lunch almost every day and saw each
other every night. On weekends we explored the city, doing
quintessentially New York things that I, a lifelong resident of the
city, had somehow never gotten around to. We rode the famed

Cyclone roller coaster and ate hot dogs on the boardwalk in Coney Island. We walked across the Brooklyn Bridge at twilight. And, after we had been together for five years, Chris asked me to be his wife. Actually, he didn't really ask me so much as tell me to do it. "I would like you to marry me" is what he said. Of course I agreed.

By this time Chris had left professional photography to help run his father's construction business in Manhattan. He had been working there less than a year when his father became very ill and had to retire unexpectedly. Chris took over and ran the business successfully for six years, until the recession of the early 1990s hit the city's construction industry like a wrecking ball. By that summer day in 1994 when he visited the Staten Island farm with his client Dan, Chris was finding that many of his customers couldn't pay him for work already done. The pressure was tremendous: If he could not keep money coming in, there would be no way to buy construction materials for new jobs. It was financially risky to borrow but completely unpleasant and ultimately unproductive to hound people to pay up. The money just wasn't there.

Stuck in a no-win situation, the person I had come to know as lighthearted and adventurous became crabby and withdrawn. Chris was miserable all the time. Little did I know those flowers in my dining room were inspiring him to come up with a plan for something completely different.

CHRIS: It wasn't that I'd ever fantasized about being a farmer. That thought was about as remote a possibility as, say, becoming proficient in Chinese and leading tour groups to see the Great Wall. But between July and October 1994, I somehow became convinced that this was what I wanted to do and this was what I would do.

It all seems to have started with that innocuous trip with Dan to

Staten Island. I'd known Dan for several years as a friendly customer. An intense, energetic man with bushy, dark hair and lively
brown eyes, Dan seemed far younger than his fifty-some-odd years.
We'd previously done several fence contracts together at the state
park there, installing split-rail fencing on horse trails and putting
huge steel bar gates on closed park roads that seemed to be mag-
nets for dirt bikers and teenage beer parties. So I wasn't surprised
when he called my office that morning.

"What are you doing today?" he asked. "Want to go to Clay
Pit Ponds this afternoon?"

Clay Pit Ponds State Park Preserve was the full name of this 260-
acre parcel, which consisted mostly of undeveloped land near the
southern tip of Staten Island, just outside smelling range of the infa-
mous (now closed) Fresh Kills landfill and a stone's throw from the
polluted waters of the Arthur Kill, a wide tidal creek separating New
York City's fifth borough from its closer neighbor, New Jersey.

It seemed that there was no particular Parks Department job for
me to look at today. Still, having nothing more pressing on the
agenda, I agreed. In fact, the agenda had been looking pretty
blank lately. My business was going down the tubes.

I had been working in the construction industry through the latter half of the eighties, and we rode the roller coaster all the way
up. I knew that if I stayed in the office until 8:00 P.M., I would probably be selling construction jobs until 8:00 P.M. Our biggest problem was getting enough men to install all the work that we sold. But
somehow, working longer hours, hiring extra help, shuffling jobs
and cash around, we got it done. For a twenty-something guy like
me, having an income just over six figures then seemed like the big
time. I was living "the big eighties."

Then came the economic slowdown of the early nineties, and I
was on the edge. There were no new buildings going up in Manhattan, and no plans to build any in the near future. The phones
weren't ringing, the customers weren't paying, and the tax man was

knocking almost every day. After seven years in a booming construction market, the chill of this recession was like nothing I'd experienced before: in eighteen months, I went from no bonuses to no assistants, then no offices, and finally no salary. It was obvious that someday very soon I'd have to come up with a new plan.

On this particular day the sun was out and the cumulus clouds were bright and puffy. Dan and I cruised under the steel cables of the Verrazano Bridge on a concrete roadway suspended a hundred feet over the shining water of the Narrows, the strait that separates Brooklyn from Staten Island and New York Harbor from the Atlantic Ocean, and coasted down the long ramp, descending toward South Beach.

"You know, I used to do farmers' markets every year with Jack and his wife," Dan said, referring to another state employee. He told me how, first with his ex-wife on their little plot on Shelter Island, and later at his aunt's big garden in New Jersey, he had grown flowers and vegetables, tilling, planting, and weeding on spring weekends with the other couple.

It seemed like a demanding hobby—if it could be called that. I had no idea he was so industrious in his spare time.

Later in the summer, Dan would load up his old Dodge van with tomatoes, peppers, leeks, zinnias, sage, cosmos, and sunflowers, along with any weeds he found growing on the side of the road that looked interesting or edible.

"We got a break on the rate for the stand because we agreed to park the van away from the market," he said. "So I'd get in the back and throw together bouquets as fast as I could while the others watched the stand. By the time I got over there with an armload of bouquets, the ones we had on display in the buckets would be almost gone and people would be taking the bunches out of my hands. Then I'd run back to the truck and do some more." By the end of the day, he said, they'd have taken in more than a thousand dollars.

It sounded like fun, I said, but wasn't it hard work? Not really, he said. "It's a lazy man's life: work a few hours in the morning; read John Burroughs on the porch in the afternoon. I don't know about large-scale agriculture, but I can show you how to make ten thousand dollars a year on a half acre, working part-time."

"You know, Dan, I'm really interested in this," I said. "Tell me more."

Right after we passed Fresh Kills landfill on the Staten Island Expressway, our exit came up, and we followed a series of back roads to the park headquarters, and finally to the Gericke Farm, a tiny part of Clay Pit Ponds State Park Preserve. It had been one of the last working farms in the five boroughs of New York City, taken over for back taxes in the sixties.

After a brief official inspection of the farmstead buildings, now State Parks' responsibility, Dan led me up a short trail behind the ramshackle gray barn to a small, flat field.

It did not bring to mind the amber waves of grain; in fact, it looked minuscule. Grass, brown-red dirt, and maybe fifteen rows of crops. It was one of the few times I'd seen so many cultivated plants up close. As we neared the rows, I noticed that the plants seemed to be growing out of some kind of black plastic garbage bags tucked into the dirt.

"That's mulch," Dan explained, "plastic mulch. Keeps water in the soil, cuts down on weeding. A good system."

The ground looked very dry, but the plants were surprisingly big and bushy. I didn't know what any of them were at first, but finally I recognized that some were tomatoes, others squash. Dan began pulling baseball-size tomatoes out of the vines and stuffing them in some paper bags that he'd brought with him.

"It'll just go to waste otherwise. I mean, they do sell it, but. . . . Anyhow, they've got plenty. You want some?"

I collected some two-liter-size zucchini and watched as he raided the row for flowers, grabbing stems and breaking stalks, gathering leaves and twigs and blooms under his arm as he flew like a cyclone down the row.

"Lots of good stuff here. Lots of stuff. Okay, let's get going."

We headed to the car toting bags of field-warm vegetables and bundles of greenery and blossoms, and made our way back to Brooklyn, feeling like we'd gotten something for nothing. And later, as we sat at the kitchen table, Dan put together a bouquet for Kim and me, and one for his girlfriend. We split the booty of vegetables, gave some away to a neighbor, and Dan left. Then Kim came home and saw the bouquet on the kitchen table, and that was the beginning.

I knew I had something to worry about when first-person accounts of novice farmers and how-to farming guides started appearing on Chris's side of the nightstand. Having at this point known my husband seven years, I was well aware that, when he starts immersing himself in a topic, it's only a matter of time before he wants to try it out. This is how a long string of renovation projects on our house had begun. First books on plumbing and carpentry started piling up. Then Chris filled notebook upon notebook with drawings of pipes and beams. And, before I knew it, a floor or wall would be torn up and I would walk into what used to be a closet only to discover it was now part of the bathroom. While I believed it was always best to rely on an expert, Chris thought he might as well *become* the expert. There was nothing he felt he couldn't learn. This was one of the qualities I most admired in him, and also the one with the most potential to drive me crazy.

"What are you reading?" I asked my husband one night a month or so after the appearance of the magical bouquet. His face was obscured by a thin volume called *Real Farm*.

"It's a book about this couple who start a farm in Iowa," Chris said. "I'm almost done. They've split up and she's trying to sell the farm, but now it's almost worthless."

"How depressing!" I remarked.

"It's actually really interesting," Chris said. "But here, you'll like this one better." He handed me a copy of *Moving Upcountry: A Yankee Way of Knowledge,* the tale of a magazine writer named Don Mitchell who gave up urban life to become a sheep farmer in Vermont. This was more my speed. Not only was I working as a writer at the time but I had also spent several happy summers in Vermont during my otherwise urban childhood.

The book was riotously funny. Mitchell described his often hilarious attempts to transform his dilapidated barn into a home for his family, learn to drive on dirt roads in Vermont in the height of "mud season," and raise, breed, and bring to market a large flock of very unruly sheep. But the lifestyle Mitchell described was not exactly one I could picture myself living. For example, there was the time he spontaneously decided to demonstrate his rural prowess to some city friends by killing their dinner—a chicken—in front of them. As he swung the screeching bird vigorously around by its neck, the body detached from the head and went flying toward his horrified guests. Not what I'd call finger-lickin' good.

Then there were the more technical books in Chris's collection. The commanding yet optimistically titled *Grow It!,* the scary *Homesteading,* the hopelessly out of date *Five Acres and Independence,* and the comprehensive *Successful Small-Scale Farming: An Organic Approach.*

But the most far-out book had to be *The Ex-Urbanites Complete & Illustrated Easy-Does-It First-Time Farmer's Guide: A Useful Book.* This was a self-proclaimed bible for the back-to-the-land movement of the 1970s and was very much of its time. The book featured advice on "How to Grow Money" and "Free

Foods," which contained a tasty recipe for acorn paste. "Before all those people came over here on the *Mayflower* and assorted ships and ruined this country, other people with a sense of oneness with nature enjoyed a healthful diet that fell out of the trees," the author explained. The book included many photos of half-naked hippies performing various farming tasks, such as a skinny, long-haired, bearded man wearing only cutoffs, pushing a wheel hoe (a kind of human-powered plow) down a field. Nearby, a topless woman with hairy armpits sat in the dirt playing some sort of lute. This was *definitely* not my style.

As the book pile grew, so did my alarm. So one night in early fall, I got up my courage and asked the obvious question. "You're not really thinking of taking up *farming*, are you?" I asked.

"Why not?" he replied.

"Well," I said, somewhat floored, "how about the fact that every time we buy a houseplant it dies?"

"That's because you kill them," he said.

I did indeed have the thumb of death. I had been killing plants for years. But that seemed exactly the point.

"Do I seem like a farmer to you?" I asked my husband. "Do you? I mean, be for real! We don't own land, we have absolutely no experience in rural living, and we don't know a single thing about farming. We wouldn't have a clue even where to begin."

"I've been talking to Dan about it," Chris said. "He can help us get started. There's lots of land available near him, in the Hudson Valley. We can go visit him and see some parcels. Anyway, just think about those tomatoes we grew on the roof last summer. That wasn't so hard!"

Chris was referring to our urban rooftop garden of the previous year. He had gotten it into his head that we would grow everything needed to make one of his favorite dishes—gazpacho—on the tarry roof of our Brooklyn row house. This involved lugging about ten wooden pallets and twenty-five five-gallon buckets full of dirt up a rickety iron ladder, through the roof hatch, and onto the sticky, sweltering asphalt. Everything was then arranged in a neat line and planted with seedlings grown in Chris's darkroom or purchased at the neighborhood hardware store. Tomatoes, basil, cucumbers, peppers, and parsley improbably flourished on the hot Brooklyn roofscape, and by the end of the summer we had indeed dined on one batch of the luscious, spicy soup, buying only the bread and garlic from the local supermarket.

"I grant you that was a successful experiment," I said. "But it's a giant leap from scoring a bowl of soup to earning a living!"

"Don't be so negative," Chris said, a constant refrain of our daily life together. "It's really just a matter of deciding to go for it. You love the country. You want to own land upstate. So we'll just have to learn some new skills."

That all was true. Chris and I had both gone to school in the largely rural and scenic upstate region of New York that spreads north and west past the metropolitan area's suburbs. We returned every fall to watch the leaves turn. Every time we took a trip north we fantasized about owning property there.

I did have to admit, also, that under Chris's tutelage I had actually become marginally skilled in a field I had never envisioned myself attempting: construction. When we'd first moved into our Brooklyn home five years earlier, it was a disaster from head to toe. Even my husband's relatives were alarmed at its condition. His aunt Sue was the first to visit us in our new abode. "Girl," she said to me as she marched down our lopsided staircase after her tour, *"head for the hills!"* I was tempted, but I didn't, and slowly we rebuilt every room. Chris was the construction foreman, and I was his hapless crew, whose prior experience with hammer and nails consisted of hanging the occasional picture. But Chris's imagination and sheer will never failed him, and I somehow muddled along. Five years later, our town house was completely unrecognizable. It had changed for the better and so had I. Learning to construct my own living environment felt very empowering, though at times I admit I would rather have just taken a nap.

But at this point Chris said he was not contemplating my giving up the home and career that had both taken such hard work to build. Neither of us was thinking of that yet.

"This could be your weekend thing," he said. "I'll do it full-time, if that's even necessary. Dan only farmed on the weekends, and look what he was able to do."

I had to admit it did sound idyllic. Improbable, but idyllic.

"It would be great to spend more than one week a year upstate," I said.

"So you'll consider it?" Chris asked.

It was almost impossible to imagine us as farmers. In fact, it was such an absurd idea that I could hardly take it seriously at all. And, since it was so remote, it wasn't difficult, as I listened to the screech of traffic and thumping of boom boxes on the avenue below our fourth-floor bedroom window, to agree to think about it. Farming? Sure, why not?

"I'll consider it," I replied. "But under no circumstances will I stop shaving my armpits."

Chapter 2

the perfect farm?

CHRIS: On a rainy Tuesday in February I was traveling north in the car again, watching as miles of unfamiliar brown and faded vegetation rolled by the rain-spotted windows in the flat, dull midwinter light. Looking for land—at least I had a goal.

I'd begun my search for the ideal farmstead in September; I don't really know when I went from thinking This is a fun idea to This is a plan, but it had happened sometime that fall. I'd spent the summer reading everything I could find on farming and gardening at my local library (actually, there was plenty on gardening but hardly anything about farming). I also searched for likely titles at any number of used bookstores or yard sales, sometimes coming up with gems like the later half of 1975's issues of *Mother Earth News* or the 1950s vintage *Your Dream Home: How to Build It for Less Than $3,500*. And all of these books seemed to have just one message for me: It can be done.

As *The Ex-Urbanites Complete & Illustrated Easy-Does-It First-Time Farmer's Guide: A Useful Book* put it, "We hope you . . . have been helped to understand how really simple farm life can be. If one were to state a basic principle of the agrarian way, it would be this—just cool it and let Mother Nature do practically all of the work for you." I could dig it.

Of course, optimistic statements alone didn't convince me to chuck it all in favor of the "agrarian way" and move to some upstate farm-topia. I'm not actually sure what made up my mind, but it might have had something to do with all the paperwork I was creating.

I still have a time line, printed in choppy type on my old Apple dot-matrix printer from this period. It shows the months July 1994 through December 1996, and for each quarter of the year there's a two- or three-sentence plan of action and a one-sentence goal. My wife says that I am an obsessive list maker. But for me there is a quality of lists that is something like magic. Items on lists can acquire a certain inevitability. These are things that are supposed to happen, that will happen if given time and effort. And perhaps the gradual accumulation of books and lists had reached some critical mass that made the decision inevitable: write something down enough times and it becomes a fact. Talk about something enough and it becomes real. This farm plan was becoming real.

Besides, this idea fit into some interests I'd always had. As a kid I was fascinated by nature; I collected butterflies, beetles, and tadpoles from the fields, ponds, and parks in our well-groomed Westchester suburb and went on nature walks and camping trips whenever I could. In college one of my majors was biology. Admittedly, though, plants were not high on my list of things to study. I was more interested in what a graduate course I took described as "the ecology of aquatic microfauna" or, in other terminology, pond scum. I did an undergraduate thesis on an organism called *Heliophyra burbanki,* which is essentially a one-celled, star-shaped slime sucker that lives, among other places, in the effluent from sewage treatment plants. And even after graduation I kept, from time to time, samples of water replete with tiny organisms from various local puddles. I could take these out, when the mood struck, and examine them under my microscope ("Call them pond life," I told Kim. "They don't like to be referred to as scum.") So, I thought, how much different could crop plants be? They didn't really move or eat anything or have complicated interactions. I could understand them.

And I liked being outside. In summers, I had worked as a life-guard, swimming instructor, construction laborer. Even now I spent a good deal of time "in the field," at job sites in remote corners of New York City's outer boroughs. It was better than being stuck in an office, although I tended to have allergies, get sunburned, and have to urinate frequently.

By winter of 1995, Chris had convinced me to borrow money from my company retirement plan to put a down payment on farmland in upstate New York—even though we still didn't really know jack about farming.

It's difficult to explain exactly why I agreed to do this. For one thing, my husband is an extremely persuasive person. It's impossible to overstate this. When he bombards you with facts, figures, drawings, and even 3-D scale models, it's very difficult to resist his pitch. Besides, he won't take no for an answer.

For example, over the seven years I had known him at this point, he had convinced me to do the following:

1. Catch and eat bottom-feeders on a fishing trip in the polluted waters of New York Harbor
2. Sleep on a platform supported by wooden stilts jutting mere inches above an alligator-infested Everglades swamp
3. Attempt to hold up, by myself, a heavy and unwieldy four-by-eight-foot piece of drywall balanced on a pole so he could screw it onto our bedroom ceiling.

I was quite sure I would be killed doing all of these things but came close only when the aforementioned piece of drywall came crashing down before the first screw was in (the fish, by the way, was delicious).

But this farm idea was growing on me. It still sounded like an improbable career choice, but I was extremely relieved to see

Chris emerging from the funk he had slipped into during the close of his fence business and becoming so enthusiastic about a new venture. Only a short time ago he had called me at work in tears.

"I feel like I've let everybody down," he said as he sat in his quiet office, tying up the last loose ends of the enterprise that had supported his family's very comfortable lifestyle for as long as he could remember.

I knew he was thinking most of all about his father, who had worked at the firm since before Chris was born and bought the New York branch of the company when Chris was in high school. But Jim Losee remained a very active consultant and had endorsed all of Chris's decisions, including the one to shut it down.

I, too, reassured him that there was nothing he could have done to save the business short of pouring tons of money that nobody had into it, and he knew that. But what really made him feel better was planning his farm. I didn't want to stop his momentum.

And there was something else. I may not have been able to put my finger on it at the time, but watching someone attempt to take control of his or her own destiny is an exciting and inspiring thing to see. There are many people who want to make major changes in their lives but few who actually do it. I, too, wanted a different work situation but was always hesitant to take risks. I started to make a few bold moves of my own.

Dan encouraged me to look for farmland in the mid–Hudson Valley, near his weekend home. The Hudson River runs almost due south to New York City from its source high in the Adirondack Mountains, and along its lower half the river's narrow valley stretches a few miles beyond its banks. This occurs mostly on the eastern side, where it isn't penned in by massive rock outcrops or mountain ranges like the Catskills, but the valley gives its name to the whole region. The river itself is a tidal estuary for about 150 miles of its length, or up to the Troy Dam. In that stretch it passes through some of the loveliest scenery in the eastern United States: from the sheer basalt cliffs of the Palisades to the rugged peaks of Storm King and Dunderberg, and the rolling hills near Rhinebeck, the Hudson's vistas inspired schools of painters and storytellers. This beauty, combined with its proximity to one of the world's great centers of commerce, did not escape the notice of New York's wealthiest inhabitants. Generations of Astors, Vanderbilts, Livingstons, and other families passed through the great houses they built by the river, halfway between New York City and Albany, and a few still haunt the old mansions today. I could understand their attachment to the Hudson, having never lost the vivid childhood memories of standing on my grandfather's wraparound porch high above the river in Tarrytown and gazing at the tiny white sails of boats slowly crossing the shimmering bronze waters of the broad Tappan Zee. But aside from the aesthetic charms of the Hudson Valley, there turned out to be practical reasons for living within its domain.

"You want to be near the river," Dan stressed. "It really moderates the climate so much that you'll have an extra two or three weeks of growing season on either end of the summer."

So the location was just fine with me, even if, as an aspiring lazy farmer, I didn't understand exactly why an extra couple of weeks in late spring and early fall were so important to the success of the whole venture. The trouble was, everyone else, from the Vanderbilts on down, wanted to be by the Hudson too. There seemed still to be a handful of working farms near the river, although it was clear that many of these were maintained as showpieces for their wealthy owners. But most of the open land had already been subdivided into housing developments, three-acre "country estates," and even strip malls along old U.S. Route 9, the continuation of New York

City's Broadway that parallels the river's eastern bank up through Albany, then, switching banks, almost to the river's source. What hadn't yet been carved up was selling at prices that were far above what I could conceive of paying. Still, Dan claimed to have found a few good possibilities among the dross and, knowing his record—he had bought several marginal properties at bargain prices that later turned out to be quite valuable—I went along unquestioningly.

It was on these trips I realized that the power of Dan's imagination was almost hallucinatory—he was seeing farms where I couldn't possibly imagine putting them. In truth, he had a definition of *farm* that went way beyond a field with a big red barn, and a flexibility that was far greater than my own. He stressed that his choices were all great bargains.

Choice 1: A very run-down former boardinghouse on four acres of land across from a juvenile reformatory. "What would they want from you anyway—to steal a couple of vegetables?" Dan asked rhetorically.

Choice 2: A cottage on eight acres—of dense woods. "A guy with a bulldozer can do an awful lot in a couple of days," Dan pointed out.

Choice 3: A flat, treeless ten-acre field through which ran a major nexus of high-voltage power lines.

"It's cheap!" Dan declared.

I decided it was time to seek professional help.

Some real estate agents showed me charming houses: Greek Revivals and Craftsman bungalows, with stone walls and metal-roofed barns, but nothing was in my price range, and none seemed to say "farm."

But I did have a few close calls. Replying to an ad in *The New York Times*, I'd found two agents who seemed to understand what I wanted to do, and as we looked we moved further and further from the river and seemed to get closer to my goal. Once, we almost found it: seventeen acres that had been part of an old dairy farm. The land was beautiful, green and rolling, and it had an enchanted quality—a tiny pond and stream, outcrops of granite and shale, groves of trees, cleared meadows. If you were going to keep the Hobbit in a zoo, this is where you would exhibit him. Alas, a soil survey revealed that the land was rocky and poor and the soil shallow—good for grazing, not for crops. Reluctantly, we let it go.

We'd also seen a beautiful bottomland parcel with a stream running through, about twenty acres, but it had no readily buildable area for a house or septic field.

So by now, late in the year, I at least knew what I was looking for. As I drove past acres of potential farmland, I could recite it like a mantra in time with the wipers tapping on the windshield: It has to have good fields. It has to be flat or rolling, not steep. It has to be off any major roads, preferably with no houses visible. It has to have at least five acres, preferably ten or more. Preferably it has a stream or pond. Preferably it has an old house and/or barn needing cosmetic renovation. It has to cost me less than $100,000, renovations included.

And, reaching the destination on this particular day in December, I stepped out of the car into the light rain, in front of some buildings that seemed like they might be our future farm.

In midwinter, Chris found what he thought should be our farm. I couldn't wait to see it. After a three-hour drive from Brooklyn, the last fifteen minutes of which took us through some very scenic farmland, we pulled into a short asphalt driveway next to what looked like the perfect Hollywood haunted house. Actually, it looked like two haunted houses stuck together. One had a skimpy front porch filled with abandoned furniture and shaded by a rotting roof; the other was taller, with half of its grayed-white paint peeled off. All the windows were dark. It looked as if no one had lived there for decades.

"I'd like you to go in, look around, and just not say anything for a few minutes," Chris said.

We opened the door, which was unlocked. When I stepped inside, I saw why: There was nothing to steal but mold.

The first thing I noticed was the smell—an overpowering animal stench. As I walked in the dark from room to room, taking in the large holes in the wide pine floors and the plaster falling off the walls and ceilings in chunks that exposed the wooden laths beneath, I tried my best to hold my tongue. Finally, I couldn't stand it any longer.

"May I speak now?" I asked Chris.

"Yes," he said expectantly.

"*Aaaaaaiiiieeeeeeeeeeek!*" was all I could manage.

"Oh come on, it's not that bad," Chris said.

"It is absolutely that bad," I said. "How many animals have died here?"

"Actually, I think they're still alive," he posited. "But we can evict them."

Chris then took me to look at the land and outbuildings, and I saw immediately why he wanted to own this property. It contained two barns filled with junk—old windows, doors, and all the other kinds of stuff I am constantly begging Chris not to buy at barn sales. Now he could simply buy the whole barn. Two of them. I am in hell, I thought.

Okay, so maybe the place was in bad shape. And maybe it did smell, though Kim is overly sensitive to odors. But at least this place had actually been a farm and the soil was good. I think we could have done a lot with it. As it happened, though, the owner and I couldn't agree on a price for the parcel I wanted. So I kept looking. And then I got some very good news from my agent: the owner of the bottomland parcel that Kim and I had both liked when we saw it six weeks ago now proposed to include another small piece of land across the road that would be much more suited for building. This time I was sure Kim and I would agree that we had finally found our farm.

I went to see this new parcel with Chris for the first time in early April. It was on a steep hill covered with cedars. We looked out across a narrow, grassy valley between the road and a winding, rushing stream. On the far side of the stream was a series of higher hills covered with maples, beeches, and pines. There was no sign of human habitation as far as the eye could see. As a light snow fell, I watched this scene and felt my heart swell. It was hard to believe, given the congested environment in which we currently lived, that we could ever own something so vast and beautiful and peaceful. I thought of how much fun it would be to explore these fields and woods with the children I hoped Chris and I would have someday. And I knew it would be worth trying just about anything to make it ours.

It took months for our purchase to be complete. The land, which had been part of a large old farm, had to be subdivided, and all parties had to agree on the boundaries. But by the fall it was done. In the end, we settled on about thirty acres. Seven of them were up on the cedar-covered hill, which was where we would build a house. This piece was mostly wooded, although there was one small field that had most recently been planted in corn, judging by the old stalks and occasional cob we saw lying under the weeds and dirt. The rest of the acreage was down in the valley across the road. This part also had old cornfields on the near side of the stream. On the other side were wetlands and woods, through which a defunct railbed ran. And in the stream there stood a beautiful dead, white tree that looked like it belonged in a Georgia O'Keeffe painting.

We signed the papers on a bright September day in the tiniest law office I had ever seen, in a two-story frame house on the main street of the town nearest to our land. The office belonged to our seller's lawyer, whose brothers ran a nearby dairy farm. I had seen their milk for sale in fancy glass bottles at our local supermarket in Brooklyn.

Though I still had some concerns about whether we could afford a new country home, I thought we had gotten a terrific piece of land at a very good price. I just hoped my husband really knew what he was doing and wasn't literally leading me down the garden path of some sort of early midlife crisis.

But then I got a signal that things were happening exactly as they were supposed to. At least that was how I interpreted a truly auspicious development in the summer of 1995: a reporting job opened up at my paper's Albany Bureau—about an hour from the land we were then in the midst of negotiating to buy.

If I moved to Albany, not only would I realize my goal of becoming a reporter but Chris and I wouldn't have to be separated during the week while he worked on building a house (he had decided he wanted to attempt to do this himself and arranged to stay at his parents' home an hour north of Brooklyn to make his commute easier). When the house was built, we could live there full-time and I could commute to Albany from there. We were already renting out part of the Brooklyn house and could rent more if need be, so we wouldn't have to sell it.

And, as it happened, the Albany position was proving impossible to fill because most *Daily News* reporters find northern New York State about as tantalizing as Fargo, North Dakota. I knew I had a good shot at getting the job, but I didn't want to jinx it by seeming overly eager. So when I went to speak to the managing editor about becoming a reporter, as I had planned to do soon anyway, I tried to play it as cool as possible.

"You know, I'd even be willing to take that job in Albany," I said as casually as I could manage.

"You would?" the editor said, his whole face lighting up like a slot machine registering the jackpot.

I knew right then the job was mine. What I didn't know was that my colleagues were avoiding Albany for reasons other than the weather.

# Chapter 3

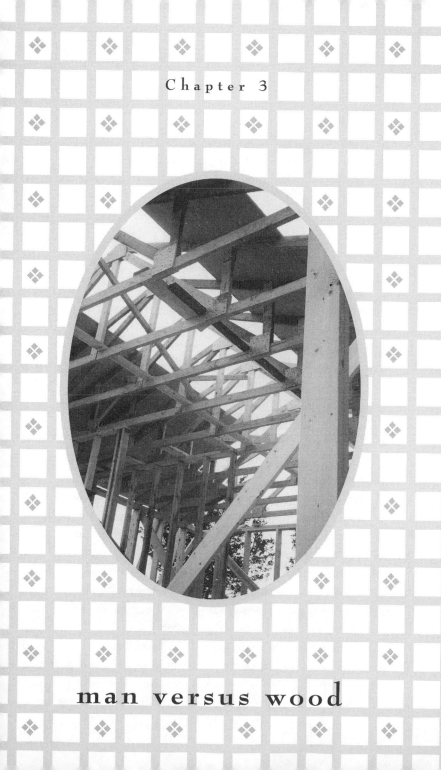

## man versus wood

CHRIS: So, a little over a year after my trip to the Gericke farm, I actually owned one myself—or at least the means to have one. It seemed odd that a few minutes in the tiny, dusty attic office of the town's only lawyer could actually put one in possession of something as vital as a good parcel of farmland, but there it was, on paper. Of course, there would still be a lot of work to do before the first row could be planted. It was time to get started.

The first things we needed were a road and a house. I already knew before I signed the papers where I would put the house. In fact, I'd visited the land many times during the summer, walking the stone ledges among the cedars on the upper part and, in the lower field, wading through waist-high foxtail grass, slowly going to seed in the August heat. There were lots of idyllic spots on the property, and I'd even toyed with the idea of building on a level area across the stream from the field, in a beautiful grove of tall maple trees near an abandoned railroad bed. Of course I'd have to pave a half-mile road through flat bottomlands likely to flood; and build a bridge over the stream; and find a place farther back for the septic; and get a permit, because it was a designated wetland.

Common sense killed that idea. Then there was the upper field from which, in a certain corner, you could actually see part of a Catskill mountain all the way across the river. The seller assumed that that was where anybody would want to build the house. But a

new house smack in the middle of the field felt wrong somehow—
too exposed, like an ominous new growth sprouting from the skin
of the land. In the cedar woods, not far from the border of the upper
field, I had found a small, flat clearing. It was a grassy, sun-dappled
spot with a few shale outcrops colored white and gold by the crusty
rings of old lichens. Deer had found it too, as evidenced by drop-
pings available in bulk, fresh or dried. And maybe a hiker or a
teenager had left the candy wrapper I saw under a stunted cedar,
when he paused to sit here and look at the sky. It was a good place
to watch the clouds, and I thought that if we could get up maybe
six or eight feet, there would probably be a nice view right across
the small valley where our farm fields would be. This was going to
be the spot. It was near enough to the upper field to run a septic
line out there if there was noplace closer. And there was bound to
be a point nearby where a well driller, if he dug deep enough,
would hit water.

But figuring out where the road was going to go was another
matter. There was no obvious path up the hill. I had scrambled up
all different ways, straight up over ledges and outcrops, around the
back and up in a spiral, before finding the best way, diagonally up
the face of the slope through a tangle of prickly blackberry bushes.
Mostly it was deer who'd been traversing this land for years. We
would have to make it more accessible to us two-legged creatures.

A colleague of Kim's who lived about half an hour north of our
land recommended a local excavator who could put in a road and
a septic system, and dig our building's foundation. "He did our
road, and ponds too," Bob said. "He's the cheapest guy in town."
This contractor sounded like someone I ought to meet, so I called
him, and about a week later he met me in the morning on the side
of the town road across from the bottom field. Ed was a stocky man
about my age with a beard and a flannel shirt, driving a new red
diesel pickup with an orange safety flasher on top of the cab. After
a pleasant exchange we began walking up the hill, and I described

my plans for the building to him with a mixture of excitement and anxiety, lest he tell me that, for some reason, things couldn't be done as I'd hoped. When we got up to my chosen place, he looked around for a moment.

"Nice spot," said Ed. "Up here in the cedars. Well in away from everybody. Sure." I felt a surge of relief. We talked about whether the shale ledge just below the surface of the thin soil would interfere with the excavation ("it runs in veins, and if you rip it right or get lucky, she'll come out just like dirt") and where the septic field would be. But when it came to the road, he refused to be specific. "We'll get you up here, sure. Be a little steep, maybe, in spots. Can't tell just how we'll go until we get started." We shook hands on the deal.

A few weeks later, on the day Ed's crew was to begin, I thought I'd go up and have a look. Arriving in the late afternoon, I encountered a hale but somewhat elderly man with a generous belly and a big chain saw. He appeared to be felling certain individual trees in a fastidious manner, cutting them into log lengths and stacking them in little piles, then pausing to reflect on the natural world and his place therein. He introduced himself as Ed's father, though I later learned that he was universally called Pops and was a retired short-haul trucker. "Nice spot," he said, "you'll be well away from everybody." We talked for a while about wood: "Locust burns real good, but it's some tricky to split," he said. "Thorns, too. Wood's the best heat, you see, 'cause it heats you twice: once when you cut it, again when you burn it." But as I walked through the blackberries up the hill, I couldn't help wondering if this was why Ed's rates were so low: Was Pops going to lovingly cut each tree into logs and split it for kindling as he worked his way up the hill, then start shoveling dirt? At this rate, I thought, it's going to take years. Now, I knew nothing about road construction except that my tax dollars were at work every time I saw an orange sign on the thruway, but it seemed that there should be a faster way.

So I was even more surprised, a day or two later, when I returned to find what looked like a completed road running straight as an arrow up the hill, with a quick buttonhook turn to the building site. It was obviously not the work of an old man with a chain saw. There was dust everywhere, trucks (including Ed's snazzy Dodge) parked randomly among the trees, and a huge yellow bulldozer idling near the bottom. Ed, seeing my slack-jawed gape, explained that he'd gotten started early in the morning and had made good progress. "Can I drive up there now?" I asked hopefully. Ed just laughed, explaining that not even a four-wheeler could get up through the deep dust made by the bulldozer until the surface material, a "dirty gravel" called Item Four, went on.

That gravel was laid in the coming days, along with a hole for the massive concrete septic tank and a clear, leveled area for the underground pipes of the leach field, where the tank would drain its liquid effluent into the earth. And then, one day, it was time to pound in the stakes that would mark the extent of the excavation for our house's foundation. The house was going to be a barnlike structure, twenty-four by thirty feet, with a bottom floor consisting of a garage and workshop, and living space on top. It would be partially bermed into the hillside: this meant that, by cutting away the earth across the slope of the hill and setting the structure into the cut, the garage on the lower level would be belowground on one side, while the floor of the living space, just a few feet above grade on the high side of the hill, would be a full ten feet above the ground on the low side.

In fact, one benefit of all the delays in closing on the property was that I'd had lots of time to draw up building plans and then go to the site to see if they'd work. I had drawn a two-story house, a saltbox, and then a gambrel-roofed barn, settling on the last as the most practical and economical structure. It seemed to me that, for now, it was more important to have lots of utility and storage space and less living space—after all, aren't barns always bigger than farmhouses? Although I didn't know exactly what one kept in them, I was confident this barn would soon fill up with something I needed. Someday, down the road, I hoped we'd have enough money and time to build a big house—but for now a multiuse barn would have to do.

Because the size and cost of the house were below a certain threshold, I didn't need to have my plans stamped by an architect, though I still needed a building permit. This was obtained at town hall, a converted one-room schoolhouse, for a fee of fifty dollars. Then I was ready to go, and the prospect filled me with excitement. Finally I could take some concrete action toward fulfilling the dream I had been pursuing. After the long months of searching and planning, designing and arranging, talking on the telephone and riding in the car, I would soon be spending some time out on my hillside in convocation with a stack of wood, a saw, and some nails. It sounded like paradise. There was just one task left to be done before I could begin.

Pouring the concrete foundation was a critical job, because the entire wood frame of the house would rest on this rock-solid slab. If it were off square, if its walls weren't thick enough to resist the pressure of frozen earth that splits stone, if it settled on its footings, then the rest of the house would follow it to ruin. Ed recommended a fellow named Tommy to do the pour, and I arranged to meet him one Sunday in mid-October. Kim and I decided to camp out on the site the night before the meeting—it would be the first time we'd spend the night on our land. We set up our tent on a level spot on the excavation, sheltered on one side by the high berm and facing south, toward the low side of the hill. It was, in fact, approximately where our bedroom would be when the house was built. We unloaded our sleeping bags, foam pads, and cooking gear from the car, and started setting up camp as the sun was going behind the hill across the little valley from our homestead.

I knew from many years of moving from apartment to apartment that the first night in a new place could be either very good or very bad. I'd had morning surprises ranging from the scent of roses through a bedroom window to noisy bar fights spilling into the street, but I had no idea what to expect out here. It was far from wilderness, yet there was no telling how close the next person was. Or who the next person was. Or whether the next person might have any particular grudge against outsiders like ourselves. Or whether coyotes were really as afraid of humans as everyone seemed to think. I couldn't stop this stream of disquieting thoughts as we prepared and ate our customary alfresco dinner of home-made chili. Wasn't there a reality-based movie about something like this? In an odd way, it was much more disturbing than most nights spent in true backcountry, like the Adirondacks, the Allagash, and the Everglades. Because *they*—the rabid coyotes, the hostile locals, the entire cast of the movie *Deliverance*—*they knew* we were here. They had seen us come in. Maybe they were watching us now.

Except for the sounds of shale fragments cracking and popping in the fire, it was utterly quiet. It got dark about eight, and we turned in as a light rain began to fall. Uncharacteristically, I went immediately to sleep, and in spite of my misgivings we passed a very uneventful first night on our land, during which nothing happened at all.

The morning was gray when we awoke, made oatmeal, and packed our gear. We met Tommy at the appointed time and went over the details of the pour. He seemed interested in the project and inspired confidence in us that our house would soon be taking shape. We agreed on the work to be done: "Sounds like a plan," Tommy said. "And if you're interested, I can show you a barn a fella's building down the road that sounds a lot like yours. Maybe you'll get some ideas." We followed his tiny silver pickup along miles of twisting back roads in the rain, losing sight of him many times, certain we had gone too far and missed a crucial turn, only to spot him again further up ahead, still tooling along. Finally, almost an hour later, we arrived — somewhere — next to a new gambrel-roofed barn of approximately the same size as the one I was planning. "Well, I guess it was a little further than I thought," said Tommy, shrugging. "Anyhow, this'll be his workshop. He's almost done. He won't mind if I show you around."

The barn smelled of pine, the pleasant, resinous smell of newly cut lumber. There was no drywall on the studs, and the framing members clearly showed the skeleton of the building. The two-by-sixes, two-by-eights, and two-by-tens marched in orderly, symmetrical rows across the wall and ceiling planes, holding up the plywood on the outside, holding out the weather. It gave the feeling of being inside a wooden ship, while the steady beat of the rain outside seemed to suggest a calm but always-moving ocean. The carpentry work seemed perfect — no scarred lumber, bent nails, gaps, or patches. It was a shame to have to cover it up. It made me want to start my barn immediately. It also made me nervous. Was I really going to do this — by myself? I had done some work on houses before, and watched lots of buildings go up in the course of my business, but I'd never taken on a project of this scale before. Yet this was the next logical step, and since it was clearly delineated on my time line, it was soon bound to be my full-time obsession.

A week or so later, I found myself alone on the hill with two tool-boxes, a new generator from Home Depot, two huge green tarps covering piles of wood delivered by the local lumberyard, and a brand-new foundation in the footprint of our house to be. Black anchor bolts stuck up from the not-yet-cured concrete every six feet or so, inviting the treated wood sill plates that would form the transition between foundation and wall. It was time to get busy. The generator shattered the stillness of the cedars as I began drilling, sawing, and nailing. The weather was still fine, and the wood was going up. There was an exciting sense of progress, of things coming together, of rightness.

But it didn't last through the week.

The generator soon proved extremely annoying, revving up and down in response to whatever tool I was using with flatulent abandon. Even when idling it sounded like a chorus of outboard motors chewing up a flock of noisy ducks, with an accompanying smell of burning toxic waste. I tried to use it as little as possible, saving up saw cuts until I had enough to do several at once. Plus it made it impossible to hear the radio, which, even though it was tuned to a station of recycled rock format, at least provided some sense that there was still an outside world. And it always seemed that there was some piece of hardware I'd forgotten to order, some nail or screw or whatsit that couldn't be left out or substituted, and was needed right now, before one more single thing could be done on the entire project. This of course necessitated an immediate trip into town, where it would be discovered that the whatsit was on back order but might be found somewhere in the storeroom if only Jim would get back to the counter, but nobody had seen him lately.

Yet, gradually, a routine emerged: I left my parents' house, where I was staying, at 8:00 A.M., stopped for coffee on the way up, and began going at it in earnest by 10:00. I usually worked through lunch, taking only a couple of short breaks from work to walk around, then packed up the tools, stashed the toolboxes under a fallen tree, covered the wood piles, and jumped in the car by 6:00 for the drive back to Westchester. My mom made an extra portion of dinner, which she reheated for me, and then I had a couple of hours to check my plans for the next day's work, write memos to myself, and call Kim in Brooklyn. Finally it was time to watch my favorite TV show, *Beavis and Butt-head,* and then go to sleep. I'd repeat the same cycle tomorrow and the day after. I even got used to the generator, found a better radio station, and accumulated a sizable cache of odd hardware items.

❖

Liberation from *Beavis and Butt-head* was the only truly enjoyable thing about the season I spent as a construction widow. Otherwise, it was a rather lonely and frustrating time. There wasn't much for me to do but wait for my transfer to Albany to come through.

While I had indeed been promised the job by the top editors ("I have no idea why you want to do this, I'm just glad you do," said the editor in chief), my immediate supervisor had not taken the news of my departure well. "Why Albany?" he kept asking me.

I suppose I could have told him that my husband and I were secretly plotting to become farmers. But, even if he believed me, that reason was only secondary to me at the time. I wanted to go because I thought this job would bring me closer to the heart of a profession I planned to be in for a long time. And state government seemed the perfect place to start working on the more informative and objective pieces I hoped to do.

Though he failed to talk me out of going, my editor did extract a promise from the higher-ups that they wouldn't move me until he found someone to replace me. And, for a while, the search did not appear to have much urgency.

So every weekday during the fall of 1995, I would wake up in an empty house and get on the Manhattan-bound subway in Brooklyn while Chris was getting in his car in Westchester for his daily northern drive. I'd spend the rest of my day constructing with words while he built with wood. And, I must say, he had far more to show for his efforts.

That little clearing in the woods inhabited only by deer and bunnies was slowly transforming into a place that humans could call home. It was now possible to stand on wooden girders ten feet above where we had cooked our outdoor chili dinner and gaze toward a series of tree-covered hills about five miles away. It truly felt like walking on air. Not that it was so high up—it wasn't even above the tips of the surrounding cedar trees, which are pretty puny as far as trees go. And certainly I was used to living in far higher places, having spent my entire childhood on the fifth floor of a twelve-story apartment building. But, somehow, that didn't seem as impressive. The thing was, I had never seen what was there before my apartment building existed. Here I had seen what was there only a month before: nothing.

After a few weeks I could say I was making some progress. I'd put up the high south wall and the half-height east wall on the bottom floor, bringing these sides up to level with the concrete foundation on the high north side of the hill. I'd installed the six-by-six posts that held up the massive girders running lengthwise down the house. Now I was ready to put in the floor joists—the big two-by-ten boards that would hold up the plywood floor deck for the living space and walls on the second floor.

And I'd had my first visitor: standing on a girder one afternoon, I heard noises that sounded exactly like the approach of a posse in a Western movie, followed with the close-by whinny of a horse, and I watched incredulously as a middle-aged cowgirl appeared in a cloud of dust in the middle of the driveway. She seemed as surprised as I was to see another human in this spot.

"I live in town," she said, "behind the cemetery—you know, where the little barn and corral is? I used to come up here and ride all the time—would you mind?"

I had no idea where her house was, or that you could keep a horse in town, but told her that she was welcome to ride on the land anytime, then preposterously added, "Uhh . . . as long as you don't shoot anything."

"Don't worry, I won't," she replied. "I hate those hunters, killing deer for no reason. They oughta be shot themselves." Then she gave her horse a carrot and headed up the hill. I never saw her again.

Even with so little experience of the place, I was certain her view was very much in the minority around here. In fact, I knew that at this time in the fall, every member of Ed's and Tommy's crew would be getting ready for the start of deer season. As surely as Friday is followed by the weekend, the October bow-hunting season is followed by black powder and antique firearm season, then the opening of rifle season across the upstate counties, usually a few days before Thanksgiving. The occasional, startling crack of rifle shots in the distance was now a signal that guns were being cleaned and sighted in, and posters announcing hunter education classes and big buck contests were appearing in the local stores. The falling of leaves in this part of the world was enduringly bound to the season of hunting, in a largely (but not, as I learned, exclusively) masculine ritual whose roots go as far back as one cares to look.

Although the season was progressing, the house seemed to show very little change as the days passed. I was coming to the realization that it was one thing to draw the location of a wall neatly on a piece of paper, another to build the thing from nails and sticks. Pencils, after all, have erasers. And all the supervisory experience I had gained working at the fence company really didn't help when I needed to know what kind of fastener was going to hold a piece of wood where I wanted it, or how strong was strong enough. What kinds of cuts should I make at a dormer? Which, of all the ways to make a corner in a wall, was the best? Would the walls really hold up the roof when the wind blew a gale? Would this piece of wood really hold me up while I stood on it? What would it feel like to fall ten feet onto a poured concrete deck?

As the two-by-six, two-by-eight, and two-by-ten boards slowly came off the pile of wood, I came to feel that each one had a unique, and usually ugly, personality. They were sometimes straight but more often slightly crooked, and came with an abundance of splinters, sticky sap pockets, and the occasional centipede, spider, or ant colony attached. By the time the pile was halfway gone, I came to know the common lumber defects—the kind you can find illustrated in a book about wood-frame construction—on a first-name basis.

Bow (as in the propeller of arrows): A situation where the piece of wood, laid on a flat surface with its wide side down, will spring up a few inches in the middle while its ends touch the floor. Not an extremely serious problem, but annoying because it throws your measurements off.

Crook: Same thing on the skinny side of the board but a worse problem, because walls and floors are expected to be flat, and they get that way by lining up the skinny sides of lots of boards; if one board in the middle of your wall has a crook, it makes the wall . . . crooked. Pick another board.

Twist: If you could clamp one end of the piece of lumber in a very sturdy vise, take a huge monkey wrench to the other end, and rotate it about thirty degrees, you'd have a twisted board. (Is this what they do for laughs at the lumberyard?) Forget it.

And we haven't even covered checks, splits, and wanes (when a two-by-four suddenly shrinks to a two-by-three-and-a-half).

It was frustrating not to know whether these boards were really any worse than average (as it turned out, they were better). How much bow is acceptable? How much wane? There wasn't even anyone to growl at when I cut something wrong, or cut myself, or bent the third nail in a row, let alone discuss the finer points of lumber grading.

And there were some jobs that went excruciatingly slowly that I knew should have been quick: for example, those three walls I'd just finished framing. Now, you can cut all the pieces of lumber to size and nail them together flat on the plywood floor deck of a new house, making all the openings for windows and doors, even putting on the outside plywood skin; then you can simply tilt the whole unit up vertically into place and nail it to the floor. This was, I understood, a quick, easy, and accurate way to get the walls up. But I wasn't able to do this on the bottom floor, and it would be out of the question on the second floor, since there was no way I was going to be able to lift a thirty-foot length of two-by-six wall by myself. That would take two people. Meanwhile, I was getting tired from just moving each floor joist from the pile to the cutting area, then to the second floor, and finally into place.

These walls had to be framed stick by stick: First, the lower end of each stud would be nailed to the bottom sill plate—the flat board bolted to the foundation—while each floppy upper end was held upright by a temporary brace. Then, when enough eight-foot-tall studs were standing vertically, like teeth in a comb, I could nail a top plate horizontally across the upper ends and hope that a wind didn't rise until the next wall could be attached. It was going to be a long, tedious few months, and knowing that there was a better and faster way to do the framing job wasn't helping my mood.

Meanwhile, I was still putting up the floor joists. It was lucky they overlapped above a beam in the center, because some of my earliest cuts were so far off that if they'd actually needed to meet up with one another, the house would have cracked right down the middle and crumbled to the ground.

If it had seemed so easy to me a short time ago to conceive that a few hundred pieces of different-size wood could be exactingly cut, fitted together, joined, and fastened, the reality was now proving to be quite a different story. One-eighth of an inch was a small error, but it would look like a big hole in the floor. Now I knew why carpenters earn good money.

Eventually, I began to wonder if I would ever complete this job. With small gaps in the walls, would the house whistle in a light wind? Would it list to one side like a barge about to sink? There wasn't even anyone to ask. And there always seemed to be another joist waiting to be put up, until finally they were all done. The house now looked like a skeleton, with thin ribs of vertical two-by-sixes holding up more massive horizontal bones, the two-by-tens that would support the floor and form the base for second-story walls. It was a relief tinged with dread at the thought of more framing adventures to come.

The next task, after the floor joists were in place, was to actually install the floor deck. I'd installed it before, many times, in my head. Simple. You take the four-foot-by-eight-foot piece of fir plywood, place it accurately on the perfectly aligned and very square floor joists, and nail it in place. Then take the next one, slide its tongue — a small protuberance in the three-quarter-inch dimension of the plywood — into the thin groove provided specifically to receive it in the first sheet of ply, align it precisely, nail, and so on. And don't forget to stagger the joints so that the cracks between two sheets don't fall next to each other on a joist.

But I found that getting these big hunks of fir to French-kiss on the deck was another monumental task. Heaving these massive sheets of wood and glue onto the deck was trying enough: they weighed about thirty pounds each and were just big enough to be completely awkward for anyone with typical human proportions — a strain to pick up, difficult to carry, and easy to drop. But positioning them on the joists was a real nightmare: If the long side lined up with the wall, then the short side would invariably be just off the centerline of the joist, and usually at some diagonal, when it should have been centered and straight. If you straightened the short side, then the long side would overhang on one end. But if you dared to reposition the joist, the next sheet would have an even worse misalignment, maybe missing the joist altogether. And the tongue would just not go into the groove the way I wanted it, and not for any good reason: One time it was because the groove was bent by being dropped on a rock, another time the tongue had been deformed by the metal bands that strapped the sheets together. Or a nail was right in the groove, blocking the tongue's entrance. Or a splinter of wood, a bug, or something else.

I spent hours cleaning grooves, banging on reluctant sheets of plywood with a block of wood between my hammer and the ply, trying to keep the precious edges from splintering under the hammer blows. Then watching with delight turning to disgust as the last tap, meant to send the final part of the tongue slipping perfectly into the groove, resulted in the other end of the sheet, formerly tight, popping right out of the groove and off the joist . . . And then starting again. And when a plywood sheet ended up in its final position, it took about sixty nails just to hold it to the deck. I was developing forearms like Popeye's, and a bad attitude. It was time to get help.

I had none of the qualifications Chris was looking for in a helper, except for the most important one: I was available. And although Chris would have loved to take a break while he looked for a more experienced assistant, there just wasn't any time. Winter would soon be here, and Chris needed to have the structure closed in with a roof before the first snow fell. I could see that he was completely fried working alone in the woods, yet I knew that he wanted to keep going. So I did the only thing I could think of to ease his frustration. I asked Chris if there was anything I could do to help until he found someone more skilled.

"Actually, there is," he said, after giving it a few moments of thought. "You can help me build a staircase. That's not a very strenuous job."

So the following Saturday morning, instead of heading to our favorite Brooklyn diner as was our custom, we picked up some bagels to go and headed toward our land. I hadn't been there in a couple of weeks and was very interested to see how things were shaping up.

As our dumpy station wagon bumped along the rocky road

that went straight up to our building site, I asked Chris, "Do you think we should pave this driveway?"

"We'd only have to keep redoing it when it froze and cracked," he answered. "I think we should try to live with it like this for a while and see how it goes. Besides, paving is expensive."

"Okay." I sighed as I held on to the dashboard to keep from bouncing up and down in my seat. I wasn't looking to invest any more money in this project at such an early stage.

When we arrived at the little clearing at the top of the hill, parked, and stepped out of the car, I immediately felt the upstate temperature difference—about ten degrees chillier than the city air. That put us in the upper forties. I was glad Chris had told me to wear lots of layers, including a red union suit with a little buttoned flap on the bottom.

Our house so far looked like a wooden box perched on top of a concrete box. The latter was the garage and the former our living space. The structure seemed to be rising out of a low pile of crumbled shale and reddish dirt in a cleared space among the thick cedar trees.

We stepped into the garage, which had large rectangular cutouts for doors and windows. It was covered over by Chris's new second-floor deck. This deck had just one rectangular hole, about three feet by ten feet, which we stood beneath, looking up.

"This is where the staircase goes," Chris said. "Our first job is to measure and cut all the pieces of wood that we'll need for treads, risers, and the carriage."

"The what?"

"The things you step on, the little vertical pieces that go in between them, and the big sawtooth-shaped thing that holds it all together on either side."

"Thank you," I said, finally understanding what he was talking about.

Chris handed me a tape measure and pencil and said my first

assignment was to mark off three-foot sections on a two-by-ten-by-ten-foot board for the treads.

That seemed like too important a job to give someone as clueless as myself. "What if I make a mistake?" I asked.

"Don't," he said. "I don't have any extra to play around with."

Great. I hooked the tape measure to one end of the long, smooth board lying on the garage floor and pulled it to the other end. Then I went back and put a mark every thirty-six inches. Then I checked it and rechecked it.

"How do you know what size everything should be?" I asked.

"Well, stair width is pretty standard. For the other dimensions, you have to use three different mathematical formulas to see what dimensions will fit the space you have for the whole thing. The formulas are based on what most people expect when climbing up or down a flight of stairs."

"I didn't think I was expecting anything in particular."

"Well, you are," Chris said. "Do you remember how we were both stumbling when we walked up that staircase at Dan's country house?"

"That was unbelievably steep," I said, recalling the steps leading up to the second floor of Dan's historic Rhinebeck home.

"Exactly. Our brains were assuming one thing while our feet encountered something completely different," he said. "That's why we were spazzing out. You shouldn't have to pay that much attention when walking up stairs."

I had no idea so much thought went into protecting stair climbers from thinking. "Interesting," I said.

When I finished my markings, Chris powered up his generator by pulling a lawn-mower-type cord on top of it. The noise was horrendous, like someone trying to drive a speedboat over concrete.

"How do you stand that?" I asked Chris, when I felt safe to take my hands off my ears.

"I'm sort of used to it, but I take a handful of aspirin at the end of every day," he answered.

We spent most of the day marking and cutting, until we had all the pieces we needed and could begin nailing the big zigzaggy boards that formed the two sides of the staircase to the floor joists at the top of the stairwell opening.

"Let me do that," I offered. I figured it would be a very low-pressure job. After all, it wouldn't much matter if you didn't hit the nail exactly right every time, as long as you didn't land the hammer on your finger.

I took a few swipes at the first nail.

"Try holding the hammer farther back along the handle," Chris suggested. "You'll get more power that way."

I looked down and saw that my hand was way up toward the head of the hammer. I moved it back and tried again. It did feel like I was getting more power this way, but also like I had less control over where the hammer landed. "This feels awkward," I said.

"You'll get the hang of it," Chris said, and started nailing the other side. He could do each nail with two blows, while it took me about seven to get the nail head flush with the wood. How embarrassing, I thought. But at least I can't get fired.

When we were finished, a few hours later, I had cold hands, sore arms, and a very rudimentary looking but functional staircase.

"After you," Chris said as we began our ascent.

Standing on the plywood platform that made up the second-floor deck gave a whole new perspective. I was able to get a feel for the dimensions of our living space and a peek at the view we would have from the big picture window Chris planned to install in the front of the living room. While this apartment was quite a bit smaller than the house in which we were now living—only two rooms as opposed to eight—it somehow felt more spacious.

That's because the panoramic view of rolling hills and puffy clouds seemed to add about five miles to the living room. From my Brooklyn living room, I could barely even see the sky.

"I can't wait to live here," I said.

After some anxious calling around, I was able to line up my old friend Andy to help me with the framing. Andy had quite a varied work history, including a position at a major record label and a brief stint with my fence company. He'd also worked for a roofer, which gave him some experience in house construction. He was now working on a tugboat that hauled gravel up and down the Hudson River and on the Long Island Sound. He worked a full watch on the boat, away from his home for a week or two at a time, then off for the same period, but he said he could give me a couple of days every other week. We started working together the next week.

The routine was basically unchanged, except for picking him up in the morning, and an earlier stop for coffee. But the work was infinitely more pleasant. We talked nonstop for as long as we were in the car, rehashing stories from our college days, tales of the tugboat and the fence crew, discussions of obscure postmodernist philosophers and unappreciated musicians. This conversation continued on the job site, together with a running commentary on the work and salty obscenities directed at errant nails. I think I understood then why cavemen formed tribes instead of going freelance—it was just better to have some company. On days when Andy wasn't there, I precut and stockpiled wood, made sketches and measurements, and did some detailed, tricky jobs, like building the roof trusses.

There are two ways to build a gable roof: rafters and trusses. Rafter construction, the more traditional method, involves placing a long ridge beam at the peak of the roof, then running plenty of smaller, riblike boards (the rafters themselves) down from the ridge to the tops of the walls to support the roof structure. The trouble is, the heavy ridge beam must be put up first, and the integrity of the whole construction depends on a great number of precisely cut and notched rafters fitting together perfectly. It's a challenge for two experienced carpenters working in harmony to execute the fancy aerial joinery; for a novice builder like myself, it sounded like a nightmare.

Trusses, by contrast, are prefabricated triangles of wood made in the exact cross section of the roof. They are built flat on the deck and, even with the additional bracing they require (forming triangles within the triangle), they're easier to assemble and move around than beams and rafters. I had chosen this method because I could build the trusses by myself and stack them in a corner when I finished. When we were ready to put them up, a small crew could easily hoist them, swing them into place, make adjustments, and nail them down.

At least, that's what the books said. Before too long I became fairly competent at making the mitered cuts and assembling the trusses on the plywood floor deck above the garage. When Andy came up, we did the heavy lifting: putting up walls, hanging exterior plywood, and moving big posts. In a short while I had a stack of completed roof trusses waiting to be installed.

About now, we finally had to face up to a problem: although we'd each had some experience with construction, neither of us had ever put up a truss before, and we really didn't know how to do it. My carpentry experience consisted mainly of building decks, closets, interior rooms, and a basic twelve-by-sixteen addition to a summer cottage. Besides working for my fence company and the roofer, Andy was a quick study and had a good general feeling for tools. But neither of us could be called an experienced carpenter. It was frustrating to have to argue about which was the best way to do a simple framing job, but I consider it a tribute to our friendship that we never actually came to fisticuffs over the correct way to build a corner post.

Yet while disagreements about building walls could be time-wasting annoyances, it seemed that ignorance of truss installation was a serious drawback. These triangular frames, after all, not only form the roof structure and the base for plywood and shingles but also hold the drywall up at the ceilings, and at the same time keep the walls from bowing out at the top. It had been easy enough to build the trusses one at a time, using a pattern book that showed the sizes and shapes of the pieces. But if we put these things up wrong it would make this exercise very much beside the point; in fact, the whole thing could come crashing down like a house of cards. Now we needed someone with experience.

Ed, our road and septic system builder, was still working at our barn construction site on and off, digging trenches for the electrical service wires and the water line from the well, so I asked if he knew of anyone. "Yeah, I might know a guy," he said. "I'll let him know you're looking for somebody."

Later that afternoon, a battered white Toyota pickup labored up the drive, and when it stopped, a wiry figure with a dirty blond ponytail emerged from the driver's side, followed almost instantly by two big dogs. As the man walked toward me, I recognized him as one of the helpers from the day Ed's entire crew had muscled a huge concrete septic tank into the hole he'd dug for it. I remembered that the dogs were at his side then, too. At a quick gesture of his hands, the dogs stood instantly still and waited a respectful distance away as he approached our work area.

"Hey," he said. "Heard you were looking for some help?"

Lee was a framer by trade and was available to help most afternoons by 2:30, when he got off working for Ed. In our first few minutes of conversation, I was impressed by the precision of his speech and the exemplary behavior of his dogs, and we started working together then and there.

I was to learn much more about Lee in the months to come. His father had been a science teacher in the local high school and, with his mother, taught their children not only to speak well but also to love observing and collecting all sorts of animals. During the time I knew him, Lee had three dogs, four cats, one ferret, and a snake or two. But when he was a child, he said, it was not unusual to walk into his house and find a hog snake in the bathtub and a boa constrictor under the couch. In summers, his family traveled to the rural South, financing their extended vacations by selling the snakes and reptiles they collected along the way.

"Nobody thought anything about it at the time," he said. "We just went into the swamp with bags and filled 'em up with snakes." He could identify a Jefferson's salamander at a glance and tell the species of a hawk from half a mile.

But to look at him, you'd never know that Lee was such an experienced, if untrained, zoologist. His long ponytail was held in place with a bandanna and a rubber band, and some missing teeth gave his speech a slightly sibilant quality. He was the smallest and slightest of the three of us, but his hands told a different story: enlarged by years of wrestling with wood and hammers, they were outsized for his body and would have looked in better proportion on a more bearlike man. Lee's uniform was a sleeveless T-shirt, a gray hooded sweatshirt, and ripped jeans with basketball sneakers. His dogs went with him everywhere and responded instantly to his commands (he claimed they could count to five). Although they roughhoused and barked at the sounds of animals in the woods, they rarely behaved badly, and I never saw him raise a hand to them except in play. And I soon saw that it might take a few hours to get as many words out of him. For as much as Andy and I enjoyed yakking, Lee enjoyed quiet. That was one of the things I had to get used to.

Another was the economy of Lee's speech, when he did speak. I'm still not sure if it was New England carpenter talk or his own idiom, but I learned a host of new names for things I thought I already knew. A length of electrical cord with a plug on one end and one or more sockets on the other could be only a *lead*—don't say "extension cord." Any piece of dimension lumber that formed any part of a house's frame—a two-by-four stud, a two-by-twelve header, whatever—was a *board*. Unless it was *ply*. Those were the only two things wood could be, with *trim* a distinct subcategory. Wood that had been treated with a chemical substance to retard rotting was simply *greenwood;* why bother mouthing the syllables "pressure-treated yellow pine"? *Roofers* were nails, which were kept in the *pouch* (i.e., tool belt). *Some* was his most common adjective, as in "that concrete septic tank is some heavy." "Got it" was his most common reply.

Although he rarely spoke about himself, Lee occasionally became eloquent on the subject of framing. He was a gentle and excellent teacher, explaining things in a deliberate way and leading by example. In contrast to Andy and myself, he saw no reason to debate how to do any particular job. There was only one way—the right way—and no theorizing was needed. If he said, "You're going to bend them roofers if you don't hold your ply down to the board while you're whalin' on 'em," we would do as we were told. And it worked. He could just as easily explain why greenwood is never used for window sashes, even though, unlike pine, it is virtually rotproof (because it twists and cracks when exposed to weather). But most of the time he preferred simply to grab a hammer and get to work. Together we eventually saw the completion of the house and several other projects.

Andy continued to come up when he could, sometimes when Lee was there as well. The two of them couldn't have been more different, and they seemed somewhat wary of each other, though never unfriendly. If at times Andy thought Lee acted like a backwoods hippie know-it-all, then Lee perhaps believed Andy was something of a wiseass know-nothing. But mostly we all got along fine. When it was time to put up the roof trusses, we even added a fourth crew member.

Captain Bill was the burly young skipper of one of Andy's tugs. He lived across the river, was looking to pick up some extra cash, and was genuinely fascinated by the process of house construction. He peppered Lee and me with questions and observations, ranging from "What's this triangle thing for?" to "Don't you think an inlaid wood-paneled desk would look *outrageous*?" He was strong as a bull and a steady worker; in two days, with Lee coming in the late afternoons, we had the trusses up and were putting plywood on the roof. When we were done, I reflected that our little crew, under normal circumstances, would probably never meet in the same room together socially, yet we'd just completed the bulk of the framing of a small house.

The most interesting thing I observed was that, without any discussion but by unanimous unspoken agreement, Lee had become the leader of our crew, while my role had shifted to that of a second carpenter and, simultaneously, client. It wasn't a position I was used to. When I ran the fence company, my role on job sites was strictly supervisory: I mediated between the contract specifications, the customer's desires, and the crew chief's practicalities, but to have lifted a tool would have been quite out of character, and no one would have been comfortable with it. While I knew in theory how everything was done, I rarely got to put that knowledge into practice. Now I had calluses on my hands from holding the hammer, and for the past few months I'd been the sole authority (and often the solo laborer) on this project.

I was experiencing trade labor from the inside of the tool belt, something I hadn't done since I spent some college summers as a construction helper, and never in a position where any particular skills were demanded. And now my boss was none other than Lee, whose wages I paid each Friday. It was a unique dual perspective. But, after one peculiar incident, I knew that I was reconciled to my place in the crew.

Lee, in an unusually talkative mood, decided to give Andy and me a safety lesson. The trusses were all in place above us, but we had just begun attaching the plywood skin to the outside of the triangles; this meant that while the lower edges of the roof near the sides of the barn were covered with ply, the middle, where the roof was highest, was a Tinkertoy web of wood beams open to the sky. It was near the end of the day, and the light was quickly fading. Lee jumped up from the plywood floor deck, grabbed the bottom of a truss, and swung himself up, ape-style, into the scaffoldlike wooden framework in the attic of the barn. Using the truss members as handholds and braces, he shimmied and scrambled to the top of the structure, quickly gaining twelve feet in altitude above the deck. Then, legs straddling a bare truss at the apex of the roof, he leaned down to speak to us on the floor deck far below.

"Safety is the main thing up here," he said. "The boards will bear your weight, but once the ply goes up there isn't much to grab onto, and you can slide off the roof real easy. Many a framer's been saved from a bad fall by swinging the claw of his hammer and catching some ply. She'll go right through this five-eighths plywood if you swing hard enough, and you can hold on until you get help. But it's some high, and . . ."

With those words, he seemed to begin executing a complicated aerial ballet, which somehow took a decidedly wrong turn. He was trying to swing from atop the two-by-four framework at the peak of his truss to the plywood that covered the lower portion of the roof. But almost as soon as he let go of the truss, it became clear that he wouldn't be able to grab the piece of roof he was aiming for. The trusses were spaced two feet apart, a lacework of boards in a narrow vertical plane, with nothing but air in between. Unfortunately, that was exactly where he ended up. He managed to swing his hammer, but instead of "catching ply" it caromed off the end wall, and down he came, arms and legs outstretched. The booming noise of his hammer's impact with the plywood-skinned wall was followed by the sound of Lee's shirt tearing as a nail, partially exposed on some truss member, caught his arm, ripping the flesh underneath. He landed in a heap on the deck in front of us, followed by his hammer, which had dangled for a moment on the truss; a drop or two of blood from the nail above made a dark spot on the new plywood deck near where he lay.

Andy and I looked at each other, speechless, although on one level we were both desperately trying to hold in the laughter. Had he really fallen in the midst of an impromptu lecture on safe work habits? On another level was sincere concern for his well-being. Was the cut severe? Had he broken any bones? And if so, would he sue me? A third level involved a bit of sadistic delight at our self-assured leader's noisy downfall, mixed with some delicious guilt about those very feelings.

"Are you okay?" someone finally asked. Lee picked himself up, wrapped the tatters of his shirt around his bleeding arm, and muttered, "See. I told you. Dangerous." He seemed fine, though not in a joking mood. But, forever after, Andy and I referred to him as Roof God—behind his back, of course.

If Lee was grouchy, Andy would remind me, in hushed tones of mock appreciation, "Roof God bled for you."

If Lee insisted on doing a piece of tricky work himself while Andy stood and watched, I'd solemnly whisper, "He is indeed a jealous God."

If Lee didn't show up on time, someone was bound to say, "Who can know His ways?"

He was our leader, and we were his crew.

And so it went. October became November, and the weather turned abruptly from nippy to bone-chilling. We made fires of scrap wood in a metal garbage can in the morning and stood around them with our hands outstretched, while our breath billowed in white clouds and froze on our scarves. For several days we worked with a dusting of snow on the ground, while more big flakes gently fell from the lead gray skies. Then came a day when Andy and I watched the headlights of Lee's truck as he struggled to drive up the snow-covered hill. He tried three times, carefully backing down before revving up to speed and going for the steep part again, only to spin out before the top. He never made it; we watched him turn around and head back the way he came. I knew it wouldn't be long before we'd have to stop working for the winter.

Then a big snow dumping came in early December. We were so close to being done. Just one little corner of the roof to go—a tricky junction between a window dormer, a truss, and the fly rafter that extended past the gable end wall. When I arrived at the property that day, I had intended to brush the snow off the roof with a broom and start on the ply myself. But soon I knew it wasn't going to happen. After parking my car in a snowbank on the side of the town road, I attempted to walk up the driveway. The snow drifts were more than knee-deep; in spots they were up to my waist. It was almost impossible to move uphill against them. I soon realized it was futile. Finishing the roof would have to wait till spring. Lee had said we'd get away with some snow on the plywood deck, so I tried not to be overly worried. I turned back to the car and headed for home. It would be months before I'd see my emerging country homestead again. But one large consolation was that I would once more be able to live in the same county as my wife.

# farm in a box

KIM: My editor took his time selecting my replacement, so it wasn't until February 1996 that I left the editorial board. By then I had done such a good job of convincing the *Daily News* management that I didn't really want to work in Albany, they decided to throw in a free apartment for me to live in. It was located in a neighborhood one colleague overoptimistically described as "the Greenwich Village of Albany."

When Chris and I pulled up our rental truck loaded with some cast-off furniture to said locale one cold and snowy mid-February morning, we found a somewhat seedy section of two- and three-story row houses with a few restaurants and bars mostly frequented by college students.

Our house was a three-story wood-frame building of no discernible style with mousy gray-blue clapboard siding stippled with rusty nail heads. The extrasteep front stoop, buried in eight inches of snow, resembled a small ski jump. We couldn't help noticing, as we swept the snow off the stairs, that as the reputed Greenwich Village of Albany the neighborhood was missing one key ingredient: people. If this was such a happening place, where was everybody? Then again, the Greenwich Village of New York City never got quite this cold.

We went inside the building to have a look around. This would be our home for at least six months, until our farmhouse was finished. We climbed a staircase in a narrow interior hall-way to a good-size living room and kitchen, then up more stairs to an attic-style bedroom.

"Hmmm, yes, this will be perfect," Chris said as he whipped his ubiquitous measuring tape around the room.

"Perfect for what?" I asked.

"The flats—you know, plant trays. It's almost time to start the seeds."

"What are you talking about?" I asked. "I thought you were going to do that at the farm."

"I can't do it at the farm," he said. "We don't have any heat there yet. They have to be kept at seventy degrees at least. Besides, this space is unusable for anything else," he said, waving his measuring tape under the slanted ceiling along the longest wall.

"Just wait a minute," I said. "What exactly do you think you're going to do?"

"What I am going to do," he said, "is build some racks for the flats right here and put in some light fixtures and, when the seedlings look ready, we'll plant them outdoors."

"How many flats?" I asked.

"About eighty-five," he said.

"*Oh, no you're not!*" I yelled. "You're going to destroy this place! What are you trying to do, get me fired? The landlord is my editor's pal, remember? This is completely nuts. People don't start farms in their bedrooms."

"Why are you always so worried about everything?" Chris said. "You're not going to get fired. They'll never know it's here. When we're done, I'll remove every trace. Besides, we have no choice. If we want a farm this year, the plants have to be started right here, right now. There's nowhere else."

Since I couldn't picture exactly what he had in mind, I wasn't quick enough to stop him. I was much more focused on starting a new job and didn't want to think about anything else right then.

"Just promise me this won't be a disaster," I said.

"Don't worry, it won't be," he assured me.

It was obvious to me as soon as I saw the attic bedroom in the Albany apartment that it was the perfect place to start a small farm; in fact, it was another harmonic convergence of sorts. The room was a converted cockloft—the ceiling was about twelve feet high in the middle, tapering down rapidly to a height of only three feet at the front and back walls of the building. Three awning-type windows about one foot high by three feet wide in front and two openable skylights in the rear allowed a trickle of light into the room but provided nothing to look at. The room had a hastily finished appearance, with its drywall not completely smooth and cheap clamshell moldings just tacked onto the walls. Exposed roof beams—not the decorative type—near the high point of the ceiling and pea green high-pile carpeting complemented the overall ambience of the room: it was 1970s colonial garret.

This bedroom would be hell to live in. True, it was big—the whole top floor of the house, in fact. But, although you could walk around the middle of the room, you wouldn't be able to get closer than about five feet from the front or back walls without hitting your head. There would be no views at all—even to crank open a window you'd have to crawl on hands and knees. And it would be warm all the time, being the top floor of the house. This space was useless for just about anything.

Except for one thing.

Young plants aren't tall. They like warmth. They don't need to look at anything. And you can grow lots of them in a modest space.

Eureka!

Suddenly the room's vices became virtues: Those exposed ceiling beams would be great for hanging the banks of lights I'd need to make up for the lack of light inside — and, to be fair, few spaces inside normal houses provide enough light for growing plants from seed. The slapdash construction would no doubt hide a multitude of sins: if, for example, I needed to put up a beam or two of my own. I certainly wouldn't need extra heat to start the plants — they'd do just fine at seventy degrees, which might be the minimum temp up here. And what would be better for hiding the occasional water stain or crushed seedling than green shag carpeting? So, it was settled: I'd take this wasted space and make it bloom . . . if only I could convince my wife of the wisdom of this plan.

I considered possible avenues of approach. We both loved greenhouses. In fact, one of our favorite things to do in our city neighborhood, especially on a blustery late-winter day, was to walk across the park to the Brooklyn Botanic Garden and visit the beautiful conservatories. In the space of a few steps, we'd be transported to a tropical climate: hot, moist air condensing on the inside of the glass blocked the view of barren trees outside, while inside we'd walk the paths past fifteen-foot-high specimen banana trees climbing toward the glass roof, myriad palms and ferns spreading their frilly green fronds, oranges and breadfruit in dense stands, airdwelling bromeliads and climbing vines clinging to the trunks of their larger cousins. The air was perfumed with the musky fragrance of orchids, gardenias, and other exotic blossoms, and the sound of trickling water from a stream that ran through the exhibit added up to a sensual delight. What would it be like to have this as your bedroom?

I couldn't believe that Kim didn't see it this way at first. Of course, we wouldn't have orchids, or bananas. Or oranges, or palms, or ferns. The plan was to start with tomatoes and peppers (which, by the way, have a fine smell). I know she thought I was bound to destroy the bedroom by constructing a growing space with all of the lights, fans, benches, and miscellaneous equipment required. But I knew this was the best way to go about things, because I'd spent quite a bit of time that fall and winter learning everything I could about plants.

❖

I did not doubt that Chris had carefully researched seed starting and all the various needs of nascent flora. I just couldn't get past the fact that he wanted us to sleep with so many plants. And I was terrified that this would somehow get out of hand. How could he create an indoor vegetable patch without tracking potting soil all over the house? And how would he water it—was he going to bring a garden hose into the bedroom that would soak the carpet? I had nightmare visions of getting sent back to New York in disgrace over a landlord-tenant dispute in which no one in his or her right mind would take my side. I did not want to endure another long separation when Chris went back to working on the house in the spring, especially while making such a major job change. Right now, I needed all the moral support I could get.

Yet, in spite of my apprehension, I knew that if anyone could tuck a farm away in a bedroom, it was my husband. He had already proved himself a master at building in small spaces. In our compact Brooklyn house, for example, he had turned a tiny vestibule between two fourth-floor bedrooms into a full-fledged laundromat—complete with washer, dryer, laundry sink, and ceiling-suspended clothes-drying rack.

The first thing I ever saw Chris build was a piece of furniture for the tiny apartment in which I was living before I moved in with him. I had been complaining that my Barbie-size kitchen had no countertops and therefore no surface on which to prepare food. Chris decided to build a table to fit between my refrigerator and stove, a distance of only about two feet. We went to a local lumberyard and purchased some plywood, a few boards of various sizes, and a tiny can of maple-hued stain. Then Chris set to work. My landlady was so impressed with the result that she begged me not to take that little table with me when I moved. Apparently, her new tenant had admired it when checking out the place and was mistakenly told it came with the apartment.

Now I couldn't very well imagine my current landlord saying, upon our departure, "My new tenant simply must have those eighty-five trays of plants!" In fact, I thought if he ever happened to visit the place and saw that my husband was sharecropping the bedroom, he would flip out. My only hope was that the landlord would never know something so out of the ordinary had occurred in that house and would therefore have nothing to report to his old buddy, my boss.

Chris understood this was my one nonnegotiable condition for going ahead with the scheme and promised once again that he would leave things immaculate.

One could hardly ask for a better guide than Dan to lead a novice like me down the garden path. Having been trained as a landscape architect and specializing in park design (not to mention his experience in farming), he was an invaluable resource. Dan seemed to know absolutely everything about plants: which ones to grow, how to start them, and how to make them flourish. One day in early fall I drove him to Wave Hill, a lovely old mansion in the Bronx well known for its extensive gardens, where he showed me some varieties of plants he liked. We saw masses of tall, fragrant *Cleome*, commonly called spider flower for its spindly, multiflowered pastel blooms, and beds of spiky salvia, or flowering sage, erupting in red and blue flames. Rows of yellow coreopsis formed a blanket of brilliant color, while purple globe thistles stuck up like buoys in the floral sea. There was a greenhouse too, a basic cinder-block structure with a fiberglass-glazed roof, where they started their seedlings. It looked simple enough, and the results were certainly impressive.

We also spent a few afternoons in Dan's office—a small room in a low-rise concrete commercial building off lower Broadway in Manhattan, cluttered with scrolls of plans and drawings, samples of brick pavers and ornamental stonework salvaged from old buildings—drinking tea and talking about plants. His favorite plants seemed to be flowers, and in fact, the more we talked, the clearer it became that flowers were a predominant part of the kind of farming operation he was envisioning. It wasn't that we wished to slight vegetables, but it just seemed that Dan had more things to say about flowers. The information he had at his fingertips was almost overwhelming; he rattled off the genus and species of a dozen flowers in a breath, told me about climate zones and cultivars, cultural methods and cuttings. Pausing occasionally to flip through a thick reference book, he'd come up with an arcane fact about a well-known plant, then continue on about how great it was going to be to grow flowers.

"You've got to have cosmos and zinnias," he said. "Everybody loves them and they're so easy to grow. Sunflowers are very popular, and marigolds, yarrow, statice, and artemisia too. Those last ones you can sell fresh or dry, along with big cockscomb and *Gomphrena.* You'll definitely want to gather *Eupatorium,* and goldenrod, shining sumac, *Boltonia,* and asters. But don't overlook the things that bloom early and late in the season—you always need to have some color on your table at market. Vegetables are good for that too."

He told me his theory about "market crescendos"—plants or vegetables that would be in peak condition and high demand at certain times of the year, which, if timed properly, would make you a pile of money at market.

"Butternut squash!" he said excitedly. "Everybody wants it in the fall. Grow an acre of it, pile it on the deck of a boat, float it down the river! Just think what that would look like, docking on the West Side at six A.M. Undercut everybody, sell it cheap! You'll sell lots of flowers with it!" But no sooner would he mention a plant that I actually knew than the conversation would move abruptly beyond the paltry reaches of my floral acumen.

"The best thing for that would be *Fallopia japonica*—is that still the name of it? It's something like a *Polygonum,* you know? I don't see it here under that name in the book . . . but I know it only grows to Zone 6. Same with *Ilex,* the hollies—great for the late fall . . . too bad you didn't get closer to the river, but maybe you could find some cultivar that would take the cold, if you covered it . . ."

My head was spinning.

"Dan," I said. "I . . . I'm just . . . Could you maybe make me a list of the plants I should grow this year?" I asked sheepishly.

"Sure." He laughed.

And he did. All of the plants he'd mentioned were on it, along with a couple dozen more flowers, about twenty varieties of herbs, and some specialty vegetables, shrubs, and wild plants for collecting in fields and along roadsides. It was an impressive collection of plant material. I planned to grow them all. And I still knew next to nothing about most of them.

So I spent the midwinter months trying to learn about them. I drew pen-and-ink sketches in a notebook so I could associate the names with the plants. As usual, I read whatever books on plant propagation I could get my hands on. I pored over seed catalogs, trying to figure how many seeds of each I'd need to get a row growing. I knew from measurements taken in the field last fall how much land I could expect to start working with, and therefore I could tell how long the rows of crops would be. Using the expected germination rates of the various plants and the number of seeds per ounce, I could calculate the quantities of each I would need, allowing for thinning, et cetera. I turned the list into seed orders from three different companies and wrote the checks, totaling more than six hundred dollars. It seemed like a lot of money, but then I hoped to make a fat profit from all of the market crescendos. And I watched the mail every day, waiting for my farm to arrive.

By now it was early March, although in Albany the spring still seemed far away. But I couldn't wait. In addition to Dan's recommendations, I had done a bit of catalog shopping on my own: I'd decided to go in heavily for both exotic and heirloom tomatoes and peppers. These are varieties of vegetables that are not widely grown but are believed to be better than the commonly available types. Heirloom vegetables, in fact, are old-fashioned varieties that have never been hybridized, while exotics may come from places as far away as Thailand or Siberia.

If you believed the catalogs, my selections were going to be the tastiest things you'd ever eaten: Brandywine tomatoes, softball-size purplish globes dripping with juice that made anything else seem to taste like mushy paste; Striped German, a handsome fruit striated with yellow and red inside that would please the eye and palate equally. Sungold, the sweetest cherry tomato you'd find. And peppers: Sweet Chocolate, a dark violet ovoid with a taste of—you guessed it; Corona, Orobelle, and Lipstick, whose colors ranged from yellow through orange to bright red; Ortega, Serrano, and Paper Dragon chile peppers, whose fire ranged similarly from blazing to volcanic. I could almost taste them.

But now the seeds, due to arrive any day, would need a winter home.

I knew that at least the tomatoes and peppers would have to be started indoors. In my part of the Northeast, the growing season—the time of year when temperatures are moderate, the sun is high, the soil is warm, and there is no danger of a sudden frost—runs from about mid-May to mid-September. But for these plants, native to the tropics, that's just not enough time to germinate from seed, grow out of the ground, mature, flower, and bear fruit. So we have to help them—raise them from seed indoors, under lights and with constant temperature, until they're about six inches tall. Then we put them outside as soon as we dare, and nature takes over to complete the process, resulting in a good crop of fruit before the first frost ends the cycle for these tender annuals. I'd had pretty good luck starting seeds in the Brooklyn darkroom, getting my first batch of gazpacho ingredients by late August. Now that I had a good space for growing, I was ready to get started with the seedbeds.

I decided that I'd build benches out of plywood—a material I'd had lots of experience with just lately. Four benches would almost fill up the back side of the room. The four-by-eight-foot sheets would be held flat on simple two-by-four frames, keeping them about a foot off the floor. These frames would be strong, light, and easy to remove when the time came. There would also have to be grow lights—otherwise, the young plants, seeking the feeble glow from the skylights, would quickly become tall and spindly, eventually turning yellow and falling over of their own weight. A bright light would keep them short and bushy and dark green, with thick stems and big leaves, the perfect state for turning them loose in the fields. That's what all the books said.

The best lights are fluorescents. Special types are made just for growing plants that emit light of certain wavelengths, but ordinary cool-white bulbs are said to be almost as good. The cheapest way I found to buy them was as shop lights, complete with bulbs, sockets, transformer, and housing; I then proceeded to take them apart, throwing away the metal carcasses to get at the workings inside. I salvaged the ballasts, sockets, and wiring, then strung four two-light units together on a wood frame to make an eight-tube light panel that was about the same size as the growing bench. I made four of these, one for each bench.

These would need to hang from the ceiling yet come as close to the plants as possible for maximum light. As the plants grew, the lights would have to be moved higher. I came up with a system of chains to hold the end of each panel nearest the wall, which could be moved up link by link as the plants got taller. A two-by-four board attached to the rafters in the low part of the ceiling provided all the support needed to hang the chains from. For the ends of the panels nearest the center of the room, where the ceiling was highest, a rope attached to the lighting unit, running up over a pulley bolted to the exposed ceiling beam, would enable me to raise the lights as high as I wanted—I could even pick the lights all the way up, sit on the bed, and watch the plants grow. Strips of aluminum foil taped to the wood frames behind the fluorescent tubes would be my reflectors, shining light back on the plants and giving the tubes the electrical ground they'd need to work properly out of their metal cases.

I set the light banks up to run off four timers. They'd come on at, say, 8:00 A.M. and run until 8:00 P.M., shutting off automatically. I could also override them manually if necessary. Finally, a set of four small fans salvaged from some old electrical equipment supplied a steady current of air across the benches. These were important, everyone said, to prevent molds and fungi from settling on the seedlings, leading to the dreaded plant disease known as damping-off, which is invariably fatal to young plants.

Now I was all set, and I sat back to watch the system run. The fluorescents buzzed and flickered a bit on starting but soon settled into a steady hum, as the fans quietly stirred the air until the clicks of the timers shut it all down. It seemed to be working perfectly. How hard could plant growing be? By this time, of course, I was pretty well versed in basic construction methods, so nothing I'd done was particularly difficult or unfamiliar. In fact, it was quite a bit simpler and less frustrating than building the new house—to which I was still prevented from returning by the frigid, wet early spring weather. Still, I felt quite happy that the dilapidated Albany apartment would provide such a good growing area for the seedlings, and I was all set to get started.

One day in mid-March I came home to find a package at the door. It was the farm. About the size of a shoe box, or maybe a boot box,

it was sitting on the top step of the steep flight of outside stairs leading to the front door of our apartment. It was much smaller than I
expected—after all, this box was supposed to contain practically
everything I'd need to plant about three acres of intensively spaced
crops. And it had cost me about six hundred dollars—was this all I
was going to get? I looked up and down the street, perhaps to check
whether any covetous would-be farmers were eyeing the box (don't
they steal seed packets in rough neighborhoods?), then grabbed it
and ran upstairs. Opening it immediately, I found that it did in fact
contain almost everything I'd sent for. A few vegetables were on
back order, and some live mint plants were being sent separately.
The few packets of seeds I'd ordered from the other companies had
already arrived in Tyvek envelopes, so this was just about it.

There they were: packets of Pac-Man broccoli, Fortex pole
beans, and King Richard leeks. Nine varieties of peppers and eight
of tomatoes, plus one tomatillo. Anise hyssop and summer savory,
herbs I had no idea what to do with. Are they for cooking, eating
raw, or making tea? And lots and lots of flowers with wonderful,
romantic, and silly names. I'd memorized these names, Latin genus
and species as well as common, last winter—sometimes without
ever having seen the plants—but here was concrete evidence that
they really existed.

Perhaps it doesn't matter what you call flowers, but it seems to
me that you have to love some varieties just for their names. There
in the box was *Celosia cristata*, the cockscomb. There was
*Centaurea cyanus*, the bachelor's button, and *Nigella damascena*,
also called love-in-a-mist. The wonderful *Amaranthus caudatus*,
known to many as love-lies-bleeding, and its cousin *Amaranthus
hypochondriacus*, known to some as Pygmy Torch. Was there a
theme here?

I had *Gaillardia*, the blanketflower, *Helichrysum*, the straw-
flower, and *Helianthus*, the sunflower. Plus *Ammi majus*, the bishop's

weed, *Coreopsis,* the tickseed, *Asclepias,* the butterfly weed. Also *Zinnia* the zinnia and *Cosmos* the cosmos. And there were about twenty more.

I opened a few packets to look: some of the seeds were as big as — well, sunflower seeds. Others were smaller than punctuation marks. Some, such as cilantro and dill, had an incredibly pleasing smell, like the most freshly ground spices you could imagine. Most had no smell at all. They all rattled around in the packets when you shook them like sand in your shoe.

There was one more thing, though, that I had to do immediately: find something to grow them in.

I knew that the plants you buy at the hardware store come in cell paks, thin plastic extrusions like tiny egg cartons, holding six or eight seedlings, with their root balls and some growing medium. I knew that a bunch of cell paks are carried on a plastic tray with two-inch-high sides and a mesh bottom called a flat. And when you buy the grow-your-own kit, you get a flat, maybe eight cell paks, and a tiny bag of soil mix, for about ten bucks. And I figured I'd need, oh, about eighty-five of them. I knew farmers were getting into debt a lot, but it wasn't my idea to start that just yet.

So I went to garden centers, looking to buy in bulk. "I'm starting lots of plants — about three thousand," I'd say nonchalantly. "What can you do for me on these seedling kits and two-quart bags of peat moss?" I was met by blank stares, mostly, and mumbles about "checking in the back," until a kind soul took pity on me.

"What're ya doing — starting a farm?" he asked.

"Uhh . . ."

"Well, don't tell the boss I told ya," he confided, "but what you wanna do is go to Griffin Greenhouse — they're out by the airport, look 'em up in the yellow pages. That's where we get all this stuff from. They got what ya want."

I thanked him and raced to the nearest phone book. The next day I followed a maze of back roads to an industrial park well within teeth-clenching range of jet takeoffs, and came to a metal-skinned warehouse with a tiny office up front: the promised greenhouse supplier. I was driving my old pickup, wearing a baseball hat, and feeling thoroughly agricultural as I strode through the glass door and up to the counter, and boldly stated, "I want to buy some *cell paks.*"

"What's the stock number?" the clerk mumbled.

"Uhh, I don't know," I replied.

"What size?" he continued.

"Well, what do most people get?"

He looked up at me for the first time, with a tepid sort of amazement.

"We have thirty-seven sizes," he said.

"Oh," I said. There was a moment of silence.

Deciding to try again, he asked in slow, precise tones, "Well, what are you planning to grow?"

I knew the answer to this. "Tomatoes and peppers!" I announced.

"How many times are you gonna transplant 'em before you put 'em out?"

"Before I put them out—in the field? Well, I wasn't planning to transplant them at all until I put them in the field. That's what I'll do. . . . Isn't that okay?" I asked desperately.

"Sure," he said. "You'll just have to get big ones."

"Okay. Big ones then."

"Look," he said, "do you get our catalog?"

I confessed I did not.

"Okay, well, the first thing we're gonna do is get you on our mailing list. You'll get the new one in a few weeks, and you'll find all of the sizes and everything listed in there. What'd you say the name was?" he asked.

"Silverpetals Farm," I announced proudly. This was the name Kim and I had come up with a few nights ago. The land was within the boundaries of a former hamlet that still shows up on some road maps as Silvernails, but any actual town had long since gone the way of the mastodon. We wanted to suggest a relationship with the specific place, but Silvernails Farm was taken already. We also wanted to say something about flowers in the name of the farm. And there was a silvery-leaved artemisia we both liked a lot and were planning to grow. Also, I knew we were going to make lots of money. Maybe not gold-type money, but at least silver. I wanted the name to suggest that, too. I thought it was a great combination of all three ideas.

"Uh huh," said the clerk. "Address?"

I don't know whether he thought it strange that I gave him an address in the heart of downtown Albany or not, but it didn't seem to matter. We spent the next hour or so talking about soil mixes, pak sizes, time-release fertilizers of different compositions, and various other minutiae of seed starting. It was a crash course in plant propagation, and it was immensely helpful; after all of the theory and the abstraction, here was the actual mechanics of the thing, in concrete terms. This was the real deal. Finally, we were down to what grade of flat I should get.

"You want the good ones or the cheap shit?" he asked.

"Gimme the cheap shit," I replied.

"All right!" he said. "Then, that's it?"

I thought about it for a while. I had purchased two huge boxes of extralarge cell paks, holding thirty-six plants to a flat; a carton of the flats themselves; four five-cubic-foot bags of preformulated soilless mix including slow-release fertilizer; some plastic liners, tags, and a few odds and ends. What else could there be?

"Is there anything else you'd recommend that I might need to, you know, get started?" I asked.

He paused for a moment.

"Yeah . . . a hose."

Seeing that I was thinking hard, he went on: "Every farm needs a hose. Just think of all the things you do with a hose! This one here is the best hose you can get. It's guaranteed for life, no matter what. If you run over it with your tractor, you can bring it back and we'll replace it for free! You can drive over it full of water on a gravel driveway and if it breaks you'll get a new one, for free! But we don't get many back, 'cause it's a really *good* hose."

I thought about it some more. It all made perfect sense. "I'll take it!" I said.

And driving home with my booty in the back, ready at last to start the seeds and my new life as a man of the land, I couldn't help thinking, This is great. I'll grow tons of stuff and sell it all. I'm gonna be rich!

# gardening at night

KIM: As all-consuming as my new job as a reporter was, I never forgot about the farm. There was no way I could. I woke up with it every morning. It is no exaggeration to say that, by early April, there was a field of vegetables growing in my Albany bedroom.

Sure, the room Chris and I slept in had all the usual things one associates with a bedroom: a futon bed about a foot higher than the carpeted floor; two matching dressers with lamps on them; a clothes closet with accordion doors. But it also had more than three thousand tomato and pepper plants invading like a vast, green infantry.

Row upon row of small stems topped with triangular leaves saluted from shallow plastic trays that filled four large platform beds across from our own. Above each platform hung a bank of long fluorescent tubes that buzzed and glowed with white-purple light. Small, round metal fans whirred and swung on thin chains screwed into an exposed roof beam that jutted from the atticlike room's slanted ceiling. The temperature was usually about ninety. The humidity was almost 100 percent.

It began one March day when I came home from the state capitol and saw that Chris was in the kitchen stirring a thirty-gallon trash can filled with dark brown muck with a big stick.

"What in the world is that?" I asked.

"We're planting today," Chris announced. "This is the dirt we're using. Actually, it's soilless mix."

"Do we have to do this now?" I asked wearily, not wanting to hear the obvious answer.

"Yes," he said.

"I'll have to change," I said. "You know, I'm really tired."

"You'll love it," he said. "It's like making mud pies."

Great. I dragged myself upstairs, put on some jeans, and gazed ruefully at the empty wooden platforms Chris had built in our bedroom to hold his trays of plants.

I didn't feel I had the energy for whatever midnight project my husband was stirring up. My job was using up everything I had. Not that I was exactly setting the world on fire with my reporting. In fact, I wasn't getting many stories into the paper at all.

As huge and complicated as the state government of New York is, my primary duty as statehouse correspondent for the New York *Daily News* was simple: to make sure I was always with the governor when he made any public appearance and to tape-record everything he said. Because George Pataki was the most powerful official in New York—not to mention the state's first Republican governor in twenty years—the slightest peep from him might signal a new policy that could affect the lives of millions. We couldn't afford to miss a word.

At first I thought keeping such close tabs on the head of the state would be very exciting. And my first stint covering Pataki a few weeks earlier had indeed been engrossing. Or at least very gross.

I followed the governor to a correction officers' convention at a hotel a few blocks from the capitol. When I got there I saw him standing on a dais in front of the room. He had just started speaking. He thanked the assembled crowd of more than a hundred officers for the great job they were doing and discussed the recently approved labor contract. He was answered periodically by polite applause. It sounded like boilerplate stuff, but I took notes just to be sure.

Then he turned to a familiar campaign theme—that the rights of criminals should not be held in higher regard than the rights of others.

"The same rule that applies on our streets must apply in our prisons," Pataki said. "Correction officers have rights too. Principal among those rights is the right to be free from some-one else's bodily fluids!"

Huh?

Freedom from someone else's bodily fluids. I had never given this much thought. But sure, now that he mentioned it, who wouldn't want this particular kind of freedom? But was Pataki saying the Founding Fathers had actually anticipated the threat bodily fluids pose to individual liberty and taken appropriate measures? Or was this his own between-the-lines reading of the Constitution? And which fluids were we talking about exactly? I didn't have much time to ponder these questions, because as soon as the words "bodily fluids" left Pataki's lips, the officers jumped to their feet and started cheering wildly.

"Inmates, I am told, call it defecation education," Pataki continued. "I call it a felony, and one that should be punished by consecutive time." The rousing applause continued.

Oh. So there was the pronouncement of the day: He wanted to outlaw the hurling of turds by prison inmates. This was not the kind of profound policy initiative I was expecting.

"Last year, bodily fluids were thrown at correction officers on an astonishing 218 occasions," Pataki went on.

Wow. Here I had thought prisons were such orderly places, but dung was being flung on a regular basis. Who knew?

"I am confident that if the target of those assaults were legislators, a felony statute would have been enacted long ago in this state," Pataki exclaimed. The officers cheered as if the governor had proffered an ingenious new lobbying technique they were all too eager to try.

I stifled a laugh at the thought of a few particularly pompous senators running for cover as the shit literally hit the fan, or whatever method of propulsion was selected.

When the speech was over, I raced uphill to the state capitol like a disoriented town crier to relay the news to my editor at the city desk in New York. What luck, I thought, landing such a great story my first time out. I was eager to pass on what I had learned to the *Daily News* readership. Through me, they would get a rare peek behind the brown-stained walls of our state's penitentiaries. I figured I could easily have this written up in time for the early edition's 5:00 P.M. deadline.

But, to my great disappointment, my editor wasn't interested. Apparently this wasn't the first time Pataki had launched his missive. What was news to me wasn't actually news at all.

"We did that one already," he said. "Forget it."

This was a refrain I began to hear often. Because my life in Albany soon started to resemble the movie *Groundhog Day*, in which Bill Murray, playing a TV journalist, finds he is caught in some kind of strange time warp in a small town where the exact same thing happens day after day.

Likewise, George Pataki's remarks were so scripted it wasn't unusual to see reporters mouthing the words along with him. Rather than stop campaigning for one day—even for the office he had already won—he stuck with the strategy that had gotten him elected: repetition of simple themes with a minimum of detail. The more controversial the issue, the less forthcoming he became, and the less interesting it was to listen to him. His comments had all the spontaneity of pro wrestling, with none of the entertainment. Rather than write down a nonanswer I already had in my notebook a dozen times, I often found myself staring into his hazel eyes as we reporters packed tightly around him, trying to make contact with the person I knew must be in there. He must have thought I was incredibly rude. Or maybe he just thought he really turned me on.

But Pataki was hardly the only Albany politician operating on autopilot. The practice was rampant in the state legislature, among Republicans and Democrats alike.

One of the first things I learned on my new beat was that, in New York, most of what the legislature does is a foregone conclusion. The truly significant bills that become law, including the whole state budget, are voted on only after Pataki, the Senate majority leader, and the Assembly speaker agree to pass them. More than two hundred rank-and-file legislators then vote to pass the legislation when it is called by number, often in the middle of the night and without getting any time to read it.

The so-called leaders' meetings take place behind closed doors that my colleagues and I would stand in front of for hours, days, or even weeks hoping to glean what was going on from the cryptic comments of those passing through.

A more senior reporter I worked with in Albany finally explained this undemocratic insanity to me in a way that made sense: these negotiating sessions weren't just about three powerful politicians getting what they wanted from one another; they were also about getting what they wanted from lobbyists and the special interests they represented—namely, big campaign contributions. Drawn-out, secret debates proved a great way to up the attendance at a governor's or legislator's fund-raiser. Many of these were held on negotiating days right in the capitol's underground complex, without anyone being the wiser about what was being asked for or promised, and by whom. Information was quietly traded with the people who truly mattered to these pols— those who gave campaign cash—while the larger public was kept in the dark. By the time the details emerged publicly, the deals would be done and virtually unchangeable. This also was why the governor and legislators built expiration dates into certain laws. What better way could there be to keep the landlords and HMOs, unions and business groups, anteing up year after year? It was like scheduling a shakedown in advance.

Where did all this secrecy leave us reporters? Usually languishing on the red-and-gray sandstone staircase just outside the trooper-guarded doors of the suite of offices known as Fort Pataki, reading discarded newspapers, eating junk food from a nearby vending machine, and pondering the futility of our existence.

As maddening as their secretive behavior was, and as great an impact as it ultimately had on public policy, it was hard to make the case to any editor who had been around longer than three seconds that it was "news."

"We'll take a story when something *happens,*" they'd all say.

So instead of writing, I'd continue to stand in the hall, doing my best imitation of an umbrella rack.

Maybe planting seeds would be a better use of my time in Albany after all.

I came back down to the kitchen with an attitude adjustment in progress.

"Okay, here's what you do," Chris said as he sat me down at the pink Formica table we had purchased at a New Jersey junkyard and showed me several stacks of trays lined with tiny square plastic plant pots. In fact, the trays were everywhere. I figured he must have bought extra. Surely he didn't expect us to plant them all.

"I'm going to fill these flats with the soilless mix. Then you make a shallow hole in each compartment with this Popsicle stick and then put two of these seeds in each hole and lightly cover it up. Ya got that?"

"Yeah," I said. "But first, I think we need some music."

I went to the living room and put on an R.E.M. tape, starting with the song "Gardening at Night," a peppy number from the band's first EP with incomprehensible lyrics like all early R.E.M. songs have. The manic strumming of electric guitars perked me up somewhat.

"Okay, I'm ready now," I said, taking my position in the assembly line.

Chris handed me a tray, and we began. As soon as I finished my first tray, Chris handed me a new one that he had just filled with the brown muck, and I seeded that one. He kept filling and I kept seeding. I found the work totally absorbing. When four flats were done, Chris and I carried them upstairs to the plant beds. Chris had lined these wooden platforms with black plastic garbage bags so nothing would drip on the carpet.

We kept going into the wee hours. I completely forgot about the governor and the legislature, as well as the looming state budget deadline, which was about to be missed for the twelfth straight year, and the fact that I was supposed to care about it.

When we had done as much as we could stand—about fifty of the eighty-five flats he intended to plant, or approximately 3,600 seeds—we went upstairs bleary-eyed, and Chris covered the beds with large sheets of clear plastic.

"We'll leave them like this until they germinate," he said. "Then we'll take off the plastic and turn on the grow lights."

I didn't say anything. He was speaking as if piling up an acre of wet dirt in one's bedroom was perfectly normal. But, in truth, he had just turned our lives into one of his undergraduate ecology experiments. Here we were, two giant mud puppies in a barely adequate terrarium, about to embark on a symbiotic relationship (we hoped) with thousands of tiny new roommates. Would it be a success?

Chris finished planting the remaining flats the next day while

I was at work, and a few days after that we did indeed see a carpet of tiny green plants poking out of the dirt. Hooray! Chris took off the plastic and turned on the enormous bank of grow lights he had constructed to hang over each of the four beds. He also rigged up a watering system, a sprinkler-topped hose attached to the bathroom sink downstairs, with which he sprayed the plants twice a day.

As I adjusted to my new habitat, I soon found that there was one tremendous side benefit to having a bedroom farm, particularly in such a cold climate. With the constant watering and heating of the plant beds, the room became quite warm and humid. It was easy to forget I was in an icy northern city, and instead to fantasize that I was vacationing in the tropics.

The plants seemed to like it, too. In a week or so they went from tiny green specks to spindly little stalks supporting two leaves apiece. When they reached one and one half inches tall, Chris said it was time to thin them. I asked what he meant.

"We have to go into every cell of every tray and pluck out the seedlings until there is just one in each space," he said.

"What do we do with the ones we pull out?" I asked.

"Throw them out, I guess."

"But that's such a waste!"

"Yeah, but it will be more of a waste if you leave them in," he said. "There won't be enough room for them to grow, and they'll all be stunted and won't fruit. But we had to plant more than one to make sure we got at least one good plant."

I guessed he had done his homework on this.

"How do I decide which ones to pull out?" I asked.

"It doesn't much matter," Chris said. "They all look pretty healthy. Just try to leave the one you think looks the strongest."

We brought our four dining room chairs up to the bedroom and used two as seats and two as tables, which we placed directly in front of us. We each worked on one tray at a time, plucking out the extra seedlings, watering the tray, and then putting it back on the platform. I did not like this job at all. I didn't want to decide who should live and who should die.

But in a few days I saw the point. The plants were totally transformed. With the extra space and less competition for water and nutrients, they shot up and became thick and bright green and fragrant. As a notorious killer of houseplants, I couldn't believe my eyes.

Chris continued tending the crops twice daily. The morning waterings were performed naked. As soon as he woke up, Chris would hop into the plant beds with his watering device and slowly crawl through the rows as I dozed in bed. I often wondered if agriculture had ever been performed this way as I watched my husband weave through our indoor jungle like a modern-day Tarzan badly in need of a tan and a loincloth. After the watering was done, I'd get up and walk to work while Chris drove to the country to work on our house.

As bizarre as our greenhouse-boudoir was—and as worried as I was that my landlord would find out and tell my editor I was a freak—this life somehow started to feel surprisingly normal. Besides, when viewed against the more typical backroom dealings of the capitol's inhabitants, my transgression appeared truly minor. Practically every night I would watch legislators slink off to myriad fund-raisers, where they would put the touch on all the lobbyists who had been asking them throughout the day to endorse or block particular bills. And I was supposed to be embarrassed about a few thousand plants growing in my bedroom? Please.

Plus, I really had to hand it to my husband. His methods may have been unorthodox, but they produced the desired result. With so much loving care, our indoor farm was thriving.

But so were other creatures, as we found out one night while eating dinner. Chris and I were having a quiet conversation about the events of our day when all of a sudden he stopped himself in midsentence, stared past my head, and silently mouthed the words *"Oh, shit!"* I whipped my head around to try to see what he saw, and I couldn't miss it: a very large bat was flapping noiselessly in figure eights around the living room. Without further consultation, we both dove under the small dining room table.

"How the hell did a bat get in here?" I asked.

"That's no bat, that's Mothra," Chris answered, invoking Godzilla's giant winged nemesis.

"What do we do?" I asked. There was a moment of silence.

"One of us has to go into the kitchen and open the back door so it can fly out," Chris answered.

"That would be you," I said. The bat continued to fly around the room, passing over the table every few seconds.

Chris looked at me as if he was about to argue, but my expression must have told him the point was nonnegotiable. He began to crawl toward the kitchen while I continued to cower under the table. He flung open the back door and then quickly slithered back to his refuge. We waited a few minutes. The bat flew into the kitchen.

"I think it's gone," he said, climbing out of his hiding place to take a look. "Yeah, it's gone."

"But how did it get in here?" I persisted.

"Uhh . . . maybe it was the other day when I opened the bedroom skylights to let all that plant vapor out."

Great. It was probably hanging upside down in my closet à la Grandpa Munster for the last three days. I wished I hadn't known that.

"When are we going to get these plants out of here?" I asked.

"It's almost time," Chris said.

About two weeks later, in mid-May, we began dismantling the bedroom farm. The plan was to move the plants to our land and harden them off in cold frames before putting them out in the field. By now they already seemed quite hardy; they looked like they could make it on their own. And, though I had gotten used to having them around, I was not sorry to see them go. After all, a plant belongs outdoors.

Chris parked the beat-up blue pickup truck left over from his construction business in front of the house, and we carried the plant trays down two at a time. It seemed like we traveled up and down the stairs inside the apartment and outside over the stoop hundreds of times before they were all gone. My arms and legs ached till I thought I would collapse. Then we drove to the country and put them in the cold frames Chris had constructed out of cinder blocks and old storm windows.

We repeated this process over the course of four days because we had four full truckloads. It seemed impossible that all this could have fit in an average-size bedroom. On the last day, we were greeted by our stunned downstairs neighbor, whom we affectionately referred to as The Shnooper.

"What are you doing?" she inquired of my husband, whose face was peeking out from an armload of leaves.

"We are transferring our crops to our farm in Columbia County," Chris answered matter-of-factly. "Soon we will move out there and never come back. Have a nice day."

I wondered if she would tell our landlord. But even if she did, I wasn't worried—we would just say she'd gone crazy: there was no evidence to corroborate her story. True to his word, Chris had dismantled the whole works and patched up the few small holes in the wall left by the screws. A quick vacuuming of the rug and it was just an average bedroom again.

❖

By this time it seemed more than likely that we would have something to sell at the farmers' market this summer. But planning for the market had been under way since late winter. There was really only one marketplace—actually, a group of markets—that we considered. It was the same place Dan had sold his produce and flowers, and still spoke of fondly and wistfully: the Greenmarket of New York City. Admittedly, it was a long way from our farm, and there were the issues of traffic and parking and fees and a mess of logistical problems to unravel, but Greenmarket ("the market," Dan called it, as many call New York "the city") seemed the best choice for a number of reasons.

For one, familiarity. Dan had sold at the market in Brooklyn Heights for a number of years and was friendly with the managers and administrators. And nearly every local farmer I spoke to (I was making a point of finding them and chatting them up at every opportunity) was involved in the market, or knew someone who was. If you mentioned another grower's name, the response was likely to be "Oh, yeah, I know him from Greenmarket." There seemed to be a strong connection between local agriculture and the city markets.

Greenmarket has been around for a long time. In the mid-1970s an architect and city planner named Barry Benepe conceived a plan to take the farm stands he loved to visit near his weekend place in the Hudson Valley and transport them to New York City. He felt that not only would the availability of fresh food and the ambience of a genuine farmers' market add to the urban environment but to do so would also help preserve open space in the exurbs by giving farmers a viable alternative to selling their land to developers: namely, making a living from their farms. Despite a mountain of red tape and bureaucratic regulations, he persuaded the city to go along with his plan to site weekly farmers' markets on city sidewalks and lots. In 1976, the first market opened for business on Fifty-ninth Street and Second Avenue in Manhattan. By the end of that summer, two more sites were in operation, one in downtown Brooklyn and the other the now-famous Union Square Market. The markets were so successful that the program has expanded every year since then, both in numbers of farmers participating and in numbers of locations.

And most everything I heard about it was good—from the written accounts, like *Giving Good Weight* by John McPhee, to the stories people told me. "It's a great market," Dan said, "you'll see. People are just hungry for garden flowers and fresh produce because they're not so easy to get down there. And they want an experience of the country, they want to talk to you about it. Why would somebody buy wildflowers up by you when they can walk outside and pick them themselves? Anyway, that's where all the money is."

The economic argument seemed to clinch the deal. Although the fees were higher and the logistics more difficult, the promised rewards were far greater in the city. "We could make over a thousand dollars in a day," Dan said. It sounded good to me.

I called the Greenmarket offices in February and spoke to a pleasant, well-informed fellow with rapid-fire speech named Tony. It turned out that Greenmarket was presently operating at nearly twenty locations, mostly in small neighborhood squares in Brooklyn and Manhattan. The program was very selective, admitting only sellers who grow all their own produce. And the farmers' average take, I quickly ascertained, was between five hundred and a thousand dollars a day. "But some do fifteen hundred," said Tony, "or, if it's a bad day, a couple hundred. It depends on what you have, what the weather's like, the market. It varies."

I had already been told that a market assignment at Union Square was out. "I've been on the waiting list since '82," one local tomato grower told me. "I ain't heard from them since." Tony quickly and tactfully confirmed this.

"I don't know if you, as a new grower, would have the resources—the size truck, the manpower, the equipment—to really supply that market," he said. "It starts early—about six A.M.—and it runs all day, and once your vehicle is in there, you aren't getting out until it's all over. And if you run out of flowers at eleven o'clock—well, let's just say your regular customers can get pretty upset, and they don't mind telling you how they feel."

Tony suggested some up-and-coming neighborhood markets to consider, and we talked a little about strategy. Saturday is the best day to sell at market, because more people are free to shop and tend to have pocket money; a Saturday market is a must. Some weekday markets can be good too, especially if they attract lots of office workers at lunch, or if you can supply a particular thing they need. The Tuesday market by City Hall, for example, was said to be good for flowers because of the large number of civil wedding ceremonies performed in the building.

And, as far as varieties of vegetables to grow, Tony was strongly in favor of heirloom tomatoes: he suggested Brandywine, Striped German, and any of the purples, along with yellow cherry tomatoes for color and reds for flavor. He said that yellow and red peppers were big sellers, along with hot chile peppers like habaneros, and specialty vegetables like fennel. Thinking about the three thousand seedlings happily cooking away in my bedroom, which included almost all of the varieties he mentioned, I smiled like a sixth-grader who gets his homework back with a gold star on top.

He said I needed a letter from the county agricultural extension agent stating my bona fide intention to become a farmer. "Okay, I'll meet the agent so he can get you the letter," I said. "Then I send you back the completed application and that's it?"

"Yep. We'll let you know your market assignments in March or April. We try to make the assignments by product category so every market's got a good mix," he said. "Good luck."

A couple of weeks later an envelope arrived from Greenmarket. The application was six pages long, asking for everything from a map of the farm to a comment about whether, and if so how, the Greenmarket program had helped the applicant personally to make a viable living from farming. "I don't know," I wrote. "This is our first year." After pondering the list for a long time, I filled in our first, second, and third choices of location for one Saturday and one weekday market, and sent it back with a check for the deposit toward market fees, which were around fifty dollars a day.

Now there was nothing to do but wait until we were assigned our two markets—and, in the meantime, make sure we had something to sell.

Chapter 6

mulch this!

CHRIS: A good reference book will tell you that an acre is equal to 43,560 square feet. Why it should be this peculiar not-quite-round number they don't say, but it seems to have something to do with rods, chains, and furlongs. When you consider that an average house comprises about 2,500 square feet of floor space, an acre starts to sound like a pretty big number. And when you're looking at a wintry stretch of bottomland stubble that size, you might say, "The hell with this, I'm moving to Florida." But I was envisioning it colored green with rows of crops. This verdant carpet stretched in my mind's eye from stone wall to tree line, from stream to road, rolling over ditches and rocks, covering the barren earth with lux-uriant growth. The numbers didn't seem to mean much, at least not then.

I was dreaming in green that fall when I surveyed the bottom-land where the crops would go. Armed with a cheap telescope, some wood planks, and a long tape measure, I set out to get a rough idea of how much land — leaving aside wet areas, groves of trees, and other obstructions — would be available to actually grow crops. The answer: of the twenty-acre bottomland parcel, about six and a half acres were now cultivable.

It seemed, at the time, vaguely disappointing — after all, the other way to look at an acre is as a square measuring about 213 feet to a side. When you put it that way, it didn't sound so big. Ten acres seemed a more reasonable amount of land to farm. And farms in the Midwest could be upwards of a thousand acres. Regardless of that, these six acres would have to do, because that was what we had.

As the time neared when the carefully tended plants that had grown so well in Albany had to be put into the ground and left to make it on their own, my ambitious designs were coming back to haunt me. Because now, standing at the edge of my field and gazing at the faraway margins of trees, I began to realize how small the human scale truly is. An acre seemed enormous. Also, there remained several major jobs to be done with the land before a single plant could be put in the ground.

The first job was fencing. I had been warned by the county agricultural agent, among others, that the deer in this area were voracious and spiteful: they would chew your most beloved plants down to frayed stubs in the dirt—but usually not until the night before you wanted to harvest them. Twenty-four-hour guard dogs and well-timed shotgun blasts were supposed to be the only really effective remedies, but, the agent explained, some people opposed these solutions on moral grounds: the dogs, with a duty to remain near the fields at night, might not feel that they got enough human companionship, and might become anxious and depressed. And shotgun ammunition was getting more expensive too.

However, if nothing else worked, a fence might mitigate the damage. Mine was to be eight feet high along the road, with a potentially movable electrified section on the other three sides in a configuration the agricultural agent called a slant seven. While the roadside fence was a straightforward wire mesh, the slant seven was far more sophisticated: it worked via a kind of operant conditioning. For some reason of gross anatomy or the wiring of their brains, deer seem unable to perceive the depth of an obstacle and at the same time its height. The slant seven exploits their weakness via the arrangement of its seven horizontal wires.

Instead of being hung from upright poles, the thin metal strands are strung between posts that slant in toward the center of the field; the wires then form a barrier at a forty-five-degree angle to the ground. If you were outside the field, walking toward the fence, you would first bump your head on the topmost wire, at about eye level. Standing there, you could reach forward and touch the second highest strand about a foot in front of your shoulders, the third roughly two feet away from your navel, and so on down to the lowest of the seven, about six feet in front of you and just six inches off the ground.

These wires alone may confuse but won't stop a hungry deer. However, starting at the top, every other fence wire is charged with 10,000 volts of low-power alternating current. That's not enough juice to injure a deer (or human) fool enough to touch it, but it's not an invitation to stay for supper either. After a few zaps, they get the idea.

Knowing something about fencing from my previous job, I felt this was a task that could be tackled right away, so as soon as the snow melted in March, we got to work. Rather than the round metal posts that are the stock-in-trade of fences in urban areas, I decided to use the one natural resource I had in great abundance: cedar trees. They were everywhere on the hillside, growing at every angle without regard to the ground, trunks crossing, under and over and around one another, making a walk in these woods seem like a Marine Corps training ritual.

"Hate the damn things," said Lee. "Worst trees in the woods."

"They're pretty in the winter though," I demurred. "They smell okay. Sort of a shame to cut them down."

"Ain't gonna cut enough of them down, I'd say—just culling the leaners will give us plenty of posts. But just wait: after you get poked with enough branches—they got about a thousand apiece—and they drop that itchy shit that passes for needles down your back, see if you change your mind. Ought to clear this whole hillside and plant maples—when you and I are old men, they'll be tall enough so we can sit in the shade."

Lee, uncharacteristically, seemed to take the cedars' offenses personally. And after a half day I was ready to agree that they were the nastiest, scraggliest, itchiest plants on our land. But by then we had thirty-five straight, thick posts loaded in our pickups, along with some pressure-treated boards for the corners of the slant seven, and we were good to go.

"You got four-wheel drive on that Dodge?" asked Lee.

"Uh—no. Why?"

"Might be muddy down there. Better let me do the driving in the field," he said in a tone that warned it was pointless to argue. I hopped in my truck and followed behind him to the edge of the field.

We started digging, with a rented earth auger and an old pair of clamshell-type post-hole diggers, into the just-thawed soil. Out of the holes came a mixture of brown loam, bluish clay, and fine gray gravel. Then, after a foot and a half, water. The earth was soaked, and the holes soon filled to within six inches of the top with a silty brown liquid. The auger blades made sucking sounds, and the diggers just splashed mud around. But posts sunk eighteen inches deep would be enough to hold up the fence. We plopped the cedar logs into the holes, then filled them in with the clay and stomped it until it sucked our boots as we lifted our feet from the mud. The posts held fast.

When we had finished posting the section nearest the road, using up all the posts on my truck, it was time to move into the middle of the field. Lee gingerly let up on the clutch, propelling his battered Toyota across the muddy stubble. The truck's wheels began throwing up showers of mud; soon we skidded sideways and stopped moving forward. Then, as the engine raced, we started moving down, sinking into the mud with an awful slurping sound. Lee took his foot off the pedal and turned off the ignition. His voice broke the silence.

"Frickin' commie! We framed her!"

I wasn't familiar with the second part of Lee's exclamation, but it soon dawned on me what he meant: the truck was, in fact, sunk frame-deep in the muck, and my door, on the uphill side, wouldn't open far enough to let me out.

"What do we do now?" I asked. I'd read about such mud, mostly in stories about World War I, but I'd never seen it devour a truck. I wondered whether we would have to get a tow truck—or a crane—and whether Lee would be mad if his Toyota became a permanent field ornament.

"Have to dig it out. What else can we do?"

He hopped out into ankle-deep mud, and I followed.

We each grabbed a shovel from the truck bed and started digging and digging. We buried pieces of posts in front of the wheels and behind the wheels. We bounced on the truck bed and raced the engine and popped the clutch. We finally dug two sloping trenches downhill, off-loaded the remaining posts from the truck bed to try to gain an inch of ground clearance, and slowly pushed the Toyota, its wheels in the trenches, down and out of the swampy mire. Once the truck's frame was above the mud and it was rolling, Lee jumped in the cab, started up, and headed straight for the tree line nearest the stream. He drove as close to the trees and as fast as he dared, hoping that their roots would give some support to the soggy soil. I watched as he raced past the scrubby brush, across the lower part of the field, then safely back toward the town road. I walked across the wet field to meet him.

It was dark now, and we were covered in mud.

"I guess that's about all for today," I ventured.

Lee just nodded in silence. Finally, he spoke. "Good thing it wasn't your Dodge. We'd still be there."

"Right. Well, see you tomorrow."

"Yep."

The sun rose and the sun went down. The days lengthened following the vernal equinox, and increased solar energy warmed the soil, which gave up its trapped moisture and dried. One day a man from the local tractor dealership came up the road on his huge machine and plowed our stubbled field. When he drove back a few hours later, he left behind an expanse of dark brown, crumbly earth, as distinct from the rest of the landscape as a lake from a shore. Weeds and stalks were now deeply buried, and soil that was recently about eight inches underground had been turned over. It formed the surface of this rectangular pond of dirt. Nutrients from decayed organic matter and broken-down minerals were now available to the shallow roots of new plants, and the life cycles of weeds had been disrupted, their seeds turned under and possibly killed. This field was ready to be planted.

There would be forty rows. This number was nice and round and a little arbitrary. It would give me plenty of room to plant the dozen or so flowers I felt were essential, along with some standard vegetables, and enough rows left over to try out all of the exotic tomatoes and peppers I had started in Albany, plus maybe some surprises. The rows would run across the field the short way, perpendicular to the town road. Each row would then be about 170 feet long. And every last row would be covered with plastic mulch: a sheet of two-mil-thick PVC plastic, which comes in rolls four feet wide by two thousand feet long, blanketing the bare earth.

I was a convert to plastic mulch before I ever put a plant in the ground. It just sounded so right: a low-tech material that simultaneously

1. Warms the soil beneath it, helping seeds germinate and transplants root in the early season
2. Chokes out weeds without chemicals or mechanical devices, effortlessly

3.  Keeps water in the soil, preventing rows from drying out dur-
    ing rainless spells.

This was especially appealing to me because I didn't
1.  Live in a warm climate
2.  Own a tractor, or
3.  Have any means of irrigating plants.

And all this from something that looked like a giant roll of Hefty bags. The idea was simple: Roll the mulch out flat on the ground where you want to put the plants. Bury the edges in dirt, leaving a three-foot-wide swath of uncovered plastic that the wind can't lift. Poke holes in the plastic wherever you want a plant to grow, and stick the seeds or transplants in the holes. That's it. Water can't evaporate through the plastic. The sun warms it. Weeds can't grow through it. It's just like the easy-does-it first-time farmer's guide said: "Just cool it and let Mother Nature do practically all of the work for you."

Another thing I liked about plastic mulch was that it works best with the bed system of growing. Also known as the intensive planting method, this is different from the typical way many farm crops are grown: in a series of long, straight, parallel lines (furrows, or just rows) with very narrow spaces in between. When you look at a field of corn, for instance, it's hard to distinguish the individual rows because they are all so near one another—maybe just eighteen inches apart, with one corn plant for every linear foot of row. But, using the bed system, the plants are concentrated in a growing strip (bed), while the beds are separated by broad medians. Looking at a field planted this way, you can easily see the beds with plants and the medians without because they are both so wide.

For example, you might have a three-foot-wide mulched bed for zinnias with a two-foot median in between as a walkway. The growing strip would be filled with plants spaced as closely as possible, just far enough apart so the leaves would not touch one another. A field that has been newly mulched with plastic appears striped with black and brown bands: the black stripes are the plastic mulch, in which you will poke holes for seeds or transplants, and the brown stripes the dirt medians in between.

A seed catalog will tell you the minimum distance apart you should put plants in your beds. Then you can play mathematical games to figure out what geometrical arrangement lets you cram the most plants into the least space. For example, I figured I would plant the zinnias in a hexagonal pattern to keep each one fifteen inches away from its neighbors and fill up my thirty-six-inch-wide bed with lots of plants. (Tomatoes, which are bushier plants, would need more space between them, while herbs would require far less.) But no matter what the spacing, one of the main advantages of the bed system is that you can reach all of the plants from the median, which makes it possible to cultivate and harvest by hand. With row crops, you would have to either weed and pick mechanically or waste lots of space by putting the straight-line rows far enough apart that you could walk in between them.

Plus, with mulched beds, you wouldn't need to spread fertilizer on the whole field—only the area under the mulch. You could even mow the grass between the rows like a mini golf course. At the end of the year, plow the grass under to decay and enrich the soil, use the medians as next year's beds and the old beds as next year's medians. The more I heard about mulch, the less I could imagine doing my planting any other way. According to my scheme for the field, a three-foot bed would be followed by a three-foot median. Forty times.

That added up to more than a mile of mulch. Perhaps that distance should have given me pause. Maybe I should have paid more attention to how I would actually get this done—the books were a bit iffy on that aspect. The fact that I did not is the best illustration of how ignorant of mulch I was at this time.

Besides, I had help. Kim was available on weekends, possibly (though she didn't know it) evenings, too. Dan had agreed to come up and help do the mulching as though it were the most ordinary thing in the world for someone to do on his day off. Surely others would leap at the chance for a bracing day in the outdoors. As far as I was concerned, the mulch was a done deal.

I called Dan the night the field was plowed, in mid-May. "They finally came around and did it. The guy had only one arm, and he drove the tractor and everything," I said.

"Mmm . . . great!" said Dan. "How does it look?"

"The field—it looks great! It's . . . all brown, like dirt, and there are no weeds. But—um, well, the soil, it's in these big . . . clods, you know, it's all in clods."

"Clods?"

"Yeah, they're like . . . clods."

Lacking better descriptive vocabulary for the soil texture, I couldn't take our conversation much further. We nevertheless agreed that the following Saturday would be the beginning of our actual farming adventure: we would lay mulch. Four rolls of the black plastic had arrived the previous week on a truck from Griffin Greenhouse, and Dan, on a previous visit, had dropped off a vintage Troy-Bilt rototiller, a two-wheeled, self-propelled device that resembled a cross between a lawn mower on steroids and a predatory insect. A thirty-six-inch-wide rotating shaft supported a dozen cruel-looking hooked blades that spun viciously into and out of the ground in a direction opposite to its forward-moving tires. The machine's purpose is to loosen compacted earth, creating a light and soft seedbed, and to work fertilizer into the soil. But I didn't like the looks of it, and I hoped it might not have to be used. In fact I was almost glad when, shortly before we were due to start mulching, it steadfastly refused to start.

When Dan arrived early Saturday morning, I was happy to see that he was excited, too.

"Wow," he said, taking off his shoes. "This really looks great."

He walked around barefoot on the sun-warmed earth as if he could absorb its fertile essence through his feet.

"This is so rich and loamy. Bottomland! Our soil was almost all sand."

"So you think it's okay?" I asked nervously.

"Oh yeah, it's great!"

Dan scuffed at the soil with his foot, and it stuck to his big toe. He kicked a clod, and nothing happened. The big clump of earth did not even move. He kicked harder, and it reluctantly broke into smaller clods, the size of a large clenched fist.

Since he was getting nowhere with his feet, I reached down and broke off a clump with my hands. It was tough stuff, in consistency something like a stale loaf of bread. I looked up at Dan, who had put his shoes back on.

"Yeah," he said. "Where I was it was all sand—hardly had to plow it at all. Just run over it with a disc harrow to work the dead plants into the ground. This soil has lots of clay. Good thing we have the rototiller."

Dan must have noticed my expression, because his optimistic grin changed to alarm as I sputtered, "Oh. Yeah. I meant to tell you. The thing is, I can't get it started. I know the machine worked the other day, but I've been trying to start it ever since then and it won't turn over. I don't know what's wrong with it. Do we really need it?"

"Well," he said, "I guess we could dig this stuff out with shovels. But, look, we'd be here all day just to do one row, and anyhow, the plants need this earth to be broken down much finer so their roots can grab the soil particles and get water and everything."

"Oh. Okay, I guess we'll have to rent one then." I reluctantly agreed to go to the lumberyard, where a tiller was available at forty-five dollars a day, plus tax. When I got there, it turned out their machine was free but had to be returned by 4:00 P.M. because someone had reserved it for Sunday. The ungainly contraption was loaded into the back of the truck, and when I got back to the field where Dan and Kim were waiting, it was after 10:00 A.M.; at least, I thought, we'd have the rest of the day to knock out some rows of mulch.

By this time, our other helper had arrived. Our neighbor Perry was big for his thirteen years and seemed interested in earning some pocket money. With his bright yellow hair, he would not be easy to lose in the field. At Dan's direction, we formulated a plan: I would walk the tiller as straight as I could across the field. Kim would walk before me, scattering fertilizer from a cut-off laundry detergent bottle so the tiller would work the nutrients into the soil as it chopped up the clods of dirt. When we reached the other side, we'd move over three feet, then make another pass back toward the road. When we were done, two rows would be ready for mulch.

I yanked on the starter cord, and the machine growled to life. Eagerly, I squeezed the hand control that started the tiller moving forward, and when I reached the beginning of the row, I moved the lever that activated the tines. Spinning and clacking and screeching like a wounded boar, the revolving blades cut into the soil, pulling the rest of it behind. The machine promptly dug itself into a hole eight inches deep, then refused to move forward. It was stuck as surely, if not as deeply, as Lee's truck.

Damn. It was not going to be an efficient morning. I turned the tiller off and planted my feet, grabbed the handles, and pulled backward with all my might. The cumbersome apparatus came reluctantly out of the hole. Then I turned it on and tried again and again.

The trick to keeping the thing moving turned out to be a delicate balance between maintaining pressure on the handles to prevent the blades from digging too deeply and physically holding the machine back, which, for some reason, kept it from bogging down as much. Finally we made it across the field and back. It was about 11:00 when we prepared to lay the first rows of mulch.

By now, Perry was sweating, the beads collecting on the downy hairs of his forehead and upper lip, and Dan was growing impatient, having been waiting since 8:00 A.M. with practically nothing to do.

"Okay," he said as we gathered around in a huddle. "Here's what. Somebody gets on each side of the roll of mulch. You roll it out a few feet, then bury the free end deep because you're pulling against it. Then, use the spade like a plow, push the dirt to one side to make a furrow. The long edges of the mulch roll sit in there." He gestured excitedly with his hands and resumed speaking in a commanding tone, as if he were addressing a larger group—perhaps a gang of petty criminals sentenced to a few days of community service.

"The thing is, you don't have to bury the edges very deep. I don't know if it's the airflow over it or what, but even if you spread an inch of dirt over the sides, it will hold. Use your spade like a bulldozer and push that soil over the edge of the mulch. Don't try to dig up dirt and throw it at the plastic—it'll take too long and it won't cover. If you spread it evenly, once it's rained a couple of times the soil will harden and the mulch will never come up. But the important thing is that you stretch the mulch evenly when you roll it out between the trenches. See—like this."

Dan dropped to his hands and knees, and a flurry of activity ensued. With deft movements of his trowel, he dug a six-inch-deep trench, slipped the short end of the roll of plastic in, and buried it, firming the soil around it with quick, jabbing motions of his hands. He scrambled around on his knees, unrolling the heavy cylinder of mulch and pushing it down the row, evening it up so there were no wrinkles across the black plastic.

He soon gave up on the cheap trowel I had provided and simply used his hands to bury the edges of the length of plastic he had rolled out. Moving them through the soil, clawing, pushing, smoothing, fingers pressed tightly together and now caked with dirt, he had quickly produced about six feet of perfectly mulched row. We gazed at him, if not in awe then at least with the seriousness one reserves for police, clergy, and the truly insane.

Because it dawned on us that *this* was how he proposed we do the entire field.

❖

This is the moment when the farm became real for me. Because growing plants in your bedroom, no matter how many, cannot be considered farming. The working conditions are far less taxing.

But as I moved through the crusty dirt on all fours to roll out my mulch, I realized I had a basic conceptual problem with this. I had always seen farmers working their land with tractors. So why did I have a little yellow spade?

I twisted my head over my right shoulder to look at Dan and Chris, who were rapidly digging their trenches and packing dirt around the mulch edges—Dan with an almost ferocious intensity. I didn't think I would disturb him with my question just then. After all, Dan had done this before; he had made money at it, and he was obviously very serious about it. So this had to be legit.

Still, I had trouble keeping up a good front for Perry, who was looking to me, as the responsible adult in this situation, for direction. And, I suppose, a tacit assurance that this was really okay, that we were not going to collapse there in the dirt. But nothing about it seemed okay, and I was embarrassed to have to pretend that I fully supported it.

Perry and I were facing each other across our four-foot-wide roll of plastic, which couldn't have been more than a foot in diameter but was so resistant to being pushed it felt like it was wrapped around a cast-iron spool. We grunted and sweated as we tried to move it forward. I considered initiating some cheerful conversation. But what in the world was there to say? Besides, after only a few minutes we were both breathing so hard I doubt we could have sustained a dialogue. Little did I know this was the easy part.

"This looks good," I said when we had about six feet rolled out. "Let's see if we can get it to stay down." Perry just sort of grunted, and we walked back to the beginning of the roll, which was buried in the dirt. He was extremely fair-skinned and had probably not bothered to wear sunscreen. I was concerned about the color his skin was beginning to turn. We again dropped to our knees.

"Okay, I guess we just have to do what Dan showed us," I said as brightly as I could manage, and we began digging with our pathetic little trowels. Once you broke through the crusty outer layer, the dirt beneath was softer, but also surprisingly resistant to being moved. You had to throw your whole weight into this to make sure there was enough dirt being scooped over the mulch edge to keep it down. It was a sort of scoop-and-shove motion.

The high noon sun offered no escape. This was about the last thing one would come up with as a weather-appropriate activity for an unusually hot May day. In fact, "Mayday" was exactly what I felt like yelling right then, as I struggled over the stones that were buried just deep enough to be invisible yet shallow enough to cause a jolt of pain every time I landed on one with a knee or the heel of my hand.

As difficult as I was finding this, I could see Perry was having an even harder time. He was lagging behind me, and our row was starting to veer off course and wrinkle. When we got back to where our mulch roll was waiting, I stood up and looked at what we had done. Not too pretty. I guess we'll have to do better next time, I thought.

We inched our roll forward again. I made the mistake of looking straight ahead toward our goal, which was about half a football field away. Good Lord. I vowed not to do that again until I was actually there, should I ever be so lucky.

Our second pass was not much better. As I looked over at Chris and Dan, whose row was coming out nice and straight, I felt like I was in a very strange relay race. I looked back at the purple, panting Perry. My team was definitely losing.

About an hour into this activity, I noticed my clothing was literally disintegrating. My leather-palmed work gloves were coming apart at the seams, allowing the dirt to jam my fingernails and chafe my hands. The canvas pants I was wearing, which had held up on several rugged backpacking trips, were being pounded and scraped to the consistency of tissue paper. And there was nothing on me—including my hair, face, and eyeballs—that hadn't been covered with what looked like instant hot chocolate powder.

And did I mention the heat? I kept taking my gloves off so I could use my hands to wipe the sweat off my face and neck, though there was so much dirt on my hands I'm not sure why I bothered. I kept sneaking peeks at Dan and Chris, hoping that I would see them hurl their trowels over the fence and then rush toward me to say this had all been a terrible mistake and what were they thinking. But it never happened.

We had been at it more than three hours by the time we reached the finish line. Perry and I shoved our mulch roll one last time like two weary oxen. I struggled to rise from the dust, more exhausted, hot, and filthy than I can ever remember being, and took a look back over our row. It was a zigzagged, wrinkled mess. Dan was shaking his head in disgust, silently adding up the demerits. Perry immediately mumbled something about having to "take my medicine" and limped toward home. What had we done to this child? What had we done to ourselves? And were we really going to attempt this another thirty-eight times? Just shoot me, I thought.

❖

By now it was 3:30, and the lumberyard closed at 4:00. It was time to pack up the tiller and trudge back to our makeshift quarters in the still unfinished house. We said good-bye to Dan, who was heading back to his weekend home in Rhinebeck. He seemed glad to be leaving but offered some encouragement: "You'll get the hang of it after a while. We used to do our ten rows in a weekend. But our soil was a lot different."

Before leaving, I took a last look at the field. After a day that was one of the most physically exhausting I can remember, we had something to show for our efforts: exactly two rows of mulch, two shiny black ribbons running in parallel across the grainy brown dirt.

It had to get easier. At this rate, even with a working tiller, it would take us until September to get the field ready to plant. Still, I was sure that after we had done it a few times we would learn better and more efficient ways to lay down mulch. Our bodies would not ache in places we did not know the correct names of, or painfully remind us of damage done to muscles we didn't know we had. Our hands would not crack and blister. Our skins would not turn bright red in angry sunburn. We would be rational, sane individuals at the tail end of the twentieth century.

But these things were not likely to happen this week.

down & dirty

KIM: The next day Chris and I were back in the field at 9:00 A.M. We had no helpers this time; it was just the two of us. We were going to attempt to mulch as many rows as we could bear.

An obvious question is, Why was I going back for more? Hadn't I learned anything the previous day? Well, yes. I had on sturdier clothing and kneepads. But the truth was, I felt there was no way I could get out of it. More than a year of planning had brought me to this field. I had selected it over a dozen others. I had borrowed money to pay for it. I had moved out of my native city to live near it. And I had endured a very strange existence in order to have enough crops to plant in it.

At this point, we were really only just getting started. It was both too early and too late to back out now.

The sun was already blazing, just as it had been the day before. I was sure we would be back around ninety degrees by noon. Though I didn't know it then, a heat spell in May is actually quite common in this area of upstate New York around planting time. I thought we were just incredibly unlucky that year.

"It's going to be another hot one," Chris said as we plopped down in the dirt at the foot of a row we had tilled the previous day, before Chris had returned the rented machine.

"Oh, joy," I answered as we buried the short end of the dreaded mulch roll and started pushing it up the field. It was a little easier today because the roll was now smaller. And the rocks were not hurting my knees nearly as much. But I knew these would prove to be minor improvements. Nothing could really make this job less than excruciating.

We returned to the beginning of the roll and started digging. Silently we dug and pushed and dug and pushed until we were sweat-soaked, filthy, and exhausted again.

About half an hour later, as we shuffled along like two warthogs, Chris turned toward me and spoke. "Farming sucks," he said.

"Farming *sucks*!" I enthusiastically agreed.

We kept digging.

"There's *got* to be a machine that does this," I sputtered a few passes later.

"Oh, probably," Chris agreed, without the enthusiasm I felt this idea deserved.

"So why aren't we using it?" I inquired.

"We don't have time to look into any alternatives, and I doubt we could afford a machine even if it existed," he said. "We have to make it work this way. Try to keep up with me or we're going to get wrinkles," he added.

"How about you slow down?" I asked as I crept forward, but an answer was not forthcoming.

When we got to the end, Chris sliced through the mulch with his trowel to free the roll and buried the loose end in the soil. The roll was getting a lot lighter now, and he easily carried it a few paces over to where the next row should start, buried the other loose end, and started rolling back in the direction from whence we came.

"Can't we take a break here?" I asked in disbelief as I stood and stretched my arms over my head.

"Don't you want to get this over with?" he replied.

"More than anything."

"So let's go—chop, chop."

I somehow managed to aim my trowel at the dirt instead of his head.

Going back to the edge of the field where we had started was better psychologically but worse physically. The achiness and tiredness was cumulative, the heat unrelenting, and the dirt, well, dirty. When we got back to the north side, even Chris was ready for a break. I was ready to throw in the trowel.

"There is no way I can do any more of this," I declared, as we sat in the grass that bordered the plowed field and sucked down the last remnants of our water bottles.

"We need some more help," Chris agreed.

"Who in the world are we going to get?" I wondered aloud as I looked westward over the unmulched expanse of plowed earth, which seemed to go on forever. Who did we know who would be willing to do hard manual labor under the burning sun for no pay? Who could we possibly exploit so sadistically?

"I'll ask my parents," Chris suggested.

Both Chris and I are lucky enough to have parents who would do just about anything for us and often have. But while my mother is a very frequent flower buyer and my father is a genius at raising houseplants in their New York City apartment, it was obvious my parents would not be right for this task. They would no doubt deride it as too much *klopping* and *chocking*. I don't know the literal translation of this Yiddish phrase but have always taken it to mean something like "hopping around madly while hurling heavy objects." Besides, when my parents made trips to the country, they wanted to go antiquing, eat fine food, and maybe sit under a shady tree. They already thought that since I liked to sleep in the woods on my days off, I was becoming some sort of barbarian. I'm sure they assumed that my weekend farming, which I described in only the sketchiest detail so they wouldn't worry about my physical safety, was just another outdoorsy hobby I had picked up from my energetic husband. I didn't want them to know how truly out of hand the situation had gotten.

Chris's parents were more rugged, their idea of fun being to sail a boat up the Hudson River for a week. And Chris's mother could even be said to have relevant work experience. Granted, she farmed only a hundred square feet of her suburban backyard, but at the rates we were paying, we couldn't afford to be too picky.

Still, Chris did not feel the need to burden them with an accurate description of what we needed them to do. He had merely told them over the phone that we needed help with the "planting."

They arrived the following Sunday morning, dressed for a few hours of light gardening. Jim, a tall, thin, balding man with a fair complexion and a ready smile, was wearing khakis, a short-sleeved button-down shirt, and a baseball cap. Ethel, who is small but solid, with soft brown hair and pale blue eyes, was in yellow slacks and a crisp, white shirt. She, too, looked like she had never had a tan in her sixty-some-odd years. And with the sun just as brutal as it had been the week before, this was certainly not the time to try to get one.

"So where are the plants?" Ethel asked when we drove them down to the field in our truck and showed them our four mulched rows. She had a strong voice, perhaps from years of commanding the attention of her junior high school English pupils.

"Oh, we're not ready to plant yet," Chris said casually, as he executed the ultimate bait and switch on these kind, unsuspecting people. "We have to put more of this plastic down first."

I looked anxiously at the two of them, certain they would balk, but they didn't.

"Kim and I will show you what to do," he added, and we took

our places at the foot of the next row. We mulched a few feet, and then Chris got up, started a new row for them next to ours, and handed them their little spades.

"You've got to be kidding," Ethel said.

"Come on, try it," Chris urged.

They are going to walk right off this field, I thought. Instead, they just stared at Chris and then looked at each other, Jim with a half smile and Ethel with a half frown. And then, amazingly, they got to work.

Mulching family style was almost fun, except I couldn't help worrying about the health and safety of my in-laws. If Chris had any such concern, he had a funny way of showing it.

"No, no, Dad, don't throw the dirt on the plastic," he called over to the next row. "You have to use your spade like a bulldozer and push the soil over the edge of the mulch. That's what holds it down." Gee, where had I heard that before?

"Okay, Chris," Jim said in his patient, fatherly tone.

Ethel just sort of wheezed. I was really starting to worry about her.

"Chris," I said quietly, "your mother is turning a shade of red I've never seen before."

"Oh, she'll be all right, she's tough," Chris answered.

All the way down I kept stealing anxious glances at the two of them, but to their credit, they kept going.

Maybe this is where he gets it from, I thought.

When we got to the ends of our rows, about two hours later, the two of them could barely raise themselves up off the ground. Their nice clothes were filthy, and they were both perspiring like mad. Jim was wiping himself with a handkerchief, but Ethel hadn't thought to bring one. And why should she have?

"All right. We'll start another one," Chris said.

*"Oh no we won't,"* his mother answered and began to storm off the field. Then she stopped. "I think I'm going to faint," she

announced. Jim hopped over the mulch and took her by the arm.
He gingerly walked her back to the truck, put her in it, and drove
up the hill toward our almost completed house. As I watched the
truck disappear, I felt completely at a loss as to how we would lay
all this mulch in time to plant our crops. But Chris would have
to figure that one out. Tomorrow would be Monday, time for me
to return to my other job—the one where I wore nice clothes,
stood upright, and even got paid.

When I got back to Albany—after having applied several coats
of opaque nail polish to hide the dirt that couldn't possibly be
extracted from my fingernails—I felt like I had been furloughed.
Since the state budget was now two months late, the secret leaders' meetings were proceeding apace. But for once I really didn't
mind. A lot of sitting around in cool hallways outside the locked
doors of power this week would suit me just fine.

By this time I had been working as a reporter for about four
months and had already formed some strong likes and dislikes
about the job. I loved the camaraderie of the capitol press corps,
which was assembled in a windowless two-level suite of cubby-
holes in the old stone capitol building. With its ripped armchairs,
old upright piano, and full-size pool table, the pressroom resembled a dilapidated cocktail lounge more than a serious place of
business. We even had live piano music, supplied by a particularly
talented radio reporter.

The best thing, though, was that I did occasionally get to do
what I had hoped: explain to my readers what was going on in a
place where important decisions were being made about how we
all would live our lives. By this time I had even gotten my first
real scoop: I had discovered a new development in a story all the
papers were following about a controversial move by the governor to take away power from the Bronx district attorney in a

high-profile murder case. I was truly proud when I saw my super-serious partner in the Albany Bureau beam at me as he said, "That's a great story."

But far too often I was chasing sensational and basically inconsequential stories featuring sex, violence, and/or celebrities. If anything grisly, salacious, or scandalous happened outside the New York metro area, I was the one dispatched to cover it; I was the closest person the news editors could send.

I had gotten my first taste of this in April, when I was sent to stake out the home of the Unabomber's brother. David Kaczynski broke the eighteen-year-old case of the mysterious mail bomber who attacked university professors and business executives out of a bizarre hatred of technology. Kaczynski noticed that the published rantings of the so-called Unabomber resembled letters he got from his estranged brother, Ted. By making what must have been an extremely painful decision to turn in his big brother, who had killed three people and injured dozens more, David Kaczynski had undoubtedly saved lives. I was one of the people sent to punish him for his good deed.

The assignment took me to the nearby city of Schenectady, where I easily found the Kaczynski home on a quiet, residential street. It was the one surrounded by the tall, white spires of television satellite trucks and an army of reporters pacing around with cell phone antennae protruding from behind their ears. David Kaczynski was holed up inside with his wife and mother and would not say a word to the media. My orders were to wait outside until he changed his mind.

I got out of my car and greeted the few reporters I knew. Since the Unabomber was a national story, many were from out-of-state papers. There was also a small, enterprising contingent of neighborhood kids doing a brisk business Rollerblading to McDonald's for tips.

The adults were far less enamored of us. "You're sick, all of you!" one shouted from his car as he drove past. Some just angrily honked their horns. "It's about time you guys call it quits!" another yelled from his doorway.

There was no sign of life at the green-and-white Kaczynski home, which had every shade pulled down. It looked vulnerable and forlorn.

I leaned against my car and began my vigil. The minutes ticked by slowly. Out of boredom, some reporters started interviewing one another. The only one who appeared to be doing any real work was the fellow from the AP, who was interviewing passersby. That seemed like a good idea, so I decided to do the same. The first couple I spoke to were neighbors. They told me David Kaczynski was a social worker at a battered women's shelter. Oh, great. I was stalking a saint.

"They did something that was so morally important for the sake of the community at large," the woman said, "and what they're getting for it is their lives put out on a platter. I don't think it's right."

I interviewed a few more people and observed four very small children, escorted by their parents, walking by with handmade signs. "Media go home," read one. "You are wrong," read another. Part of me felt annoyed at adults who would use their kids this way. Another part wondered if maybe they were right.

After two hours, I drove to a pay phone and called my editor. "Give it two more hours," he said.

When I got back, the scene felt edgier somehow. The pack had resumed its pacing. Now the movements were quicker. Boredom had given way to hunger. It was time to move in for the kill.

I don't know who started it, but someone thought they detected movement in the backyard and hurried toward it, pulling the rest of us along as if by magnetic force. We found ourselves surrounding a small, sealed-up white plastic bag with a paper bag inside it. Camera crews began filming it. Reporters took notes. But what was it?

"I think a neighbor brought them food!" one reporter said excitedly. "I saw a loaf of bread!"

"I saw a banana peel," said another.

Great. Our thrilling discovery was garbage. And so, I decided, was this assignment. I got in my car and drove to the pay phone.

"Nothing's going on here," I said when my editor picked up the phone.

"Okay, you can pack it in," he said. "But write up what you have. We'll use it as a color story."

What I had? What in the world did I have?

I drove back to the capitol, sat down in front of the computer, and did the best I could, describing the scene and the neighbors' reaction to it. I couldn't imagine what the editors would do with this.

I'm afraid that with the deadline pressure and my usual performance anxiety, I was completely oblivious to the irony in what I was doing: writing a story about people not wanting me to write a story about them. But I now realize why I felt so confused doing it. I was telling only one side. As an article about a media feeding frenzy, what it really needed was a quote from the paper's management explaining why we were doing the story at all if we hadn't really garnered any news. But I never thought to ask that question.

By the end of my nearly three years on the state government beat, the assignments tended to get more pointless, grotesque, and/or ridiculous. Though I didn't know it yet, I would: stake out the home of a well-known doctor so I could ambush his mistress; join police on a hunt for the missing body parts of two teenagers; and try to track down a transvestite jailbird known as Peaches.

After wading through rubbish like that, I was always happy to get back to a different kind of dirt when the weekend rolled around.

❖

Chris finally solved the mulching problem by getting more help from Dan and Lee. He also had the good sense to abandon the hand-propelled tiller in favor of a second paid visit from the tractor dealer, who tilled the entire field with his tractor in a few hours. By early June there was a total of twenty plastic-covered rows—half of what we wanted. But Chris decided to move on to the planting because there just wasn't any more time to spend on this if we wanted to have anything to sell at market this summer. There would be no more mulching. I was tremendously relieved. Sanity had been restored to Silverpetals Farm.

I was eager to try my hand at planting. This had to be better than mulching, especially since the heat wave had mercifully broken. We were going to begin by planting some flower seeds that were not started indoors. These supposedly wouldn't take as long to grow as tomatoes and peppers and therefore didn't need the head start we gave to those crops. Since we had had such success with the bedroom farm, I figured we already knew something about getting seeds to germinate.

On the appointed day, Chris and I drove down to the field and took our places in front of the first row of mulch, in which Chris had already poked holes with a bulb planter (a metal cylinder with teeth on the bottom and a handle on top) so we could reach the soil below. Then he handed me a little white paper envelope of seeds that was no bigger than my hand. I looked out at the acres of mulch. I looked at the little seed packet in my hand.

"Now wait a minute," I said. "You are not going to tell me that farmers jump off their tractors and race around their fields with little seed packets."

"Well, obviously not if they're planting acres of corn in an unmulched field," Chris answered. "But we're doing something totally different. We could never use some kind of machine to plant in a mulched bed system."

Another reason to hate mulch, I thought. Mulch is not my friend. I studied the holes that had been poked through the plastic, creating a pattern that looked almost like a vast line of dominoes all turned to the number five.

"How many holes are there?" I asked, quickly adding, "You know what? Don't tell me."

"Right, let's get to work." Chris explained that the first thing we were going to plant was a fuzzy, relatively short, burgundy-hued plant called Pygmy Torch, a type of amaranth.

"Do you remember what this one looked like in the catalog?" Chris asked.

I said I didn't.

"It's kind of bushy and small," he said. "That's why there are so many holes in this particular row. We can put the plants twelve inches apart. Let's work across from each other again."

We assumed the position.

"Try to loosen the dirt in each hole with your trowel, tap three or four seeds in, and then pat it down lightly with your hand," Chris instructed. "The seeds only need to be covered a little bit, so don't dig a hole, just scrape the soil a bit."

I opened my seed packet and looked inside. The seeds were so small you could barely distinguish them individually. I took out a pinch and put them on my palm. They felt hard, like bits of glass, and when held to the light were a transparent red color like tiny garnets. I put them back in, put my gloves on, and then raked the hole in front of me with my trowel. Then I tapped my packet and about thirty seeds came out.

"This is impossible," I announced.

"Try creasing the packet like this," Chris said, folding the little envelope the long way, "so there's a little channel for them to flow through one at a time. And I think it works better if you dig as many as you can reach at one time and *then* plant them, instead of doing just one hole at a time."

"Okay, but let me just finish this one," I said, trying to pick out the extra seeds.

"Don't bother with that, we don't have time," called Chris, who was already a ways ahead of me. "And I don't think you should be wearing gloves, they're just going to get in your way."

I didn't want to give up my gloves. My hands were a part of my body I particularly liked. They were exactly the same as my mother's and my grandmother's, only the fingers had grown longer with each generation. I enjoyed noticing this whenever the three of us were together. I had hoped to get through the farming season without getting my hands destroyed. But as I patted down my first planted hole with my glove on, I saw what Chris was talking about. The glove seemed to be picking up too much dirt, and probably some seeds with it. If that was really happening, all this work would be for nothing, and that would truly be a disaster.

I took off the glove and put my hand on the dirt. I was amazed at how warm it was. A little farther through the hole under the mulch, it actually felt steamy.

"Wow, that is warm," I said, enjoying the sensation of moist heat on my skin.

"That's one of the reasons we mulched," said Chris, who had come back to the start of the row to fill in some more holes closer to me. "The seeds should love this. It's like a hothouse for them."

I scraped a few more holes, and then realized I had a problem: because the width of the row was covered with holes—some close to me, some close to Chris, and some in between—I couldn't always tell if he had already done the ones in the middle or if I should do them.

"This is very confusing," I said to Chris.

"Let's try something different," he said. "Why don't we each do a whole row by ourselves? That way we won't be tripping over each other."

"Yikes!" I said.

"Let's just try it. The next row is another kind of amaranth called love-lies-bleeding."

"Do we want to sell something that sounds so violent?" I joked.

"You've got to love that name," he said. "It's got drama." He went off to the next row, and I tried to get into a groove with my seeding. His technique of creasing the package was definitely helpful, as was getting rid of the gloves (though as the dirt on my hands dried it assumed a sort of baked-on quality). But I still found I was having a hard time keeping track of which holes I had planted in and which I hadn't. And then I did something really stupid. I looked up toward the end of my row. Now I felt sure I would never have the patience to get to the end of it.

I got up and walked to Chris's row to see how he was doing it. He had come up with a great system. He would place a small stone on the plastic as far away from himself as he could reach. Then he'd scrape out all the holes between himself and the stone, plant them all, and then cover them all up. Then it was time to move over and put another stone down. The stones served not only to mark off the area that was being worked on but also to hold down the mulch, which was rustling a bit in the breeze.

I went back to my row and tried it. Not only did it solve my problem of keeping track of what I was doing but it gave me a little goal I could congratulate myself for reaching every few minutes. My job satisfaction rose tremendously.

Another thing I liked was that, without the enormous physical strain of mulching, my mind could wander to things other than pains in my body. In fact, there was nothing to do but think, and when had I last had so much time for that? So while my body crept along a narrow, straight line, my mind pranced around freely. I was amazed that something that had once seemed so improbable to me was now a reality. Chris and I were farmers. Almost.

Looking back over the finished row a couple of hours later was gratifying (after all, it was done!), but I had no idea whether I could really expect anything from it. This was a lot more questionable than planting at the kitchen table in Albany. There I knew the plants would get enough light, heat, and water. Plus, the light yellow tomato and pepper seeds were very easy to see against the black soilless mix. Tiny red seeds against reddish soil are nearly impossible to see. And would they really be warm enough? When would it rain again? Would it rain too much? Who could say? The suspense of this really will kill me, I thought.

Planting seeds might be called the ultimate act of faith. On the other hand, it may also be thought of as a kind of slow-paced suspense thriller: you just never know beforehand what, if anything, will come up out of the ground. Even the ancient Greeks, an essentially agrarian people despite their regrettable penchant for disastrous wars, were well aware of this fact and celebrated it in several charming myths. One of my favorites is the story of Cadmus, which seems to speak directly to one's agricultural anxieties.

Cadmus's sister Europa had heard that the flowers in her favorite field by the sea were at their absolute peak for cutting and went to gather some with her maiden friends. While she was there, in the way that only a mythical Greek heroine can, she fell in love with an attractive bull and jumped on his back. To her friends' dismay, the bull carried her off over the sea, never to be seen again. Her father, on hearing what had happened, sent his sons out on search parties with instructions not to return unless in possession of the unfortunate young woman.

While his brothers simply set out in various directions on their quest, Cadmus had the good sense to go first to the temple of Apollo in Delphi and submit a query as to Europa's whereabouts to the god of truth. Like the Internet of ancient Greece, a priestess of the temple soon relayed an answer back from the god: Forget about Europa, boy! The bull in question is, of course, none other than Zeus, and the girl is living large on her own island and in the process of founding a dynasty. Instead of meddling with her or slacking around the temple, why don't you go out and found your own city? Just follow the cow you'll see on the road out of town, and where she stops to rest is where you can start building!

Cadmus did exactly as he was told; unfortunately, the cow chose to stop at a spring that was guarded by a fierce dragon, which promptly dispatched all of his companions. It was up to Cadmus himself to slay the beast. But no sooner had he done so than the goddess Athena appeared and instructed him to plow the land all around, sow the dragon's teeth in the furrows, then wait to see what happened. Once again he did as he was told, but to his dismay what sprang up from the furrows was not a crop of snapdragons or small scaly lizards but a myriad of angry warriors, armed to the teeth.

This myth clearly shows the ancient Greeks' insight into some basic agricultural truths:

1. Farm at your own risk
2. Never follow a cow if you don't know where it's going, and
3. You never can tell what you'll get if you plant unfamiliar seeds.

Fortunately for Cadmus, the armed warriors immediately took to infighting, and all but five quickly slew one another. Enlisting the survivors' help, he went on to found the great city of Thebes. So you could say that it all works out in the end if you didn't know that, while Europa went on to become a household name, Cadmus's line would soon produce the ill-starred Jocasta and her son-husband Oedipus.

Most modern seed packets are designed to produce more predictable results. Every seed catalog shows pictures of beautiful blooming flowers and ripe vegetables, and all seeds are small, hard things that come packaged in paper envelopes. The trouble is what happens between the envelope and the picture. While some have no advice at all, the better catalogs usually give oracular instructions in a kind of shorthand that can seem like ancient Greek to the uninitiated: for example, (7–14/ Sp/ d, t/ sun, part shade/ 24"/ 6") and (HHA) (G 7–30, 65–85F) (S/D) (F/E) ( o ).

(In case you are curious, the first set of markings can be translated as follows: This seed germinates in seven to fourteen days, produces flowers in spring, can be direct-seeded or transplanted, grows well in sun or shade, reaches a height of twenty-four inches, and should be spaced six inches apart. The second, from another catalog, indicates that the plant described is a half-hardy annual that germinates from seed in seven to thirty days when temperatures are kept from 65 to 85 degrees Fahrenheit, and can be started via direct-seeding or transplant. It requires a fair degree of skill to germinate but is easy to grow on after that stage, and prefers full sun.)

These kinds of instructions are the reason why the bookstore shelf on horticulture tends to be overflowing with titles. Gardening books can tell you how to decode, and under ideal circumstances control, the variety of factors—soil temperatures for germination and growth, planting media, fertilizer content, moisture, day length, and a plethora of other variables—that transform seeds from inert lumps to blossoming plants.

Yet sowing seeds in rows in a field, under the indifferent spring sun, is not an ideal, controllable environment. The ground may be properly prepared, the timing planned, the seeds carefully planted—but then nature takes over. Then it becomes a matter of faith. The seeds are in fact alive, waiting for the right conditions to grow, but whether they get them is not controlled by the one who plants the field. This has always been the nature of agriculture. If you are so inclined, you are welcome to pray to the god of your choice that your seeds will flourish.

The Greeks chose Demeter, goddess of the harvest. She favored the earth with vegetable bounty for eight months of the year, then took a vacation for four, resulting in winter and the end of the growing season. Her worship was so important to the Greeks that it took on a cult status, eventually leading, in some Eleusinian mystery rituals, to particularly nasty forms of human sacrifice. Fortunately, this practice has been discontinued (except possibly in some rural communities portrayed by Stephen King). But even today, when seeds spring up from the brown earth and fill the rows with foliage and flowers that look more or less like the pictures in the catalogs, I find it most helpful to talk in terms of nitrogen content, soil temperature, and drainage, but to think in terms of magic.

Suspense and mystery seemed decidedly lacking when we transplanted our bedroom farm crops the following week. You knew you would get a plant because that was what you put in the hole. In this case, however, we didn't think a lack of drama was such a bad thing. Because, even though it took longer and required more energy to dig the deeper hole needed for this kind of planting, the payoff was instant: there was a nice, healthy plant standing right in front of you. Rows and rows of them in fact.

The transplanted section had a very different look from that of the seeded section, and not just because there were plants in one and not in the other. The transplanted part had no lines of black plastic running from end to end, since we had decided to forgo mulching (hooray!) in this part of the field. And the plants were arranged in a very different configuration. Most of our flowers in the seeded rows could be planted fairly close together, twelve to fifteen inches apart. That's what gave rise to the domino-like pattern as the holes covered the wide band of plastic. But tomatoes and peppers are bushier plants and need more room to spread out. So we planted these crops single file, eighteen to twenty-four inches apart. The plants marched forward in one skinny line per row.

By late June all the planting was done—mostly by Chris, who continued to commute to the farm from Albany every day. We were a month late, but at least everything was in.

On the last Sunday of planting, as we headed back to Albany, we slowly drove by the field. The mulched rows seemed tidy, with their tightly tucked-in plastic and symmetrically placed stones. In the unmulched section, the tomatoes and peppers waved leafy little arms.

"This is really looking like something," I said proudly as we passed by.

Chapter 8

what now, my bug?

CHRIS: It was sometime in mid-July when we lost the crops. The exact time was hard to pinpoint, since it had been a gradual process. In fact, I watched it happen day by day and it never seemed like anything to be alarmed about, until one day none of the tomatoes or peppers were visible. It was a good thing I knew where to look for them, or they might have disappeared forever. Still, something dreadful had happened: the field was engulfed in weeds.

When I decided to abandon the idea of mulching the entire field, the planting process suddenly became immensely easier: it was simply a matter of making a straight row (since the bed system had been scrapped as well), digging a small hole with a trowel, and plopping in a tomato or pepper plant every two feet or so. Granted, there were three-thousand-plus plants (equivalent to about a mile of row) that had to be put into the ground this way, but after the mulching experience it seemed like a vacation in Bali. The sun was a gentle, golden ball, the soil a rich, fluffy brownie mix, and birdsong was again audible in the summer field. It was almost like being in love.

And, like many an almost-love, it didn't last a month.

It was true that when we put the tomatoes and peppers in, this half of the field looked like an instant farm. Against the uniformly brown, coarse-textured, and weedless earth, the bright green, young vegetable plants in their neat rows stood proudly, evidence of the care we had given them, and the order we hoped to bring to this land. Clearly, the seedlings had done quite well in their Albany home. And, after we'd moved them to the country, they had been nicely acclimated to the harsher conditions of life in the field by spending a few weeks in a cold frame.

The cold frame is really nothing more than a big box sitting on (or under) the ground, large enough to hold several flats and having a hinged, openable glass lid that functions like a mini greenhouse. In mild weather, the top is opened during the day to prevent overheating and allow moisture to escape, and closed at night to retain some heat and protect from a chilling wind or even a late frost. The temperature fluctuates here far more than it would indoors, but the plants are protected from truly extreme conditions as they grow accustomed to the outdoor life.

I had built four cold frames from scrap plywood, concrete blocks, and salvaged patio doors and windows, and the plants seemed to love them. While they didn't get bushy, the tomatoes grew to nearly two feet tall, and the peppers were almost as big. Eventually, it became difficult to close the glass without breaking the tops of the plants. This was another reason they had to be planted without delay: they were crowding all the space inside the frames, sending white roots out of their cells and into the rocky ground below, and the concentrated, resinous odor of the tomatoes was enough to knock you over when the lids were opened.

A twenty-inch transplant is a big plant, but because the roots are still confined to a two-by-two-inch pot, the pots packed thirty-six to a flat, it can't really become very bushy or woody — in other words, its stem remains fairly soft, and it grows up, not out. Ideally, tomatoes should be put into the ground eight or ten weeks after they've been seeded in flats. Then they will still be in a stage of vigorous growth in their tiny cubes of soil but small enough so their roots aren't looking to annex the next piece of earth, and their stems won't droop under the weight of their own leaves or be knocked down by a breeze in the field. But, as a result of the delays in plant-ing—namely the facts that the field hadn't been tilled until mid-May and the mulching job had taken weeks longer than expected—these plants, like seventh-year college students, had been hanging around the hothouse too long. It was time for them to go.

To figure out when any specific plant should be started from seed, you need to know how long that variety takes to germinate and develop into a strong seedling with at least two sets of true leaves. Most seed catalogs and thousands of gardening books have this information. Then, you simply count backward from the ex-pected frost-free planting date—that is, the earliest date on which there has been no frost in eight of the past ten years—which is obtained from the weather service or local lore. In our area, the tar-get date for starting to put annuals in the ground is the third week of May. Our tomatoes and peppers had been started from seed in late March, in the expectation that they'd be planted about this time. But, in fact, the last plants didn't go into the ground until mid-June.

That was too late. Although tomatoes can develop new roots along any part of the stem that comes into contact with the soil, and can be buried up to the second set of leaves in the expectation that these adventitious roots will hold the soil and form a stronger sup-port system for the plant, doing so didn't help our plants. Their stems had simply become too tall and spindly. Within a couple of weeks after planting, up to half of the plants in each row had broken at some point on their upper stems, and the tops had fallen on the ground. Gusty winds, which occasionally blow straight down our small valley, had probably been the cause of the damage. The tallest of the seedlings seemed to be the ones that were damaged the most.

Certainly this couldn't be a good thing, but I didn't sense disas-ter yet either. After all, cutting off the tops of most plants won't kill them. And didn't lots of authorities in the books I read recommend "pinching off" tomatoes at a leaf node to make the plants bushier and higher yielding? I decided to view the wind-damaged plants as having been pinched off—by Mother Nature. Anyway, I reasoned, with twenty-odd rows of tomatoes and peppers, something had to bear fruit. But what I hadn't counted on was the weeds.

It seems trivial to observe that a piece of bare ground is rarely seen in the country, because ground doesn't stay bare for long. It may be covered by snow in winter, blasted by chill winds in March, but before spring is over the earth is certain to be greening, and by midsummer it's likely overrun with a tangle of weeds, tree seedlings, grasses, and wildflowers. Whether the weeds are carried as seed by wind, water, or woodchuck, lying dormant in the soil for years or spread by wandering roots from the plant next door, the earth tends always toward a weedy green entropy. Gardeners are supposed to know this, and to take a grim pleasure in reversing the trend to weediness, eradicating the unwanted plants by any means necessary. As a would-be farmer, I was hoping that it wouldn't come to that—not on this scale!

Still, it wasn't exactly surprising when I noticed, a few days after planting the peppers and tomatoes, that they had company. Poking through the soil in a random pattern, the first weeds seemed like puny dwarves compared with the big transplants in their neat rows. How could these ragtag sprouts threaten the crops that had been tended and planted so carefully? In the shadows of the transplants, I thought, they would never amount to any serious competition.

The weeds' secret, as everyone knows, is their rapid growth and persistence in spite of all adversity. And so, while the tomatoes were still deciding whether they liked their new surroundings, or if they should make two new stems where one had been broken, the weeds were Hoovering the fertilizer and expanding by the minute. I hesitated to take my eyes off them, because each time I saw the weeds they were bigger, while the tomatoes stayed exactly the same size. If at first it had seemed like overkill to go after a bunch of pathetic weedlings, it was now becoming a question of whether anyone had the time, patience, or fortitude to try to control their ever-growing masses. And how would we do it — with a five-dollar good (as in not better or best) quality hoe from the hardware store's annual sale? With our hands? Our feet?

Meanwhile, on the other side of the field, the situation was somewhat different. Since that side had been mulched, the weeds did not present a frightening green shag rug to be dealt with. Instead, they were confined to the holes in the plastic. However, those rows had been direct-seeded, so there were no tall crop plants to compare the weeds with. And there was the problem.

Some seeds — the cucumbers, beans, squash, and zinnias — germinated so quickly and grew so fast that it was impossible to mistake them for anything but what they were: cultivated plants, vegetables and flowers, the results of years of careful crossbreeding and selection. In short, our precious crops. But other seeds just took their time to sprout. And, since I'd never seen what the seedling stage of, say, a pomplona aster looked like, I had no idea which of the tiny plants in the hole might be asters and which weeds.

Because, at about the same time the weeds sprang up in the unmulched rows, the same thing was happening in the mulch. The geometrically spaced circular holes began to show traces of green as the tiny seedlings pushed aside the crust of soil and stood up to the sky. But who knew which ones should be plucked and which pampered? Which should be pulled up and which left to grow?

In the end, it was a matter of some educated guesswork and more than a little luck. If there were a couple of the same tiny plants in a hole, and almost every hole in a particular row had the same type of tiny plant, then these must be the seedlings and any others the weeds. Unless, of course, they were the same in *every* row — then it stood to reason that they must be the weeds, and the others the seedlings, or at least some of them . . . The sad fact was that the tiny plants all looked the same, and until they got much bigger and developed some true leaves they weren't going to look anything like the pictures in the seed catalogs. And that was the only way I could recognize most of the different plants I had chosen to grow.

But if there was still some debate about whether the weeds would catch up to the tomatoes, there was no question about weeding the annuals seeded in the plastic: it had to be done. Otherwise, the upstart weeds would outcompete the more genteel flowers and vegetables, leaving us nothing to show for our hard labor in the mulch gulag. I knew that a mutiny, a coup, a revolution, would be justified if that happened, so I concentrated my efforts on the mulched rows.

This was the kind of work that my guru Dan called meditative, his euphemism for repetitive, monotonous, uncomfortable, but not actually harmful tasks. It was a broad category that, when I pondered it, encompassed about every farming job I could think of. To do it, you simply kneel down at one end of a row (trying to avoid the long view and to concentrate on the few holes directly in front of your eyes) and pluck out those seedlings which, in your best judgment, seem most weedlike. When you have weeded all the holes that can be reached from one position, crawl forward a few feet (keeping your eyes on the area of mulch nearest you) and repeat the process. Eventually, you will come to the end of the row and to a decision: Can you make yourself do another row, or is it time to quit right now?

Let me just say that hole weeding, as we have come to call it, is my favorite farm chore. At no other time are the before and after so dramatic, as each tuft of weeds peeking out of a hole in the black plastic mulch becomes one perfect little plant. Actually, it's before and after and after. The second after comes the next day, when that tiny plant seems to have quadrupled in size overnight. You can see right away that you've really helped something grow. Now, isn't that satisfying?

Plus, this isn't muscle work, it's about dexterity. All your efforts are focused on a small exposed circle of earth measuring perhaps three inches in diameter and brimming with plant life. The faster you can move your fingers through the tiny weed clump as you kneel before it, feeling every sprout, the faster you will be able to distinguish the "good" plant—if there is one. And, for me, that surprise element is what makes it different from any other agricultural labor. It's like digging for the prize in a Cracker Jack box.

With transplanting, for example, you know you are going to get a plant sticking out of a hole because that's what you are putting it in. Rewarding, but in a boring sort of way. With hole weeding, you don't know what you're going to end up with. You may get the desired plant or you may not. Because, hole by hole, you now get to find out if your seeds actually germinated. Is there a good plant here? Yesssssss! As far as cheap thrills go, this is my number one.

And this task leaves you enough breath for conversation, so you can have someone working across from you and actually talk to him or her. One of the most pleasant days I ever spent farming was when my childhood best friend from the city came to help me weed. We moved down a row of cosmos, catching up on all that needed to be related now that we lived in different places. It was the only time I can remember actually being sorry to reach the far end of the field.

❖

Many objects, when examined closely, reveal new and unexpected aspects that the casual watcher will never notice. Looking at a great number of similar things over and over allows the careful observer to make fine distinctions between them that would otherwise go unremarked. And having hours and days to fill while doing incredibly repetitive tasks (the aforementioned "meditative work") practically forces one into an unwitting Zen-like state, where tiny details take on a significance out of proportion to their actual importance at the time. Our soil, for example: Uniformly dark brown when wet, it fades mostly to a reddish tan when dry, except for one small area of the field, where it stays almost black and mucky. It tends to have far more tiny, flat rock chips than pebbles, but most of the larger stones are very rounded, like eggs. It also has bugs. Many, many bugs.

I never disliked bugs, at least not those that were unlikely to bite or sting me. I even felt a little sorry for those I killed. I vividly remember one May morning, the early mists rising over the Potomac River as I collected dozens of specimens from the muddy stream banks and fields in a last-minute dash to complete the requirements for a college course called Environmental Entomology. At the time, I never dreamed that such arcana as the larval instars of coleoptera (beetle grubs) could have any significance to my everyday life. But now, the more I looked, the more insects I saw. They were everywhere.

There were Japanese beetles and Mexican bean beetles and Colorado potato beetles. Cutworms and hornworms, flea beetles and blister beetles, squash bugs and stinkbugs and tarnished plant bugs. Not to mention the larval forms of these insects, which, if they were magnified even to the size of small dogs, would have to be among the scariest creatures imaginable. The ground beetle larva, for example, is composed of an eyeless head that looks identical to a single large lobster claw, three small Michelin Man tires for its torso and six legs, and an abdomen resembling an orange drywall screw. If it could, it would eat you for breakfast; luckily, it is less than an inch long. By contrast, the Japanese beetle grub looks like a long gobbet of phlegm attached to six legs that protrude directly below the head of the creature from the movie *Alien*.

I saw all of these insects as I weeded the rows, along with many others: millipedes that produced a noticeably bitter smell where they congregated; white, threadlike ascarid worms that I found dead in the tiny puddles of rainwater that collected on the plastic mulch; big, daytime-flying moths that hovered like hummingbirds to collect the nectar from wildflowers; bright green mantids, silently waiting to begin preying. The names and images I vaguely remembered now were arrayed in a panoply of insect form, and I wondered why we, not they, seemed to be in control of the earth. Nevertheless, we had spent a great deal of effort on these plants so far, and now a bunch of damn bugs were about to enjoy a free lunch, courtesy of me.

The question was, What was I really going to do about it? Although we didn't yet meet all of the standards to be considered an organic farm, principally because we used regular commercial fertilizer instead of a special organic formula, I wanted us to go in that direction. And I was not about to start spraying some toxic chemicals on these thousands of plants with a squeeze bottle. Besides, many insects are beneficial — they pollinate plants, aerate the soil, and eat other, less helpful insects in great quantities. Still, some insects, like the first ten I mentioned, can be quite harmful to plants: Aside from eating foliage and fruit, they can spread disease from one infected plant to an entire field. Some even eat a ring around the base of a young plant's stem, felling it like timber to die and rot on the ground. Yet a balance between the two, harmful and beneficial, has kept things going for a few million years.

So I decided that the only thing to do was just let them duke it out. There wasn't a great alternative either way. If things got really out of control, I could reconsider the squeeze bottle — or some organic controls, like rotenone or diatomaceous earth. The former is a dusty, yellowish powder made of the roots of a South American shrub, the latter a fine, sandlike substance made up of the skeletons of tiny marine animals. Both are approved for organic pest control and reputed to alleviate infestations of particular insects. Yet, although the bugs seemed to have gotten a fair number of seedlings in a few rows, the majority were unaffected so far. Weeding the holes had an immediate effect: the seedlings shot up, almost like weeds. Some even began to look like the pictures in the catalogs. Besides, out of forty-plus rows, we were bound to get something.

But, just to be sure, I decided to give in to a sudden impulse and purchased about a dozen flats of flower seedlings from a local nursery. It was quite late in the season, and the selection was hardly the best, but I got a few varieties of flowers I hadn't seeded, at a bargain price. It made me feel better—and worse. On the one hand, I hated to spend the money on something I should have done myself, and in a way it seemed to be admitting that a "real" grower could do something I couldn't. On the other hand, I'd had no room to start anything but tomatoes and peppers in Albany, and there was no telling when—or if—my direct-seeded flowers would bloom. If some varieties take ninety days, as the catalogs said, that would put them in flower about in time for the first frost. And having no flowers would mean no market, since, regardless of what the vegetables might do, the bright bouquets would be the lure to draw customers to our stand. Dan always stressed how essential flowers are to the success of the market, and I wasn't about to deviate from his plan now. I guiltily planted the bought seedlings in some unmulched rows on the opposite end from the tomatoes, and I waited for something to bloom.

By now, in the latter half of July, the part of the field that contained the peppers and tomatoes looked from a distance like an overgrown vacant lot. The plants were almost waist-high, and any evidence of rows was obliterated in a low-lying green fog of weeds. It seemed impossible that any crops might ever have been planted here. At closer range, you could begin to make out individual plants. Foxtail grasses, with sharp sprays of tough, wide blades, formed clumps almost three feet tall scattered throughout the field. Green amaranths, relatives of the garden species, had prickly, pea-soup-colored buds springing up all over their thick, shrublike stalks, and were popping up in every square foot of earth. Canada thistle, a small but extremely nasty perennial weed with spines like needles and a habit of growing back two stalks where one was cut off, seemed to lurk behind every vegetable plant. Lamb's-quarters, milkweed, bindweed, jimsonweed, and Virginia creeper filled out the collection, pushing and climbing and poking through any spaces left between the plants. A dense and malevolent green mat had formed over the tilled soil.

The tomatoes and peppers were still there: if you stared hard enough, you could mentally connect one crop plant to the next and reconstruct where the rows had been. But if you blinked, the imaginary line would be gone, lost in a sea of weeds. Oddly enough, although they didn't seem to have grown since being transplanted, several of the plants were flowering, and a few peppers had even managed to produce some tiny green fruit. But any semblance of an organized effort at agriculture was gone. These plants were truly on their own now—if they yielded any produce, it would be in spite of anything that nature could throw at them.

But even though this half of the field seemed likely to turn out a complete failure, I wasn't devastated. True, the effort and expense of growing the transplants might end up having been for nothing, though there was still a chance that a vegetable or two might appear. But, after all, this season was primarily a trial. I had chosen the twenty-odd varieties of peppers and tomatoes mostly to see what they'd do, and to find out what to do with them. To put it in scientific terms, the experiment had been pretty successful—up to now. I was consciously trying not to have great expectations for the farm the first year, and I've found that if your expectations are low enough, it's hard to be really disappointed. But probably the main reason I wasn't crying in my Gatorade was that there were too many other things to do. The mulched rows were thriving and needed attention. The house was nearly ready to move into, though far from complete. There were details of the market operation to work out: for example, all of the details. There just wasn't time for me to be crushed.

❖

I was truly surprised at Chris's ability to put the vegetable garden fiasco behind him and concentrate on other aspects of the farm. Once it was clear the tomatoes and peppers were stalled, he basically ignored the unmulched part of the field and the hundreds of plants secreted within it. But I kept wandering through the weeds, waiting for a sign that something would happen. It just didn't seem fair. We had spent so much time on these plants and brought them so far. Was it really going to end so prematurely?

It is now my own reaction that I find ridiculous. How could I have believed nature held some sort of money-back guarantee, especially for those who had violated such a basic rule of field maintenance as weeding? Of course, by now, after five years of farming, I have had whole rows of crops drowned, devoured, and even carried off by birds. But this was not yet in the realm of my experience.

Fortunately, there was another momentous event to take my mind off the transplanting disaster. We were transplanting ourselves from Albany to the farm, too.

The *News* had arranged for me to have the Albany apartment for a year. But, by the end of July, it seemed that the focus of our existence had shifted to our land, and we were itching to live in the country full-time. Chris still had a lot of work to do on the house, but we decided it was ready enough. After all, we had plenty of experience living in the midst of construction projects in Brooklyn. So I informed my editors that I had made other living arrangements, and we excitedly packed our belongings.

On moving day we borrowed Dan's van so that, along with our truck, we could carry everything in one trip. But as we began to bring the contents of our household—which included eight pet tropical fish individually bottled in old mason jars—out to the curb, something stopped us dead in our tracks. It was an unbe-

lievably awful smell, like composting dead rats. It seemed to be
coming from a small, red pickup that was parked directly in front
of our stoop. Stifling an impulse to gag, I peered into the truck
bed and saw a large burlap bag stuffed with what looked like rotting plant material, possibly mixed with manure. There was no
writing on the bag that might identify it.

"What the hell is in there?" Chris asked, pulling his T-shirt
up over his nose.

"I think it's the proverbial sack of shit," I answered, pulling my
shirt up likewise.

"It's awful!" Chris gagged.

"I think maybe I should call the Health Department," I
offered.

"No way," Chris said. "If we stay here one minute longer than
necessary I'm going to vomit and die!"

"You're right, let's just get out of here," I answered.

We frantically ran up and down the stairs, carrying our pos-
sessions and holding our breath. I kept hoping the owner of the
putrid pickup would appear and drive its fetid load to its final
resting place, but we had no such luck. The unbearable nasal
assault continued until our two vehicles were fully loaded. Then
Chris took the wheel of the van and I got into the pickup, and we
peeled out. I don't think I took a full breath until I got to the
interstate. Being chased out by a mysterious, revolting stink was
actually a very fitting end to my residency in Albany, as I was
becoming increasingly nauseated by the far less mysterious but
equally revolting stink emanating from the capitol itself.

When we moved in, our house still had bare plywood floors,
no ceilings, no kitchen, no bathroom walls, and no paint. Living
there was more like camping. But it didn't matter. I had two
weeks off and usually went camping on my summer vacations.
The indoor plumbing made this "trip" seem quite luxurious.

We put large sheets of cardboard up around the bathroom fixtures to create the illusion of privacy. We cooked on a portable grill every night and made tea on a camp stove in the mornings. I went to sleep listening to frogs chirping in a nearby stream. I woke up to the call of honking geese. And, best of all, the air smelled wonderful.

By early August, there was one more reason not to dwell on the lost vegetable plants: we finally had some honest to God crops.

None of the tomatoes or peppers was as yet producing any salable fruit. The tomatoes simply hadn't fruited at all among the weeds, while tiny peppers, two inches long, hung from the almost-hidden plants. None of the purchased seedlings produced any usable flowers. Most blossomed shortly after they were planted, on stems only half a foot tall—too short to be of any use as cut flowers. Undoubtedly they had been sitting in the nursery too long.

But, in one of nature's offhand miracles, the direct-seeded flowers were starting to bloom, and they were beautiful. There would soon be eleven usable rows of flowers: one row each of Pygmy Torch and love-lies-bleeding, both amaranths with fuzzy, burgundy-colored flower tufts; three rows of cosmos, which looked like a child's drawing of flowers, with big, paper-thin petals of magenta, pink, and white; three rows of sunflowers, pale yellow, gold, and reddish brown; three rows of zinnias in a pastel palette; and a feathery white Queen Anne's lace look-alike called *Ammi majus*, or bishop's weed. These plants ranged in height from a foot and a half (zinnias) to six feet (sunflowers), and they were uniformly bushy, dark green, and sturdy. In fact, the only direct-seeded plants that completely failed were the two rows of asters (I never did get to see what an aster seedling looked like). Although insect damage and other causes had wiped out a lot of plants—in the worst case, nearly a third of the plants in a row—it was hard to tell from a distance that anything was missing; the remaining plants simply branched out, filling up the empty space with their stems, leaves, and blossoms.

There were the other vegetables, too: a row of purple pole beans, and one of green; four rows of cucumbers, including one the size, shape, and color of a lemon; a patch of zucchini; and a stretch of basil. All of these were among the seeds that had arrived in the big box on our snowy porch step two seasons ago. Sometime in the late spring, while we were concentrating on our ambitious plans for the flowers and tomatoes, we just plopped these seeds into holes in the mulched rows we had set aside for them, and then essentially forgot about them. Now they were rewarding our virtual neglect with an abundance of produce.

Among the things I was not neglecting was the house construction. Here, in contrast to the rows of tomatoes, things seemed to be coming to fruition. I could finally see what the interior would look like in its finished form, and I liked what I saw. Lee was now working with me nearly every day, from 2:30 until 5:30 P.M., and we were making good progress. Together we installed kitchen cabinets, hung doors, put up more drywall, and finished the exterior trim.

One afternoon we drove down to the field to repair a section of mesh fence that had been knocked down, probably by confused deer. "They don't know you yet," Lee said. "These deer have been living here for years, but they haven't figured out yet that you've put this fence across the field. Once they do, they'll just cross the road further down and go around it. They sleep in the woods on your hill, and come down to your stream to drink at night. You could say they're *your* deer, because they live right on your land, and you'll eventually get used to each other."

While I could not imagine myself being responsible for a herd of needy deer, his observation concerned me. I knew that the state legally "owned" the deer, but was he trying to tell me I had some sort of obligation to the misguided beasts? As he continued speaking, I felt relieved.

"I've hunted plenty of deer when I had to," he went on, "but I don't understand why everybody gets so excited about it. It's not like it's so hard to get one, or anything. If I needed meat, I could just sit up in an old apple tree before dawn and wait until a deer walked right underneath. Then you could practically drop a brick on its head if you wanted. The young does are the best for eating. But I'll tell you one thing—there's nothing like beef. After you've eaten deer meat all winter, you just get an urge to go out and have a hamburger."

I was hesitant to tell Lee that the few times I'd eaten venison had been in fancy restaurants, so I just nodded and looked thoughtful.

Sometime after five, a white station wagon pulled off the town road and wound down the drive into our field. It was Kim, wearing her Albany uniform: a dress, jacket, and high heels. This was one of the rare times when she'd come home before seven, and it could only mean that on this summer afternoon the state capital was virtually asleep: the legislature was out, the governor on vacation, the courts quiet, and the police blotter empty. It seemed so seldom that I saw her in the daylight, at any time when there wasn't an agenda full of tasks that required our immediate and full attention, that I was simply delighted. She could finally get a taste of how I spent my weekdays here on the farm, and she might have a chance to speak to Lee, with whom she'd probably exchanged fewer than a dozen words so far.

When she walked through the gate and came over to us, I gave her a hug and kiss. I proudly showed her the hole Lee and I had fixed, and the rows where the vegetables were ripening. She and Lee, who all at once seemed thoroughly bashful, shared perhaps another dozen words before he announced that it was time to go home for supper. As the three of us walked toward the gate, I put my arm around Kim's waist and pulled her tightly to me. She returned the gesture with a squeeze.

"Hey now," Lee said in a tone of admonishment that was obviously fake, "you'd better save that up for the winter. You're a farmer now. Got plenty of other things to be doing in the summer. Besides, you'll appreciate the warmth a lot more when it's cold out." He gave us a smile as he turned to go. "I'll see you tomorrow," he said.

He whistled up his German shepherd, who jumped into the passenger seat of his battered pickup, and they started for home. Kim and I, still arm in arm, watched in silence as he pulled out of the drive and onto the town road.

After Lee left, Kim got back in her car and drove to up the house to change. I remained in the field, walking between the mulched rows and sampling the vegetables. They were good! The purple beans were visually attractive, but the green ones were delicious. Likewise the lemon cucumbers were novel, but the Suyo Longs were crisp, sweet, and tasty.

It was time to go to market. Even though we didn't have a great deal of variety, the flowers were blooming, and the veggies were ripening. They might never be better than they were right now.

"gonna sell them
weeds?"

KIM: On August 9, 1996, the eve of our first market, Chris and I sped down the Taconic State Parkway in a van loaded with flowers, vegetables, and a few thousand of our favorite bugs. The insects cavorted merrily amongst the produce and buzzed around our heads, deftly avoiding the occasional swat. The warm night air rushed through the open windows as we raced toward the cash.

"We are going to rule," Chris asserted from the driver's seat.

"We are going to sooooo rule!" I agreed.

Our day had been a marathon of picking and preparations, as we geared up for our first Saturday market in a residential area of Greenwich Village. This location had been our first choice, based on the fact that the neighborhood residents have a good deal of disposable income, and the suggestion from the Greenmarket staff that this market needed a flower grower. Our other market was going to be on Tuesdays in a commercial area of downtown Brooklyn—the very market at which Dan had sold his produce for years. We were very pleased with these assignments and couldn't wait to begin.

Most farmers harvest the day before market and then rise before dawn for the drive to the city, arriving in time to set up their stands by 7:30 A.M. For us, this would have meant leaving our house at 5:00 A.M. (at the latest), and neither of us could quite get behind that idea. So we decided to make use of the one advantage we had over most of our more experienced market mates: our home in Brooklyn. We would spend the night before market there. This would certainly enable us to get more sleep, but it left a lot to squeeze into the Friday before our debut. Fortunately, I was on vacation this week and could help Chris with all of the preparations.

First came the harvesting of our cultivated flowers. Chris and I marched through the rows, clippers in our hands, straw hats on our heads, and empty five-gallon buckets stationed by the edge of the field. I started with Pygmy Torch, a short, fluffy amaranth with blossoms arranged in fingerlike clusters that seemed to be made of burgundy chenille and a stalk that resembled a stick of rhubarb. These had done quite well, and we had several hundred of them.

"How many should I take?" I called out to Chris, who was in a nearby row picking papery white, lavender, and magenta cosmos.

"Just get two buckets," he said. "We don't want to use them all up in one market."

"What are these things?" I asked, pointing out a light green plant growing alongside the Pygmies that looked similar but was taller and thinner.

"Those are a wild type of amaranth," Chris said. "Let's take some of those, too. They go well together."

Chris and I carried armloads of flowers to the waiting buckets, and then we moved on to cucumbers and zucchini, a tiring treasure hunt in a tangle of low, overgrown vines. Two of our cucumber varieties were rather bizarre. One looked more like a lemon than a cucumber (and in fact was called a lemon cucumber), and the other, an Asian variety called Suyo Long, looked like a twisted green tree root. But both of these, Chris and I agreed, tasted better than the standard cucumbers we had also grown.

Though harvesting was definitely hard work, taking plants

out of the field could not possibly compare with the labor of putting them in. And as the overflowing buckets filled Dan's van, which we had borrowed for the occasion, it was hard to believe how bountiful it all looked.

After we had trolled through the cultivated rows for several hours, Chris said, "Now we need some wild stuff." He headed to a patch of weeds just past the unmulched part of the field. "Let's start with Queen Anne's lace."

This tall, white, flat-topped wildflower had always been a favorite of mine, but it was difficult to pick, the spindly stems intertwining and breaking easily. Filling just one bucket between us seemed to take forever.

Having nothing yellow, we decided to pick some goldenrod, which Dan told us made good filler. We also found a tall, bushy wildflower with trumpet-shaped yellow blossoms that we both thought would look great in bouquets, though we didn't know what it was. I thought that rounded out our assortment very nicely, but Chris said we weren't done yet.

"There are two other wildflowers I want to get," he said, "and I know where we can find them."

We drove the van back up to our house and deposited our full buckets in the cool garage. Then we collected some more empties and a bucket of water and headed out to forage for wildflowers. We were going to make several stops at places Chris had noticed on various back roads we took to Albany.

The first was right along the roadside, a gravel cul-de-sac with a prominent No Parking sign.

"Are you sure we should do this?" I asked Chris.

"We're not parking, we're just stopping for a few minutes," he said.

Right. We hopped out of the van with our clippers.

"Hmmm. Not as much here as I thought," Chris noted as he looked around. "Well, we can get some more Queen Anne's lace. This stuff actually looks better than ours. The flowers are bigger."

After collecting what we could, we got back in the van, back-tracked a bit, and stopped at a triangle of vacant land near a major local intersection.

"People are going to see us if we do it here," I said nervously.

"So? We're not doing anything wrong."

"Well, I feel like I'm doing something illegal," I said.

"Like stealing weeds?"

"Yeah."

"Well, you know what? No one cares."

"How do you know that?" I persisted. "We don't know whose land this is."

"Technically, roadsides don't belong to private owners, they belong to the state," Chris said. "And the state does not cultivate roadside weeds. It mows them."

That made me feel a little better, but I was still not totally convinced.

"I just don't understand why we really need to do this," I said. "I mean, if we need this stuff, why don't we just grow it?"

"Why should we grow it if it's already here?" Chris asked. "Did you really want to do any more planting than we actually did?"

Hell no, I thought. We got out of the van.

"See these little thistly purple things? They're wild bachelor's buttons. Let's get a bucket of them."

As we clipped and snipped, I cast a few nervous glances over my shoulder, relieved not to see any flashing lights pull up beside the van.

Our last stop was a large, overgrown field running up a small, steep hill. This, at least, was somewhat secluded. We collected some bee balm, a lavender, tassel-like flower on a long stem, and loosestrife, which resembled a skinny spruce tree branch whose needles had been replaced by soft purple petals.

When we got back home it was about 5:00.

"We better get this van loaded," Chris said. Our plan was to meet Dan at our house in Brooklyn at 9:00 P.M. and go to market together in the early morning. We had a lot to pack.

There were the flowers and vegetables themselves, looking bright and luxurious in their overstuffed five-gallon buckets. A card table and matching chairs courtesy of my grandmother. A checked tablecloth and some antique galvanized metal buckets and baskets borrowed from Dan to give our stand that coveted farmy-country look. A bag of rubber bands to bind bouquets with. A big pile of newspaper—collected from a state capitol recycling bin—to wrap them in. And a chalkboard on which to display our farm name in front of our stand.

As we were arranging our equipment and wares prior to loading, Lee drove up to collect his payment for the weekly construction work he did on our house with Chris.

He sauntered over to the van and surveyed our buckets. "Gonna sell them weeds?" he asked in a half-mocking, half-admiring tone.

"You bet," Chris said, handing Lee his money. "People in the city love this stuff."

Lee just smiled. "Well, good luck," he said as he headed back to his truck, got in beside his dogs, and drove away. It was time for us to do the same.

We tossed a few items of clothing in a duffel bag, drove to the local convenience store for gas and take-out sandwiches, and headed out of town. Although our day had been exhausting, we were too excited to be tired.

"How much do you think all this stuff is worth?" I asked as we bounced along in the van with our buggy produce.

"Well, Dan said he made a thousand dollars a day," Chris said. "I'm not sure we have that, but I bet we have eight hundred."

"Definitely eight hundred," I agreed.

By the time we got to Brooklyn, three hours later, the day was catching up to me and I couldn't wait to get to bed. We pulled up in front of our house (where, miraculously, there was a parking spot) and waved to Dan, who was sitting on our stoop. We were about fifteen minutes past our agreed-upon meeting time. Chris turned off the ignition and took out the keys.

"What are you doing?" I asked.

"Parking the car," he said. "What else?"

"You're just going to leave it here? With all this stuff in it?"

"Why not?"

"What if it gets stolen?" I asked.

"By whom? A rogue florist?"

Hmm. Good point. But it felt unnatural to leave anything of value on the streets of New York overnight.

"I don't know about this," I said.

"Don't worry, they'll be fine," Chris said. "We're right in front of the house."

"Well, what about air?" I asked. "Won't they suffocate all sealed up like this?"

"They will be just fine," Chris reiterated, as he got out of the van and shook hands with Dan, who had stepped off the stoop to greet us.

"Look what we've got," Chris said proudly. "We figure it's about eight hundred dollars' worth."

Dan peered into the van. "Hmmm," he said, rather noncommittally. "I'm not sure you've got eight hundred there. We'll see when we get to market."

I thought he was being overly cautious about raising our hopes.

Once upstairs, we chatted in the dining room a bit, and then Dan retired early to our foldout couch in the living room so he could get a good night's sleep before our early-morning grand opening. This sounded good to me, but Chris had other plans.

"Do you know where my colored pencils are?" he asked.

"No, why?" I answered.

"We have to make signs."

"What are you talking about?" I asked. "Let's go to bed."

"No, we have to do this," he said testily. "Greenmarket's regulations say you have to have signs for each thing you're selling and what it costs."

"So fine, this should take you all of five minutes," I snapped back. "We have flowers, cucumbers, and zucchini. That's three things."

"It has to look good," Chris said, his voice rising. "I need those pencils!"

I don't believe it, I thought, as I suddenly realized what was going on. He had opening night jitters. I would have found this cute if I weren't so tired and humoring him didn't require energy. I helped him find his pencils.

"Now where is that rubber stamp we used on our wedding invitations and the ink pads?"

"You've got to be kidding."

"No, it will be perfect."

Chris and I had gotten married in a garden three years before and had sent out garden-themed wedding invitations stamped with a sprig of green ivy. I remembered that the stamp was in a credenza drawer in the dining room. Chris spread out his equipment and began drawing on the backs of leftover wedding invitations we found in another drawer.

"So what are we charging for things?" he asked.

"You're asking me?" I was surprised and annoyed that he had left a detail that seemed so important for the last minute.

"Well, I figured we'd charge the same thing Dan charged for his bouquets, five dollars and seven dollars."

"That sounds fine," I said, not really having any idea what they should cost.

"Well, what about cucumbers and zucchini?"

"I don't know. What do they cost in the supermarket? About fifty cents apiece?"

"That sounds good for the cucumbers," he said, "but those zucchini are really huge. How about a dollar each?"

"Sure," I said.

Chris sketched and stamped and scribbled until he came up with a set of signs he liked.

"So what do you think?"

"Lovely," I said. This had all taken close to an hour, and I was not in the mood to play art critic. "Can we go to bed now?"

"Okay," he said. "Don't forget to set the alarm for six-fifteen."

"That's harsh."

"Well, we have to be there at seven."

"I know." I sighed as I dragged myself up the stairs.

❖

When the three of us emerged into the bright morning sun on Saturday, I was relieved to see that the van and its contents were still there. Overnight, the plants had turned the van into a mini greenhouse, fogging up all the windows and re-creating the tropical humidity of our Albany bedroom. The flowers looked great.

We had taken it on faith that this market would be right for us, never having found the time on a Saturday to come into the city to check it out. So we would see it for the first time on the day we actually set up to sell there. Heading into the unknown, Chris drove while Dan navigated. He used directions provided by the market manager, who was supposed to meet us there and help us get set up. But when we arrived at about 7:30, she was nowhere to be found. The market, however, seemed to be in full swing.

There were ten or so vendors set up along a narrow street bordering a vest-pocket park filled with tall, straight, shady trees, a few benches, and a bronze statue. Seeing no available space by the other sellers, we parked the van on the street perpendicular to their trucks, walked to the middle of the park, and surveyed the scene. I was relieved, after having considered wearing a skirt, that I had instead opted for jeans and a T-shirt. This was clearly the unofficial uniform of the vendors. Most of the stands seemed to be manned by two or three people, who weighed produce and collected money. Many were sheltered by white canopies. Brightly colored vegetables abounded, and the enticing smell of fresh herbs filled the air. "We should get started," Dan said impatiently after briefly checking out the competition.

"But we don't know where to set up," I said. Though Dan obviously felt sure of himself in this situation, I had no idea what we were supposed to do and found the whole thing disorienting. Just like with mulching, I thought, Dan was expecting us to fall right in line. Didn't he realize how confusing this was for us?

Chris decided we should wait a few minutes to see if Harriet, the market manager, showed up.

I looked at the other stands again and saw something very alarming.

"Weren't we supposed to be the only ones selling flowers?" I asked.

"I thought we were," Chris said. "Other people have them?" He looked down the street and answered his own question. "Everybody has them."

Dan was tired of waiting. "Let's just pick a spot," he said. "We need to start making some bouquets."

After mulling it over a bit, we decided we would set up right where we were, in front of the statue. It was a little distant from the other farmers, a bit more in toward the park rather than out toward the street, but we figured here we would have plenty of room and not get lost in the crowd. And, given that we had no canopy, the deep shade from the park's trees would be welcome. As we were unfolding our tables and arranging our buckets and baskets into a picturesque little display, Harriet, a petite and pretty young woman with a serious demeanor, showed up.

"I was thinking I'd put you down at that end by the other farmers," she said with a wave of her hand after we had all introduced ourselves.

"We like it here," Chris said, "kind of set off from the crowd. Could we stay here this time since we've already started, and take the other spot next week?"

"That's fine," she said, and collected our forty-dollar fee.

Dan went off to the van to start assembling bouquets while Chris and I finished arranging our cucumbers and zucchini in little baskets along with the carefully prepared signage. It felt better to be doing something rather than just standing around and gaping. Soon Dan reappeared with his first bunches. Chris and I gasped.

"Wow! That looks great!" I said. His bunches were big, bright, and bushy—somewhat wild looking yet also very artful and deliberate. Not waiting around to bask in our praise, he dashed back to the van to make more.

Chris and I stood stiffly in front of the stand, rolling our eyeballs toward each other every time a potential customer approached. What would be our first sale?

Dan came back with more bouquets and sprinkled a few blossoms around the table as decorations. Back to the van he went.

Then it happened. Someone wanted to buy something! A neatly dressed woman in her mid-forties was holding up one of Dan's bouquets and a five-dollar bill.

"I'LL WRAP THAT UP FOR YOU!" Chris announced with great fanfare as he took the bouquet from her and rolled a piece of newspaper around it.

"Thank you," she said as she walked away.

"Thank *you*!" we boomed in unison.

A few more sales immediately followed.

We grinned and nudged each other. We were starting to rule.

When Dan appeared with more bunches, the stand was empty.

"We can't let that happen," Dan said. "The stand always has to look bountiful or you'll lose business."

"I'll help you," Chris volunteered, leaving me alone to wait for more product and more people.

❖

Making bouquets was something I'd been looking forward to for a long time. In a way, it represented the climax of our efforts on the farm — taking the raw materials we grew and gathered and putting them together in a form that was irresistible to the eye and, we hoped, to the customers. I had no prior experience in arranging flowers at all except for buying, say, a handful of yellow daffodils and a bunch of purple irises from the Korean deli on the corner and putting them together in a glass vase. That was easy, involving only a principle I remembered from fifth-grade art class: purple and yellow are complementary colors, which means that the eye finds them pleasing when they're put together.

But when Dan spoke about making bunches, it didn't sound so much like a visual composition as like a musical arrangement. He casually threw around terms like *rhythm, repetition, harmony,* and *punctuation* as if he were composing a symphony. I knew that he was an aficionado of classical music; it was his habit to haunt the plaza at Lincoln Center on nights when the Metropolitan Opera was performing, hoping to score an extra ticket at a drastically reduced price or, best of all, for free. But right now I couldn't see how his musical metaphors were going to help me get the job done on our first market day.

"Don't worry, you'll pick it right up" was all he'd say. "You have a good eye for design. You went to art school, didn't you? Anyway, the flowers will tell you what to do with them."

But it was early in the morning, I was nervous, and if the flowers were going to talk to me, they would have to speak a lot louder.

At first I just watched Dan work, and he tried to narrate the process of making his luscious bouquets as he went along.

"Now, look at what you've got to work with here," he said, taking in with a sweep of his hand the dozen-odd buckets arrayed around our work area. Each five-gallon plastic pail was filled with a single kind of flower that seemed to form a dense mass of bloom above its rim.

"Color—well, maybe not a lot of color, but you've got this deep purple loosestrife and this cosmos and amaranth. And the goldenrod—see how it comes in different forms? Some of it is like shrubs, some is like clouds, and some is like fireworks."

I began to see what he was talking about. Some of the plants grew in upright, many-branched tendrils covered with minute yellow florets, like a diminutive cherry tree in blossom. Others bore their flowers in a loose, misty cluster, while a few took an almost willowy form—each drooping branch seemed to trail golden sprays behind it like sparks from an earth-bound skyrocket. I realized that, although I'd picked a few hundred stems of the stuff, I hadn't really looked at it closely.

"Now think about what you're going to do with it. The spikes and blooms stand out. The looser stuff is good for filler. You've—umm—got a lot of filler here. Let's start with that."

As I looked at the buckets lined up near the stand, I realized he was, once again, right. The flowers that looked so appealing as masses of color in a tightly packed bucket were not necessarily the ones that would stand out in a bouquet. Nobody but a minimalist fills a whole vase with just baby's breath; yet it seemed that bouquet filler was mostly what we had brought to market. I vowed to do better next time.

Undeterred, Dan grabbed a handful of the open sprays of goldenrod.

"You know, they grow this as a cut flower for the markets in Europe," he remarked softly, as if reciting an old lesson that no one wanted to hear anymore. "It's only in this country where we have so much of it growing all over that it's called a weed."

Holding the stems gently in his left hand, he pulled and shook and turned the flower heads until they filled up a volume of space with a colorful but airy presence, something like a puff of exhaled smoke.

"Good. Now we'll work some Queen Anne's lace in. See how they go together?"

He reached into another bucket and loosed a tangle of the gossamer blooms. About a third of the stems immediately snapped in his hands, but Dan just shrugged and clicked his tongue. "These are so delicate. You can't avoid a little breakage."

He pushed about half a dozen of the frilly white flowers stem first into the yellow mass, where they seemed to hang suspended, filling the spaces between the colorful spikes.

"There. Now for some color."

Carefully he extracted a few of the deeper-colored cosmos and added clumps of them to the growing bouquet. It was beginning to look as if someone had seeded them all in a garden bed together, or happened upon them in a field and simply grasped the stems together and cut the plants off at ground level. The big purple blooms stood out brilliantly against the paler background, yet there was clearly something more of the country and less of the florist about this arrangement.

"Then a little punctuation. For some reason I find that odd numbers work best, but I don't know why—maybe it's just me."

Dan picked three plumes of burgundy amaranth from a bucket and purposefully set them into the bouquet. It was done.

"Boom. Boom. Boom. This will knock them out."

He put the completed bunch aside and immediately started making another, as I tentatively began picking out a few flower heads and holding them together at arm's length to see what they looked like.

His next arrangement consisted of Pygmy Torch, green amaranth, and loosestrife, tall spires of red-violet, gray-green, and purple whose shapes echoed one another while their colors differed; this, I understood, was what he meant by rhythm—or was it harmony? Whatever it was, the bouquet was completed when he layered some multiheaded lavender bee balm between upright spikes, completing the tertiary color palette. It was beautiful, and I resolved to make a bunch of flowers that was equally good.

With a mixture of deliberate and random choices, I began assembling my initial bouquet. After working on it closely for several minutes, I held it away from me for a better look. It seemed to consist of a stem or two of each one of the flowers we'd brought to market. It was arranged so that all of the blossoms were at an approximately equal altitude. It was colorful, and I thought it was pretty good. I held it under Dan's eye, looking for a reaction.

"Well," he said, shaking his head gently, "it's nice. It . . . seems to lack a concentrated focus. But why not put it out there? Next time, you know, you don't have to use every flower all at once. Maybe try to stick to just three or four kinds in a bunch."

I nodded, then gathered the completed bouquets and walked them to the stand, where Kim waited.

"Ooh, they're beautiful," she said. "Did you make any?"

I pointed out the bunch to her and again waited for a reaction.

"Wow," she said, "it's gorgeous. Exquisite. Really great."

I remembered then why I loved her.

"Go make some more like that!" said Kim, as I walked back to the van. I was determined to make bouquets that were just as good as Dan's.

For a while I tried to copy his style, with just a few minor variations. A pile of similar-looking bunches accumulated. At last the urge struck—were the flowers finally talking to me?

I assembled a small bunch: amaranths in front, bee balm behind, and a few cosmos off to one side. It had rhythm, harmony, everything. I liked it a lot. I held it up for Dan's inspection.

"Yesss," he said. "It's . . . sweet. Put it out there. Someone will buy it."

Sweet?

Well, I *did* put it out there. I kept going and eventually stopped asking for his approval. After all, people were buying them.

❖

I liked Chris's bouquets. They were stylistically different—not as bushy, a little more delicate. I was impressed that he could just jump in and do this.

"Do you want to try it?" he asked.

"Oh, no," I said, "I'll keep selling, you keep bunching. You're doing great."

Chris went back to the van again.

Our sales tended to occur in little bursts of activity followed by complete stillness. I found selling a lot more fun than I had ever imagined. For one thing, there was the perfect simplicity of it: I get what I want, you get what you want, and we're both happy—all in the space of a few minutes. And I really liked the people I met at our table. Most were professional women my age or a bit older, though there were also a few couples strolling around the market together. I enjoyed chatting with them, though it seemed that whenever someone had a factual question about our flowers, it would reveal a gap in my knowledge or my mind would go embarrassingly blank on what I did know. Which flowers were perennials and which were annuals? Which would last the longest? How late in the year would we have them? I found myself running to Chris for every answer, if I was lucky enough to have him close by at that moment. Perhaps I was more nervous than I realized. I vowed to study up for the next time so I wouldn't further tarnish the image of Silverpetals Farm.

Soon I saw a tall, auburn-haired man and a blond woman of average height waving at me as they approached the stand. They had on hats and sunglasses and the goofy smiles they always wear when they think I'm doing something cute. They were my parents.

"These look sooooo beauuuuutiful!" my mother exclaimed in her typically theatrical way as she hugged me.

"You're really doing it!" my father added as he nodded approvingly at our display.

I returned their hugs a bit self-consciously. Although I was very happy to see them, I didn't want Chris and me to stand out as the novices we were any more than necessary. And a quick glance around the market confirmed my suspicion that no other farmers had brought their mommies down to *kvell* over their produce.

"This is my favorite one," my mother said, pointing out a small bouquet of cosmos and goldenrod.

"Don't you love *this* one?" I asked her, holding up a tall arrangement of Pygmy Torch and loosestrife that I found particularly striking.

"Well, actually, no," my mother said. "That looks like something you would feed to a horse."

Just then Chris appeared with more bunches. "Hi, Gil. Hi, Michele," he said.

"Congratulations!" my mother said. "The flowers look beauuuutiful!"

"Why, thank you," he said. "So things have slowed down a bit?" he asked me, noticing we had no customers.

"Yes, there seems to be some sort of lull," I remarked.

"I guess I'll take a little break then," he said, sitting down at the table.

"Let's take a picture!" my mother suggested. She plopped down next to Chris. "You, too, Kimi," she said. I sat on her other side, and the three of us grinned at the camera my father obligingly pointed at us. After a few more pictures, some potential customers sauntered by. Chris and I sprang up, and my mother, a professional actress, walked in front of the stand. "I have never seen such beauuuuutiful flowers!" she exclaimed, as if seeing them for the first time. She proceeded to lift bouquets out of the buckets of water we had arranged and pretend to consider which one to buy.

"Ma, you don't have to do that!" I whispered sharply.

She mouthed a silent "okay" and tiptoed back behind the table, where my father was seated. Soon business began to pick up a little more and they got up to leave, wishing us luck and promising to send pictures.

Chris went back to help Dan. When the two of them finished making bouquets, at about 1:00, they rejoined me at the table, and we waited to sell our remaining produce. There were hardly any people strolling on the street at this point (someone must have rung the brunch bell), and we had nothing to do but sit and watch the flowers dry. This got boring very quickly and, feeling hot and tired, we decided to pack it in around 2:00.

"Let's count the money first," Chris said.

I figured our take must be in the ballpark of what we had expected. After all, we had sold out, except for a couple of buckets of wild stuff Dan said didn't look too healthy.

Chris took the wallet we were using to stash our cash out of his back pocket and began counting. When he finished almost as soon as he began, I knew that something was terribly wrong.

"A hundred and sixty," he said, looking pained and confused. "We made a hundred and sixty dollars."

We stared at each other, completely dumbfounded.

What the . . . ?

Chapter 10

show me the money

CHRIS: It was not a jolly ride back from New York City that Saturday afternoon. Kim and I were returning upstate with less money than we'd started with, although our special market wallet still bulged with most of the fifty dollars in singles that I had thought to pick up from the bank the day before, in anticipation of changing big bills. With a minimum of conversation, we agreed to stop at a convenience store off the parkway for two $1.25 milk shakes, then I steered the rattling van over the back roads for the rest of the trip home.

All the while, various words of Dan's kept buzzing around my head like flies above a rotting tomato:

"We used to make a thousand dollars a day."

"We were selling them so fast that I couldn't keep the stand stocked."

"A thousand dollars a day."

"They were just grabbing them right out of my hands."

"A thousand dollarzzzzz . . ."

I could hear his voice speaking, could almost picture his head on a fly's body, his tiny curly hair blowing as he circled endlessly around the inside of the vehicle.

I had now been up for too many hours, on too little sleep, and it was hot and stinky inside the van. Finally, Kim and I arrived at the house, dragged ourselves upstairs, and fell promptly into bed. Our first market was over. Had we learned anything? I will let the record speak for itself, verbatim, from my notebook at the time:

| 1st Greenmarket | SAT AUG 10TH ABINGDON SQ. NYC |
|---|---|
| Approx 13 buckets: | 2 goldenrod |
|  | 1 bach button |
|  | 1 Big Yellow |
|  | 1 Queen Anne's lace |
|  | 1 loosestrife |
| Bouquets $5/$7 | 1 bee balm |
|  | 2 amaranths |
|  | 1 green amaranth |
|  | 1 cosmos |

Mkt mgr: Harriet H
Present: Kim, Chris, Dan
Weather: fair
Visitors: Schayes, David + Alysha
Results: sold out of good flowers
(had 4+/− buckets not usable because of low quality of blooms, e.g., bach buttons, Big Yellow)

| Gross: | $160 |
|---|---|
| Expenses: | $40 market fee |
|  | $100 Dan |
|  | $20 gas |
|  | - 0 - net |

*Conclusion: Bring more good flowers*

This little document seems to capture the essence of the first market, better even than the pictures my in-laws took that day of Kim and me grinning behind a tabletop display of colorful bouquets and cucumbers at our stand in the shady park. Somehow the eleven buckets of individual flowers in the right column have become "approx 13 buckets" in the left. Have I forgotten something? Of the roughly one dozen buckets, exactly three are cultivated flowers — that is, flowers we planted and grew in rows in our field. Two of them are amaranths, and one is cosmos. The rest are wildflowers — that is, flowers that we did not plant but that somehow managed to grow anyway — in short, weeds.

And . . . what was I thinking when I wrote "Big Yellow"?

It was a start. No one actually laughed at us, to our faces. In fact, one customer even specifically asked for a bouquet of just Big Yellow (which I much later identified as evening primrose). But if things didn't pick up, we would soon go broke buying six-dollar sandwiches at the deli across the street from the market. I felt I had to talk to Dan about this.

I have in my hand one of the pictures my parents took that day. It catalogs just about everything wrong with our first marketing effort:

1. Our table is tiny.
2. Our display is tiny.
3. We have propped three zucchini in a bucket that could hold thirty-five.
4. We are selling weeds.
5. Actually, we are not selling weeds, we are posing with our relatives.
6. Our stand is in Siberia instead of alongside the other farmers.
7. We are hiding behind a statue.
8. There are at least five overstuffed buckets of tall, eye-catching, gorgeous, and perfect cultivated flowers within view of our stand. They do not belong to us.

9. What's with the chalkboard? We couldn't afford a real sign?
10. This whole thing looks about as professional as a ten-year-old's lemonade stand.

I could go on. It's all very obvious now. But, at the time, I was confused and actually panicked. We were not farming for our health, we were farming to earn a living, or at least part of one. Obviously, we were just starting out and needed time to catch on, et cetera. But we had grown flowers and gotten them to market. Wasn't that the hard part? How could we have no profit, not even a tiny one?

I was truly alarmed about what the financial ramifications of this might be. I had never wanted or expected anyone to support me, but that didn't mean I wanted to be carrying the entire financial load for a two-mortgage household indefinitely. I was feeling enough pressure from that responsibility and thought my employers already abused me enough. What if they found out how badly I really needed the job?

I have never been the type of person to say, Hey, if things don't work out with this job, I'll just get another one. I felt lucky for every job I ever had, with the possible exception of selling croissants at Boston's Faneuil Hall after my freshman year in college (I have nothing against croissants, but I hated the stupid wool beret they tried to make me wear while standing in front of a hot oven in July). Plus, as much time and energy as I had put into the farm, Chris had put in a zillion times more. He and Dan had better figure this out, I thought.

❖

"Well, you know, it was really later in the season when we made that kind of money," Dan said with a touch of defensiveness. "We had lots of vegetables, too, plus honey and some other stuff. Potted herbs. Jerusalem artichokes. And it took a while for us to get up to speed. After Labor Day it's different—people are just dying to get a taste of the country, the summer. Plus, the market was different then. There wasn't anybody else with flowers. Now everybody's got them."

I nodded my head, trying to keep up with the speed of Dan's backpedaling. Finally, he offered some encouragement:

"Look, you can say they're just weeds, but the fact is that they're not available in New York City, and you're bringing them in. People really want them, you'll see. But you've got to concentrate on getting the best-quality stuff, not just anything that grows on the side of the road."

This seemed a bit at odds with everything he'd previously told me—after all, how many times had I heard how he'd stop on his way to a market at 5:00 A.M. and pick three buckets of wildflowers in fifteen minutes from a field in Staten Island underneath some power lines; on the side of the Hutchinson Parkway, wearing his state parks department hat for cover; even by the old piers on the west side of the city. If that wasn't roadside picking, then what was?

But he went on to explain it wasn't the location that mattered, it was the quality of the flowers. Whether wild or not, cut flowers have to be picked at the right stage of growth: just before the buds have fully opened, when there are still lots of green leaves on the stem, and no traces of brown anywhere. He even drew sketches of wildflowers, along with notes on where they might be found. Some of them were very specific.

"The parking lot behind this bank, they must have dumped a load of fertilizer in the marsh, because the loosestrife there is huge and it's really *purple*. There's some eupatorium there too. You've got to see it!"

His enthusiasm was infectious. Soon, I had almost forgotten about last Saturday and was busy thinking about what flowers I'd have for the next market. And before I knew it Friday arrived, and was it really time to pick again? It seemed that just yesterday I was lifting the awkward buckets, loaded with flowers and water and weighing about twenty-five pounds each, and muscling them one by one into the back of the van. My back ached in recalling last week's adventure, an ache that was compounded by the knowledge that, after counting the lunch expenses, it was costing me money to pick these weeds. I was paying to be in pain, and it would be two full days before it was over. If last week's picking spree seemed like a treasure hunt, this week's was starting to resemble a sojourn at some low-rent S & M club.

One good thing, though, was that we had lots more flowers in bloom. Also, I had decided to follow Dan's advice strictly: No more weedy-looking weeds. A stem of goldenrod with a single brown flower or leaf would be rejected. A bushy sprig of bachelor's buttons with more than two spent blooms on the whole thing would not be picked.

I started in our rows and got two and a half buckets full of zinnias right off the bat. While they'd started blooming a week or two ago on stems too short to cut for bouquets, the side shoots that the plants formed were now about eighteen inches tall, and the flowers were big, bright explosions of vivid color. These long stems could be cut without damaging the plant, which would then send up more shoots. As long as they were picked, the zinnias would continue to flower until the first frost killed the plants.

The yarrow followed. Its woody stems held up flat, oval sprays of tightly clustered pure yellow florets, and the fernlike leaves gave off a powerful, almost medicinal, but not unpleasant odor, something like a mixture of incense, pine needles, and men's cologne. After that came the *Ammi majus,* whose loose, white florets formed misty clusters that looked much like Queen Anne's lace. Next were the delicate cosmos, with their translucent petals and clean floral scent, and last the two cultivated amaranths.

Then came the weeds: A bucket of bee balm with pale lavender, golf-ball-size compound flowers redolent of its heady, sweetly perfumed fragrance. A bucket of three-foot-tall spires of deep purple loosestrife from our stream banks, along with the huge, mauve-colored flower heads of joe-pye weed. A bucket filled with bright sprays of goldenrod, with an aroma exactly like that of fresh hay. And another of frilly white Queen Anne's lace, its paper-doily flowers supported on impossibly thin stems that were packed over a hundred to a pail. Finally, with green wild amaranths as filler and some tall yellow and gray mullein to add an architectural touch to the big bouquets, I was done picking flowers.

Today's flower harvest, while not the exciting scavenger hunt of last week, seemed more promising in terms of quality and variety of blooms. I could see that it was a better mix of showy flowers and background filler—both of which were needed to make the kinds of bouquets we liked. While I'd put in a full day in our field, I felt happy not to have had to rush around in the van gleaning dubious blossoming weeds from the sides of the county roads. There was some extra satisfaction in having picked everything, both the cultivated flowers and the wildflowers, on our own land. My goal was to create a situation in which the land could support us, and this was at least a step in that direction. But there was little time to reflect on that now.

It was getting late. Kim would be home from Albany soon, provided there was no governmental crisis, and I still needed to get some vegetables. I hurriedly picked as many beans as I could grab and filled five more buckets with cucumbers and zucchini. As the afternoon's breezes stilled, the night insects—moths, mosquitoes, and fireflies—were starting to come out. For the first time that day I noticed the rushing sound of the stream as it flowed around trees that had fallen across its low banks, and its heavy, slightly rank smell. Only a short distance beyond the fence that outlined our field, the brook's presence had been hidden all day behind a screen of willow and dogwood shrubs and disguised by the rustling of leaves in the breeze. Now it was making itself felt.

The calm of evening brought a noticeable change throughout the field, a prelude to the quiet watchfulness of night. Soon the mists that rose from the cool water would begin creeping over the ground as they often did on cloudless evenings, filling the bottom of our small valley with a low, silvery fog. I slapped a mosquito on my thigh and removed a gnat from my ear almost simultaneously. It was time to go to market again.

By noontime the next day our stock of flowers was running low. The buckets were empty, and everything we had was now out on display—a dozen or so bright, bushy bouquets, a bowl full of cucumbers, and a couple of brickbat-size zucchini. This was a good sign, even though I hadn't yet counted the money.

When we'd arrived in Brooklyn late the night before, Kim had had the good sense to go to sleep immediately, while I'd spent a nervous few hours knocking around the dusty old house that we'd renovated and lived in for the previous six years, wondering if it was too late to reverse the terrible mistake I'd made.

If last week's market was any indication, the farm business was shaping up to be a fiasco. Sure, we'd had idyllic moments amongst the weeds, but mostly it was a series of hard, hot, and boring tasks, one right after another. And, after all, our life in the city hadn't been so bad. If I didn't have to get up so early, I thought, I could walk out into the night right now and stroll the avenue, its trees and streetlamps creating a pleasantly dim glow in the cooling summer breeze. I could get a decaf latte and a cannoli at the Italian bakery up the street, or a Thai dinner at the restaurant with the deck in the backyard, where they put candles inside of brown paper bags on the table. There would be plenty of people around—I might even run into someone I knew and sit down for a chat. Anything could happen. Where we now lived, at this hour, there would be exactly nothing going on.

As I wandered through the unused rooms in the small hours, it began to seem as if my recent past had been a series of missteps, one small error leading to the next, each unfulfilled promise becoming larger the further I went on this path. At least here in the city I had lots of friends, and I'd never had trouble putting a few dollars in my pocket. What would be the culmination of this adventure—to drag Kim and me into a spiral of downward mobility and a hard-scrabble existence in the sticks? Where would it end?

After a short, fitful sleep (I was no longer used to the car horns and music from the busy avenue below the bedroom window), I rose with the sun and drove us to the park that hosted the market. I felt on edge; it was a good thing I had something to do other than sit behind the stand or I probably wouldn't have made it through the morning. Putting together bouquets behind the van and carrying them over to the stand, chatting with Dan, and rearranging the display kept my mind occupied.

Now the work was mostly done, and the three of us sat behind the card tables, selling the remaining bouquets, talking, and handling vegetables. I couldn't stand it anymore. "Okay, let me have it!" I exclaimed.

Kim, smiling, handed over the market wallet. I grabbed it and started counting. Panic moderated to relief—it was small bills, mostly, but lots of them. Well over three hundred dollars. Even subtracting our starting stash, we had doubled last week's sales. The profit was still pathetic: counting my day picking and the two of us at market for one day, we could each draw fifty dollars a day, after paying Dan his agreed upon fee of a hundred dollars. But at least we could afford lunch. More important, I thought, was the fact that we wouldn't be returning with any unsold buckets of flowers. People had actually bought every bouquet we made! It was going to be a far less somber ride home. Tomorrow would be our day of rest, followed by a day of picking for me on Monday, and the first Brooklyn market on Tuesday morning.

Making more money at our second Saturday market was some-what reassuring, but I was far from convinced that this was going to be a viable business venture. After all, $320 was not $1,000, and I was still somewhat in shock over the disconnect between our reality and Dan's stories. Though Dan had come up with some possible reasons why our take fell so far short of his, in the end he could offer no better explanation than something along the lines of That was then and this is now. But, given that our earnings had doubled, it seemed worth hanging in there to see what would happen next.

Besides, after only two markets it was obvious we were learn-ing a tremendous amount as we went along. We had picked less bedraggled-looking flowers, created a fuller, more eye-catching display, and were getting more comfortable with everything from making change to making chatter. As a reporter, I hated few things more than not being able to come up with the right infor-mation. So I had done my homework. This time, when a cus-tomer asked, I could say that eupatorium—also called joe-pye weed—is a perennial; smaller-petaled flowers like yarrow last the longest; and we would probably have a good supply of fresh flow-ers until the beginning of October.

I supposed it would take the full market season for us to be able to tell what the potential was here and whether we should keep forging ahead. Maybe the Brooklyn market, which Chris and Dan were due to start in two days while I was at work, would hold more promise. I couldn't wait to hear about it.

An asphalt plaza flanked by a city park and a small garden was the site where Dan and I, along with a dozen or so other farmers, bakers, and fishmongers, convened in the early morning that

Tuesday. We set up our stands across from a set of tall marble steps on the back side of the old Borough Hall building and prepared for the market day. By 8:00 A.M. the air already seemed stagnant, and enclosed by the six-story buildings of old Brooklyn Heights, the heat from the pavement seemed to reflect back into our bodies, as if we were inside an oven on slow roast. Dan and I were melting, but our flowers still looked good. So did everyone else's.

It was clear from the start that this wouldn't be an easy sell. Although it was Dan's alma market, and the same manager (who seemed quite friendly and remembered him well) was still in charge, I could tell from Dan's previous descriptions of it that the market itself had changed quite a bit since he'd sold flowers here. Instead of being unique, we were just one of four flower vendors: a grower from Long Island specialized in dahlias and gladioli, and had brought tens of buckets full of the showy blooms; a farmer and orchardist from the Catskill region had premade mixed bouquets packed in clear cellophane wrap, displayed around the base of a pillar near the middle of the plaza; a New Jersey greenhouse grower had seasonal cut flowers along with potted plants and hanging baskets. And we had . . . what did we have? Twelve buckets of flowers, two-thirds of which were gathered from places other than our garden, a stack of old newspapers to wrap them in, two card tables, and a hand-painted sign. At least we had replaced the chalkboard.

Dan was clearly at ease here, chatting up the sellers he remembered and whipping out bouquets for the display as I fretted and paced. Our morning sales were not encouraging: we sold about ten small bunches at four dollars each—the going rate at this market. Still, Dan encouraged patience.

"It's your first day," he noted. "You can't judge the market by that. Sure, you've got competition, but not everybody wants a bunch of flowers that look like they came from a convenience store, or are on their way to a funeral. It's fine if their bouquets stand up like little soldiers, all in a row, but you've got something they don't."

"Yeah, weeds," I remarked.

He gave me a pained look and went back to arranging flowers. Around noon, the market was suddenly flooded with people—office workers from the city agencies, the borough offices, police head-quarters, and the courts poured into the narrow plaza and strolled up and down the hot walkways between the stands. Lines formed at the bakers' tables, fruit and vegetables changed hands briskly, and we started selling bouquets as fast as we could make them. But by 1:30, the market was again quiet, and we baked in the sultry afternoon sun. Around 3:00 P.M., more than eight hours after we'd started, I decided to call it quits. Our sales had exactly tied the first day at Abingdon Square, and the net take remained exactly zero. I would be returning home with six buckets of unsold flowers, half of what I'd brought to market. The only consolation was that here I got a free lunch.

It was Eric the market manager's habit to go from stand to stand and buy just one item from each—a small loaf of bread, a tomato, some lettuce, sprouts, red pepper, whatever. These amassed food-stuffs were constructed into an immense sandwich, which Eric kindly offered to share with me. It was surprisingly tasty and did wonders for my flagging spirits. Perhaps it was just the first-day blues, and this market would pick up like Abingdon did. I had to hope it would, because as of now this was my full-time job. With a field full of flow-ers and vegetables, and the efforts of the spring and early summer behind me, there was no going back now.

By late August the market work was settling into a routine. The week began on Friday, with a full day of picking that lasted from about 8:00 A.M., when Kim left for Albany, until 7:00 P.M., when she got home. Then, as she changed into a different kind of work clothing, I loaded the truck as quickly as I could. We drove to Brooklyn in the dark, eating a sandwich on the road and talking about the day.

Arriving by 10:30 P.M., we tried to get as much sleep as possible. The market routine was the same: rise at 6:30, meet Dan at the park at 7:30, sell until 2:30, pack up and return home by 5:00.

Sunday was our day of rest. Monday began the same picking routine for the Tuesday market, the only difference being that I made the drive alone. The Brooklyn market went on the same time schedule as Abingdon, and I usually got home early Tuesday evening. Wednesday and Thursday were for weeding, mowing, and finishing various jobs on the house, like painting the walls and installing finished floors. Then Friday came around again and the cycle repeated.

The butterflies still flew in my guts before each market, although they were quieter now. But the excitement of handling the money, making bouquets under time pressure, and talking to the customers about flowers only grew. While I enjoyed them more, I was quietly adjusting to the reality that, no matter how you looked at it, my expectations had been far too high regarding the amount we could earn at the farmers' markets. Then one day in early September everything changed.

I first noticed it almost as soon as we arrived at Saturday's market. While early bird shoppers aren't uncommon—the early morning hours of the weekend are the residential neighborhoods' most beautiful, quiet, and uncrowded time—the difference was that on this day it seemed everyone in the immediate area had awoken early with the idea of visiting our stand. Until now I'd had plenty of time to spend making each bouquet, trying to concentrate on the principles of harmony, contrast, and rhythm that Dan had shown me, and feeling my way toward a style of my own. But today it would be a race just to keep the display stocked: as soon as either of us finished putting together a bunch from the buckets of flowers that bounded our work space, a square of sidewalk and street adjacent to the open rear doors of the van, someone would walk up to us and ask, "How much?" Then he or she would buy it. We soon decided that the only way we would ever have bouquets available to stock the stand was to make only seven-dollar bunches for a while. Surely some customers could be directed to the tables, where a few five-dollar bunches still remained.

Well, nice try, but no thanks. Seven bucks was no problem. Within minutes, Kim had no bouquets to sell at all. She eyed me impatiently as she bagged cherry tomatoes, which were a surprise gift from the fields just in time for the end of the season. Of all the tomatoes we started and grew, these small-fruited varieties were the only ones that did well enough to bring to market, and now they were selling briskly at four dollars a quart. But as far as delivering more bouquets now, all I could do was shrug.

Finally we hit on a workable plan to cope with the traffic: Dan alone would be the custom bouquet maker. While I ran through my limited repertoire of bouquet designs as quickly as I could, charging off to the stand when I'd completed three or four, he took care of the customers who had a special request. I watched him at work, fascinated. Instead of setting a price at the start, he'd simply start putting together whatever flowers they wanted, smiling and chatting away the whole time.

"You're starting to get up around seven dollars," he'd remark, as the bouquet in his hand took shape.

"That's fine, let's keep going. How about some more red zinnias?"

Dan complied, and the bunch grew larger.

"How's that? Does ten sound okay?"

"Fabulous. They're so pretty. Thanks so much!"

He wrapped the flowers in sheets of newspaper, shoved the bill in a shirt pocket, and went to the next customer waiting patiently outside the ring of buckets.

"Hello. What kind of bouquet would you like today?" he'd ask.

"Just make something beautiful. I love what you've been doing." This system kept things under control for an hour or so. Then the men showed up.

We hadn't been keeping track, but it seemed that up to now our clientele had been predominantly female. I assumed it might be that our flowers appealed mostly to women, or that they did more shopping at the farmers' markets than men. But now, down from the hills, away from the beaches, back from wherever they'd been all summer, singly and in groups, men were congregating at our stand. And they all seemed to want just one thing: sunflowers.

The three rows of sunflower seeds I'd planted were the only flowers that grew in the part of the field without mulch. And grow they did—the plants were now five feet high, and we'd started bringing in the big single blossoms, in autumn hues of yellow, orange, and brown, just this week. At a dollar a stem, the two buckets we had were emptied before we could manage to work any into bouquets.

But the customers kept coming anyway. They cleaned us out of crookneck squash; red, orange, and yellow cherry tomatoes; zucchini; and cucumbers. They bought zinnias, amaranths, cosmos, mullein, and black-eyed Susans. By noon we had sold completely out of flowers, and sixteen empty buckets were stacked by the van alongside a big pile of clippings. The few remaining vegetables were soon gone, and we quickly packed up the tables and counted our take: nearly six hundred dollars in cash. Bidding a hasty goodbye to our neighboring vendors, we hurriedly headed north, lest fortune somehow rob us of what felt like our first real triumph. And Dan didn't even say, "I told you so."

We didn't know it at the time, but there would be just three more weeks of busy post–Labor Day markets. Sales in both Brooklyn and Manhattan would be about double what they'd been before the end of the traditional summer season. Although it's hard to describe the exact difference in climate between a fair Saturday in late August and one in September, it seemed that the city dwellers could sense that winter was approaching, and it was time for them to squirrel away their nuts while they could. Or else their leases had run out in the Hamptons. Either way, we were enjoying the markets more than ever.

❖

By late September, I was completely at home at the market. What had first been so alien was now a comfortable routine, and I discovered many things I loved about selling.

Being outside was a welcome change from the dark, airless state capitol building in which I spent most of my time. And, miraculously, it hadn't yet rained on a market day. I loved sipping tea on the brisk early fall mornings right after setting up the stand and just before diving into the flower buckets to make my first bunch of the day (by this time, I had gotten up enough nerve to make bouquets, too).

I saw my family and friends more than I had when I lived in the city. And Chris and I made some new buddies, too. There were our immediate neighbors, also a couple just starting out, who were selling field greens and other vegetables. And, of course, there were our customers, whose preferences we came to know as well as our own.

The European documentary filmmaker loved the weedier-looking bunches, which she said looked very "French"; the psychology professor wanted all whites and pastels with the stems cut short; the redhead who worked in the fashion industry favored vibrant oranges and yellows; the short elderly man with long gray hair and black-rimmed glasses carefully selected two cucumbers each Saturday.

It was hard to imagine there would come a day when we would pack it in for the season. I would miss them all.

❖

As we slouched toward October, the signs were becoming clearer. One market was missed because of heavy rains. Another Saturday morning found us dressed far too lightly for the unexpected chill in the early morning air; noticing Kim shivering and miserable behind the tables, our market manager, Harriet, kindly took off the leather jacket she was wearing over her sweatshirt and gave it to her. Then we had to cancel a Brooklyn date because, after a marathon picking day devoted to the Saturday market, the plants were no longer growing back fast enough: there were potentially only seven buckets of flowers available, not enough to justify the trip.

On Thursday of the same week I heard ominous news on the morning weather report: temperatures were expected to plunge to the mid-twenties that night, and a freeze warning had been issued. While it was possible that a very light frost in the valley had already retarded some plant growth, a temperature below 28 degrees could mean only one thing: the growing season was coming to a close for the year. And although a few woody plants and some shrubs might continue to flower for a short time, this was it for the tender crops, like zinnias, tomatoes, sunflowers, cucumbers, cosmos — in short, everything we had. I canceled my plans to work on the house and instead went down to the field to harvest everything I could get: fourteen buckets in all, plus some vegetables. It was a bright, sunny day, seemingly no different from any other this season, and I wondered when the picking was all done whether the forecasters had made a mistake. But the buckets were dutifully stored in the garage, where the concrete walls embanked in the sloping hill would keep the temperature from extremes, and I waited to see what changes that night might bring to our fields of summer.

Looking from the window the next morning I didn't notice much difference. But the thermometer read 25 degrees, and the heat had come on inside our house. As soon as Kim left for work, I raced down to the rows to see what had happened. From a distance nothing seemed amiss. Among the tangle of stems and leaves, the flower blossoms were never the first things I noticed in the fields anyway. But as I got closer, bouncing the big Dodge down to the bottom of the valley, it seemed the foliage was darker than usual. I stopped by a row of cosmos and got out. And then I saw.

The flowers had turned completely black, as if they had been burned in a fire that didn't consume them but drained all the resilience and color of life from their petals. Many stems had broken just below the flower heads, and the blooms hung pointed at the ground, stiffly waving from side to side in the light breeze. While the plants still showed some green near ground level, all of the foliage on top had turned the crispy brown of oak leaves in the fall. The cosmos were history.

It was the same with the zinnias, the *Ammi majus,* everything. A few orange tomatoes still hung from the vines, but these were frozen solid. When the rays of the rising sun hit them, they turned to mush before my eyes. It was all over, just like that.

Our final market was on a cold and windy Saturday, but the flowers seemed to look better than they ever had before. Perhaps it was because they'd been in cold storage, or maybe it was just that we knew we wouldn't be seeing them again for a while. While this market day wasn't as frenzied as the previous few, we sold out of flowers at the end and said bittersweet good-byes to our customers and market mates. We heard that the market was slated to move next spring back to its former location a block away, and that there might be a new manager and some new vendors, while some of this year's regulars would not be returning. But next year seemed very far away. We had made it through the first season, and for now that was the only thing that mattered.

# the salamanders' dance

CHRIS: It would have been nice to start off our farming career with an unqualified success at the markets, earning the kind of money we thought was possible. It would also have been a suitable reward for all of the backbreaking labor we'd put into the enterprise. Because, aside from any personal validation to be gained from running a productive farm business, the fact was that we needed the cash.

Silverpetals Farm was never intended to be a "hobby farm," the kind of operation that generates fat tax losses and employment for locals who keep the place looking tidy in between the owners' visits. In truth, we couldn't afford to lose money at all because there simply wasn't any money to sustain an expensive hobby or a failing business venture. We were financially strapped just paying the bills.

Although Kim had a salary considered fairly high in our rural area, the fiscal taps were wide open, and for some time our funds had been pouring out like free beer on a hot afternoon. Aside from the costs of building a house, starting a farm, and paying for Lee's work and other miscellaneous bills, we were still paying one mortgage on the house in Brooklyn and another on the farmland, as well as taxes, maintenance costs, and utilities on both. The rent we collected in the city didn't cover the bills, and our tax forms showed a loss there every year. It had been a good deal when we'd lived in the place, but now the hours we spent there could be counted on our fingers.

We'd worked like dogs all summer long. Occasionally it was fun, more often just meditative, and sometimes downright oppressive. And, at the end of the season, we had exactly this to show for it: in thirteen markets, we had gross earnings of $4,435. That's $341.15 per market on average. Before expenses.

There are different ways of looking at a figure like that. For a day in the park at a pleasant market, it's not bad. But divided by three (one person one day to pick, two people one day to sell), it stinks. Multiplied by two markets as a weekly wage, it's okay. But if you can earn the money for only eight weeks of the year, it's not okay. Especially since it doesn't include any costs. Especially when you think about laying mulch. Anyway, you can't support a family of hamsters for a year on that sum of money.

Still, it was our first year, and I felt a sense of accomplishment just for having lived through it. Even though we never achieved the legendary thousand dollars a day, by the end of the season we were up around that amount per week. And people seemed to like the flowers—maybe we could work our way up to a livable return at some time in the future. The question was: How?

Clearly we were not going to do it by selling two-pound zucchini for a dollar apiece. In the first place, not everyone wants a vegetable that looks like a cudgel and tastes like—well, a two-pound zucchini. (I overheard an older Englishwoman who, after picking one up and turning it over and over in her hands, begin reminiscing to her companion about her diet during the Second World War. The memories were not entirely pleasant.) Besides, only about five would fit in a pail, meaning that the five-gallon bucket was worth ten dollars—if they all sold. By contrast, a bucket of flowers, whether cultivated or weeds, was worth an average of about twenty-six dollars. And at four dollars a quart, the cherry tomatoes would fetch eighty dollars a pail. Now, that was a crop to think about raising more of. And suddenly, without making any conscious decision, I was beginning to plan for the next season.

There were never any leftover tomatoes—the sweet orange Sungolds and tart yellow pear tomatoes were certified knockouts. We would have to concentrate on growing them and forget the zucchini, which were too much trouble anyway: Their vigorous vines spread across the medians and into other rows, and the young vegetables we wanted to pick were never anywhere to be found. They seemed to hide under the mulch until they had grown to mutant size, then emerge, daring you to pick them. We could live without them.

But what about the cucumbers? They were popular, we grew some varieties no one else had, and Kim was very fond of her old cucumber man. They were easy to grow. They could stay, but not three rows—two would be plenty.

And peppers? None of ours had grown, although you could say we didn't give them much help. But the market was crowded with green peppers, and our season was too short to wait for them to turn yellow or red, as almost all peppers eventually do. They would have to go.

It was becoming pretty clear where we stood. There were a few limiting factors: the length of the growing season, the number of rows planted, and the size of the truck. We couldn't change the first, and the next two would require major investment. There were only so many hours in a week that someone (me) could spend working on the farm, and I could see that I was already nearly at the limit of the area one person could cultivate. There was no way I was going to sink money into a bigger truck until I knew I could fill it—and bring it home empty.

The crop plan was one of the things we could change. If nothing else, the tomato and pepper trials had shown us two varieties that grew rampantly and sold like hot pretzels. Using what we had learned last season, we would stick with the good performers, chuck the bad, and leave some room to try new things. The goal would be to fill every row with a salable crop, and to fill the truck with the buckets that would bring the most money at market.

There is another aspect to the profit-and-loss equation: after gross sales come expenses, and cutting costs has the same effect on the bottom line as increasing earnings. My expenses were running from one-third to one-half of sales—and that was just in the direct costs of bringing the stuff to market. It didn't include seeds, equipment, field help, tractor work, et cetera. It was just the fee paid to Greenmarket, the gas, and . . . Dan.

Dan had gotten me interested in the whole idea of farming in the first place. He'd shown me his tricks and his picks, laid mulch on the first day, and made the first bouquet. He'd guided us through our first season with patience and skill. And now I was thinking about casting him aside like a peach pit.

But what else could I do? He was costing me a hundred dollars a day, nearly a third of the average market take right from the word go. Sooner or later I knew we would have to learn to do the whole thing on our own, and I was sure he didn't expect to come to markets with us forever. Still, the whole thing seemed cruel and callous—and it seemed that it would have to be done. I could only hope that he would take it with good grace, and that I could tell him in a way that didn't make us both feel like dirt. Fortunately, next season was a long way off, and I wouldn't have to say anything for quite a while.

To a surprising degree, the cycle of New York State farming coincides with the cycle of New York State politics. Late spring—early summer is a frantic race to bring crops to market and legislation to the floor. But by the time the first frost arrives in early fall, killing the crops, the politicians have long gone dormant (unless it's an election year, and then you just wish you could plow them under).

From around the date of our first market in August through the rest of the selling season, Albany was a ghost town. After the legislature enacted a state budget in mid-July (three and a half months late), the capitol hallways no longer echoed with the bellowing of pols, the footsteps of their flunkies, and the shouted questions of reporters. In fact, my job was quite uneventful until one early fall day when I received an urgent phone call from my editor in New York. "Did you see the Amy Fisher story on the wire?" he asked.

He did not have to explain who Amy Fisher was. At the time, everyone in America knew about the "Long Island Lolita," who, when she was sixteen, shot her lover's wife in the head.

"I didn't see it," I said. "I'll call it up now."

I typed in the command for the AP directory and found the story. "Amy Fisher testifies she was raped in prison," read the headline. Wow, this is big, I thought. But what does it have to do with me?

The story explained that Fisher, now twenty-two, was suing nearly two dozen prison officials and seeking millions of dollars in damages and a transfer out of a western New York prison because the guards there were allegedly forcing her to have sex with them on a regular basis. At a hearing before a federal judge in Buffalo that day, Fisher was giving all the gory details about the sex acts she was allegedly forced to perform by five guards.

This was tabloid Nirvana.

The story concluded by saying, "Testimony was expected to continue in the hearing Wednesday." That was tomorrow.

"You have to be there at nine A.M.," my editor said before hanging up.

Say what? Buffalo was clear across the state. It was already after 5:00 P.M. I didn't even know if I could catch a plane out of Albany's dinky airport that would fly there. I supposed if Amy Fisher was describing sex with New York State prison guards, someone had to be there. But why me?

It was pointless to ask. By now, I was well aware that when

your editor tells you to go, you go. So I called the *Daily News* travel agent and found that the flight I needed to take would leave the next morning at six. I couldn't see driving back to the farm and then having to wake up at 4:00 A.M. to get to the airport on time. So I called Chris.

"I can't come home tonight because I have to go to Buffalo for a story. Amy Fisher is having sex with prison guards," I told my husband.

"Live?" he asked.

"Yeah, film at eleven. Actually, six A.M."

"That sucks."

"I know. I really don't want to do this."

"Where are you going to stay tonight?" he asked.

"I figured I'd drive out to the airport and look for a motel. There's bound to be something."

"When will you be back?"

"Maybe tomorrow after court. I'll let you know."

We said good night, and then I left the deserted capitol building and drove in the dark toward the airport on the outskirts of the city, keeping a lookout for motels. I chose the one that I thought looked the least sleazy. As I pulled into the asphalt parking lot, I wished I were driving up the hill to my little house in the cedar woods.

After checking in, I had a chicken sandwich delivered from a nearby pizzeria. Then I washed out some of the clothing I was wearing with the tiny bar of soap that was the only amenity the place afforded its guests, hung my laundry on the radiator to dry, and went to bed. The next morning at 9:00 I was seated in a Buffalo courtroom awaiting the testimony of the star witness.

When she got up on the stand, Fisher was asked by one of the defense attorneys whether she had resisted any of the alleged sexual abuse.

"When you say resisted, do you mean did I scratch and fight

and kick?" she asked somewhat defiantly. "Or did I want it? No, I did not want it."

Just what the editors ordered, I thought. I could practically hear them drooling long distance.

She also described the loneliness of being in solitary confinement. "TV is my only friend now," she said. No wonder this girl was a tabloid darling.

When everyone was finished questioning her, the judge said the hearing would continue the next day. I called my editor, and he passed me along to a rewrite guy who took down all my quotes and information. He would be the one to write the story and share the byline.

By then the travel agent had booked me into a much fancier hotel within walking distance of the courthouse. I checked in, ate another chicken sandwich from room service, and washed out my clothes again, hoping I would be sent home before they learned to jump into the sink themselves.

On the way to court the next day, I stopped at a newsstand and picked up the *Daily News*, so I could see what they did with my story. "I've Known Only Sex Abuse & TV, Sez Lonely Lolita," blared the headline. Well, this sure ain't gonna win me a Pulitzer, I thought as I entered the building.

I checked my beeper with the officer at the door, went through the metal detector, and took my place in the courtroom along with the other reporters and a few "court watchers"—retired folk who sit in on trials for the sheer amusement of it. One local TV reporter had on so much perfume, I thought she would asphyxiate us all. Today Fisher's mother was on the stand, testifying about one guard who had called the Fisher home constantly when Amy was temporarily moved to another prison. In the conversations, many of which the mother had taped and now played in court, the forty-six-year-old guard asked for photos of his favorite nineteen-year-old inmate, and for messages to be relayed to her. In one call, he admitted his requests could get him fired.

But, amazingly, though Mrs. Fisher played these tapes for prison officials not long after they were made, the guard was not fired. He was merely transferred to a men's prison, where presumably he did not find his charges so appealing. This seemed to me a story well worth writing, but it was not to be the focus of my day's work. That came when Mrs. Fisher testified about a love letter the guard asked her to smuggle in to her daughter.

"It opened up, 'Hello, my gorgeous gerbil,'" said Mrs. Fisher.

I wondered if that salutation set Amy's little whiskers atwitter. It certainly did mine.

Just then, the *New York Times* reporter, whom I hardly knew, leaned over to me and whispered, "I hate you."

"Why?" I asked her, somewhat shocked.

"Because you're going to get that in and I'm not," she said with genuine regret.

"Damn right you're going to get that in," my editor said when I told him about the day's events. He was so pleased, he even allowed me to expense some new underwear.

So after reading my notes to rewrite—for a story that would appear the next day under the headline "Amy's Mom Bares Tapes of Jail Love"—I went shopping. I bought a long skirt, a sweater, three pairs of intimate apparel (at this rate, who knew how long I'd be here), and a knapsack to put my old clothes and court documents in. I was very pleased with my purchases. Gerbil Man was going to take the stand, and I didn't want to greet him in four-day-old underwear. Somehow I felt this would undermine the moral authority I needed to handle the encounter properly.

When Gerbil Man testified, he denied ever having sex with Fisher, being in love with her, or ever even being alone with her. "I thought I was just helping a kid," he said, blaming his over-attentiveness on too much alcohol consumption.

After his testimony the courtroom was cleared, and all the reporters went down to the lobby to wait for our own chance to cross-examine the witness. Before long his lawyer appeared, and we hurried over for a comment.

But no sooner had we done so than one of the court watchers—a short, plump man who had been at the hearing from the first day—shouted from another corner of the lobby, "He's over here!"

Everyone ran to the door and saw that, while his lawyer was distracting us, Gerbil Man had snuck out and was briskly walking up the block. Perfume Woman wasted no time. She kicked off her high-heeled shoes and gave chase, her cameraman right behind her. Well, I'd be damned if I was going to get beat on this story by a powder puff like that. I ran after her, and so did everybody else.

Gerbil Man by now was also running. He scurried into a building with the rest of us hot on his tail and leaped into an open elevator packed with unsuspecting office workers. But some of his pursuers jammed the doors before they could close and whisk him to safety, and that was it. He was cornered; this Habitrail was a dead end.

He turned his back to the cameras and tried to hide against the far wall of the elevator. But, alas, poor Gerbil Man found to his chagrin that the elevator was mirrored. He stared at the wall an inch from his face, and there we all were, smiling at him.

Then Perfume Woman made her move. Thrusting her mike practically up his nose, she demanded, through clenched teeth, *"Did you have sex with Amy Fisher?"*

The elevator passengers gasped.

Gerbil Man wasn't talking. He just stood there and scowled into the mirror. The cameras rolled for a few minutes, and when everybody had gotten enough footage for the evening news, we released the doors.

When we got back out on the street, my colleagues went wild. "You go, girl!" shouted one of Perfume Woman's competitors as they all leapt around on the sidewalk high-fiving one another.

My romp through Buffalo complete, I bid my fellow scribes adieu and hailed a cab to the airport. Yes, it had been fun. I had a great story to tell Chris and a nice new knapsack filled with party favors. But I was just as glad my days on the gerbil-sex beat were over. I needed to get to a washing machine.

As the first postmarket fall wore on into winter, and next season's seed catalogs began crowding the mailbox, I became convinced that there were two things we absolutely had to have to keep our farm venture from utter ruin: a tractor and a greenhouse.

The first project was easy. A local tractor dealer had a number of used machines in his inventory, and after a little shopping I came home with a twenty-horsepower, four-wheel-drive diesel that looked like an overgrown lawn mower. It was bright orange and came up to my waist. It wasn't what I pictured when I thought of the archetypal tractor: a green monster with rear wheels as big as a man and a muffler the size of an oil drum sticking straight up from the engine block. But mine came with a hydraulic snowplow on the front and a big rototiller attachment on the back, eight gears, and an extremely low number of hours on the run-time meter. It also came with a price tag far higher than I expected to pay for a used machine, but with the smallest new tractors starting at about the same price as a new pickup truck, it seemed like a good deal. At least I wouldn't have to pay someone to plow the driveway, and come spring I could do the field preparation as early as possible, instead of waiting for someone to put me on his schedule.

There was another thing about the tractor: it was fun to ride. In high gear it could bounce along at about twenty miles an hour, and it plowed through brush and mud puddles like a rampaging goat.

And even though the run-time meter quit advancing for good shortly after I got the tractor home, I wasn't worried. The thing was solid as a stump. I soon gave up walking and drove it all around the farm-land. Everyone who came to visit that winter had to ride it for their curiosity and our amusement, and we took lots of pictures. After all, no one we knew had ever owned a tractor.

The greenhouse, though, was something else entirely: a brand-new construction project. In order to be of any use, I figured it would have to be far bigger than our house, have more light and a better heating system. We would use it primarily to start plants from seed for later transplant into the field — there would be no more bedroom farming. Kim had extracted that promise from me, and the new house was far too small anyway.

I had read quite a bit about greenhouse design, and I was intrigued by the concept of the solar greenhouse: a structure that relies primarily on solar thermal storage to provide the constant heat needed to grow seedlings, and uses a fuel-burning furnace only as a backup. There was a whole subcategory of literature on solar building design, much of it dating from around the era of *The Ex-Urbanites Complete & Illustrated Easy-Does-It First-Time Farmer's Guide*. I saw plans for solar A-frame greenhouses and self-sufficient greenhouse–living spaces called arks. There was a geodesic solar greenhouse surrounding a concrete fishpond, and a rustic combi-nation greenhouse-henhouse-sauna. Born of the late seventies "energy crisis" and alternative shelter movements, these structures shared a common, somewhat utopian vision of self-reliance and independence. They were meant to be built by competent amateurs and to have a milder impact on the environment, in terms of both the materials used in construction and the energy used in operation. They were kind of funky. What's not to like?

Unfortunately, published information on this topic seemed to have dried up by the mid-eighties, perhaps reflecting a changing social climate, or the elimination of alternative-energy tax credits.

Wasn't anyone interested in these designs anymore? Following a lead from Dan, I contacted a geologist at a quarry that supplied stone for solar heat storage systems; he put me in touch with an engineering professor at Cornell, who sent me some of his papers and then spoke to me on the phone.

"I'm not saying she's a liar," he said of the claims made by the owner of the greenhouse-henhouse that she maintained growing temperatures in the house all winter with the sun and a flock of chickens as the only heat sources. "But I'm familiar with her story, and I'm just saying that nobody has been able to duplicate her results. Let me put it this way: We know how many BTUs of heat an animal will give off per kilogram of body weight. It doesn't matter whether they're chickens or cows, the number is practically the same. We calculated how many BTUs she would need to heat her building, and I'll tell you, those birds would be stacked three deep. She'd need hundreds of chickens. And don't forget," he told me, "here in upstate New York we can grow mushrooms as a field crop."

That was true: our winter days could be sunless for a week or more at a time. It would be foolish to design a greenhouse here without an additional source of heat. There were some sound solar design principles that could be incorporated into the structure, however, and he urged me to try to use them. But, in a nod to the spirit of self-reliance, I decided I would add a special room on one end of the greenhouse. It would be just for chickens, and if they contributed to the overall heat of the building, that would be fine. They would definitely contribute a rustic ambience to the whole enterprise.

So, it was settled: I would build a 1,000-square-foot greenhouse with attached chicken coop, oriented due south for maximum solar heat gain. It would be partially below grade and would be earth-bermed to take advantage of the insulating properties of the soil. It would look from a distance like a steep-pitched roof sitting on the ground, with hardly any walls under it. Instead of glass, the south side of the roof would consist of two layers of a special clear plastic inflated by air pumped into the space between them. This inflated cavity would keep the plastic from flopping in the wind and also provide some additional insulation from the cold. The north side would simply be metal roofing, since only dim skylight would come from that direction in winter. Holding up the plastic and metal roofs would be trusses, just like the ones I'd built for the house. These would rest on a frame of heavy posts and beams instead of a stud wall. The whole thing would sit on a perimeter foundation of concrete, with additional big concrete footings under each post.

But probably the most interesting feature of the greenhouse would be the solar thermal storage mass: thirteen cubic yards of fist-size round rocks dumped behind the posts that held up the north roof. This would be a volume equal to one and a half full-size cement-mixing trucks full of stones, and would weigh about sixteen tons.

The reason for the stones was simple. The rays of the winter sun, low on the horizon, would fall directly on the back wall of the greenhouse and warm up the rocks. After sunset, they would then re-radiate the stored solar energy as heat, keeping the temperature well above freezing. In the summer the metal roof would keep the rocks in shadow, since the sun would be much higher in the sky, but they would continue to absorb heat and moderate the temperature inside the house. Best of all, the energy was free and the heating system required no maintenance.

Of course, I would have to build it first. The greenhouse was going to cost me about the same amount of money as the tractor. I would need Ed and his bulldozer to dig a hole, dump in the rocks, and backfill the foundation with dirt. I would need some concrete trucks full of concrete for the foundation, and Lee and I would have to dig the footing trenches, build the frame, and put the whole thing together. I wanted to get started immediately, before the ground froze solid, and I called Ed the excavator as soon as I had finished the plans.

A few weeks later there was a gash the size of a meteor crater in the field behind our house. In a couple of hours with his 'dozer, Ed had created a hole with sloping sides surrounding a level area on the bottom. That area would be the floor of the greenhouse. Like our house, it was set into a hillside, so the depth of the hole varied from six inches in the low corner to nearly six feet on the high side. The earth he removed was piled high around the edges of the excavation, waiting to be pushed back against the walls when the structure was complete.

The following week, temperatures plummeted to near zero at night, the lower twenties by day. The ground froze solid enough to turn the blade of a shovel or even a pickax. Then it snowed, and then it snowed some more. Until the weather changed, the greenhouse construction would have to stop. For all we knew, that could be next May.

❖

Just go as slow as you need to, take your time and you'll be okay, I thought, as I rolled through a nighttime blizzard on the back roads that would take me home. The commute from Albany to the farm, usually an hour-and-fifteen-minute drive, was going to take a lot longer on this messy December night. Although I had on the glasses that usually helped me see better after dark, the snow was coming down so hard I could barely make out anything but the fat white flakes spinning toward my windshield. Beyond that, it was just black. Right now all I wanted was to get home safely. And to cry.

I had been trying to get the tears flowing ever since I left the office about an hour before. After a particularly awful workday, I simply needed to release the stress. It was late Friday evening, and I had just finished putting together a profile of one of the state's leading politicians for the Sunday paper. A wealthy man who lived on a country estate, this legislator had threatened to let regulations lapse that keep rents on certain apartments in New York City below market rates. The rent-control issue was huge, and it was one the entire press corps would be following until the law's expiration date in June. There was a lot of pressure to get as many stories into the paper as quickly as possible to beat the competition.

With very little time to complete this assignment, I had interviewed the legislator, read his financial disclosure filings, and written a piece that showed how different he was from the many middle and lower income people who would be affected if he had his way. But no matter how I tried to rework the story, nothing I did seemed to be good enough for my boss. He wanted more damning information, more inflammatory quotes. The lawmaker had to be richer, had to be meaner. Wasn't there anything else in my notes we could use?

After we had gone around and around on this theme into the night, it became clear that my editor wasn't going to be satisfied until we had turned this man into a cross between King Midas and the Wicked Witch of the North. I read page after page of my raw notes out loud into the telephone receiver, a completely humiliating experience for someone who is supposed to be capable of using her own professional judgment. At one point I gave him a quote that I didn't even have written down, I only remembered the legislator saying it. Or did I? Now I wasn't sure. I wondered, as I tightened my grip on the steering wheel: Was I just making something up to give my boss what he wanted? Had I sunk that low? Or was I just doubting everything because the whole episode had left me feeling completely incompetent?

Whatever the case, I had to get that quote taken out of the story, I decided as I turned an icy corner in the road. I noticed I was passing by the same intersection where Chris and I had foraged for wild bachelor's buttons four months ago.

Maybe I had remembered what was said correctly, but maybe

I hadn't. I wasn't going to take the chance. I would call the Sunday-paper editor tomorrow and get the quote removed. Of course, that meant this nightmare wouldn't be over until I could make my request in the morning. But that was my own fault, I thought, my heart jumping in my chest like a hooked fish. Why wouldn't the tears come?

Leaning forward and peering into dark, dizzying snow, I made a right onto the stretch of road by the field where we had picked the wild bee balm. I couldn't even see up the hill to where the plants were. By now they would be no more than strawlike stubble covered in snow. The wheels of my station wagon slipped but quickly regained the road. Thank goodness for all-wheel drive, I thought.

But even with a good car, there was no way I would make it up my driveway tonight. Chris had probably plowed it several times during the day with his new tractor, but he couldn't possibly have kept up with this mess. I would have to walk all the way up from the bottom of the hill. At least this time I had boots and a flashlight with me. I had only needed to get stuck down there once this winter to learn that walking up a steep, icy gravel track in the dark wearing dress shoes is a great way to set a new record for number of falls per yard. But even prepared as I was, it wouldn't be easy. An exhausted, stressed-out person can't do anything well.

I made the last turn onto our curvy little road and approached the one steep downhill portion of the drive that was always the trickiest in bad weather. In the sunshine, this was a beautiful little stretch of country, with freshly painted barns and horses grazing in well-manicured fields. But tonight it was going to be nothing but trouble.

I tried to hug the curve and keep the car from picking up too much speed from the hill. But halfway down I lost control and began skidding. Just then, from out of nowhere, a herd of deer came running single file across the road a little ways in front of me. I pumped the brakes, but the car kept going. I was hurtling toward the deer, and there was nothing I could do. *"Go, go, go!"* I urged them as I watched the white tails pass like fluttering handkerchiefs in front of my windshield, getting closer and closer until the last one seemed only inches from my face. I heard a thud as I clipped the back leg of the last deer and watched with sadness as it limped up a snowbank—the same one into which my car now plunged. It came to a dead stop with the motor still running. And then the tears came and they wouldn't stop. I sobbed and sobbed, and when I had finished the tension was gone.

But now I had a new problem. Was I stuck in this pile of snow a mile from my home? Did I have the cell phone with me? Would Chris have to come and get me out? Could anyone? I put the car in reverse and very gently put my foot on the gas. The car moved. In a few moments I was back on the road.

A short time later I pulled into my driveway and, with immense relief, turned off the car. I had made it this far, and now it was time to climb the hill. I slipped out of my shoes with a sigh, laced up my boots, and found the flashlight in my bag. Then I stepped into the cold, wet night. It actually felt good to be walking instead of driving. I was home. Everything would be all right. I would call the Sunday editor tomorrow and take out that quote. What was more, I vowed, I would never get myself into a situation where I had to make a phone call like that again.

By the first of March, winter's chill was loosening its grip on our land. It was still cold, and snow lingered in sheltered spots on the ground, but the soil was beginning to thaw. The raw brown earth in the greenhouse excavation glistened with liquid water when the morning sun hit it, only to freeze back to a dull, solid gray in the late afternoon shadow. To judge by the barren fields, spring was still a long way off. Yet counting back from the expected planting date in May, it was now about time to start the ten-week transplants. That would be a problem, since there was no place to put them.

It was still too cold to pour concrete. With nighttime temperatures well below freezing, the fluid material would not harden properly and would lose most of its strength when it finally did solidify. Although the lumber was ready and I had already fabricated the roof trusses, there would be no foundation to put them on. And when the weather would decide to cooperate—next week or next month—was anybody's guess.

Lee, however, could already sense the coming change in seasons. One evening early in the month, he and his wife, Ruth, came to our new house to share a dinner of beef brisket. It was the first time we'd had dinner guests there. The oven had been on for hours, filling the little room with moist heat and the steamy aroma of slowly baking carrots, onions, and meat. As the cold wind whistled outside, the four of us ate, talked, and played a few rounds of Scrabble, which they won so handily that it soon became pointless to continue the game.

"Well," said Lee, "it's good we had the brisket now. It's a winter meal. You'll soon be opening all of the windows when you put the oven on. That's what you get for using that six-inch insulation."

"Yeah, but it doesn't seem like this winter will ever end," I remarked. "There was snow on the ground in October, and there's still snow on the ground now."

"Not for long," he said. "Any day we'll get the thaw. Then you'll start hearing the peepers in the trees and you'll know that spring is just about here. That's the time we used to get ready to go into the woods and hunt salamanders."

"Huh?" I said. "You hunted *salamanders*?"

Lee explained that when he was a youngster, he and various family members and friends gathered spotted salamanders to sell to pet stores. A certain day in the early spring was the best time to find big groups of the amphibians in the marshy woods.

"You have to wait until the first warm rain following the spring thaw in March. That's when they come out of hibernation and start moving around. It's mating season. You can tell it's time when you hear the wood frogs—not the peepers, they start earlier and have a real high-sounding call. The wood frog's sound is lower, and when you hear it, you know the salamanders will be moving around too."

He continued in his now-familiar teacherly mode. "The salamanders come out from under rotten logs or rocks, in the woods where they've been holed up all winter, hibernating, and they head for the nearest swamp. What they're looking for is about six inches or a foot of clear water. Melted snow or big rain puddles are fine, but not a year-round pond—that might have fish that would eat their eggs. They want a temporary pond, just for a few weeks so their eggs can be fertilized and hatch.

"What they do when they get together is a dance, a mating dance. The females form a group, and the males make a circle around them. The boys swim around and around, until some girl salamander decides she's ready. She swims through the ring of circling males, and on her way she picks one of them, and they go off together."

"That must be really cool to watch," I said. "So you used to go out and look for them every spring?"

"Yep. The pet stores bought them two for a dollar. We could make a couple hundred bucks apiece in a night. But we never took all the salamanders. We always left lots of females—they're the smaller ones—and some males in every pond. They're still there, plenty of 'em."

"Awesome. I'd love to see something like that," I said.

"Will you take us?" Kim asked eagerly.

"Sure," he said. "Listen for them wood frogs."

❖

A week or so later, two days of moderate but steady rain had removed the last traces of snow from the ground, swelling the creeks into muddy turbulence. Peepers began calling from the trees. The eerie, high-pitched, insectlike cries of these tiny frogs seemed to come from everywhere at once. It was impossible to tell if they were straight ahead or to the left or right, two feet away from the listener or twenty yards distant; maybe they really *were* everywhere. I still couldn't distinguish the sound of a wood frog, but the next evening, as a light but distinctly warm rain began falling, I decided I had to try to see the salamanders dance.

Kim and I arrived at Lee's house about nine that night, wearing slickers and rubber boots. When I'd called earlier, Lee seemed at first slightly reluctant at the prospect of going out into the wet night, but the anticipation in my voice must have swayed him, and he agreed to take us to a spot where we might see some fine specimens of the slimy amphibians. We all piled into our car and headed down a back road near his home. We drove for some time, stopping frequently with the windows open to listen for the croak of the wood frog. On this foggy night, landmarks on the unlit back roads were elusive, even for Lee.

We doubled back several times, finally pulling just off the road into what seemed like a patch of dead weeds and tree stumps. With the engine and lights turned off, the darkness was total. The night's sounds became intense: a cacophony of peepers with some deeper, strangely hollow tones overlaid on the higher vibrations. Wherever he had brought us, this had to be the place.

"I think I know just where we are. We should find some water right over there," said Lee, sweeping with his hand the area past our car. "Let's go."

It turned out that the car was parked on a strip of dry land between road and swamp that was barely wide enough to accommodate it. A step away from the car doors, I plunged into clear, cold, ankle-deep water. In the glow of the flashlight beams, last fall's dry leaves were clearly visible on the bottom, amidst some fuzzy, slime-covered twigs and a rock or two. Broken trunks and roots of fallen trees punctuated the slick black surface of the water every few feet, making travel in the pitch dark a tricky business, even with our lights. We stayed close together as the water rose almost to the tops of our calf-high boots, silently following Lee deeper into the swamp.

Suddenly, we heard a splash. Turning the weak radiance of my flashlight beam to the sound, I watched Lee raise his clenched hand slowly from under the water and open it for inspection. Inside was a big, wet, and quite lethargic spotted salamander.

The beast was six inches long. Its slimy skin had the color and texture of an overcooked eggplant. It had a flattened triangular head with slightly bulbous, dark eyes, a broad, pudgy midsection, and a long, tapering tail. A dozen small, yellow polka dots were spaced across its shiny back, and a pair of stubby legs stuck out like afterthoughts from either side of its body. Like a truly prehistoric creature that is suddenly discovered alive and well in someone's backyard, it was at once fascinating and repulsive.

"Female," said Lee. "There'll be more around."

He put the rubbery salamander back in the water, and we watched it swim away lazily.

I began to play the light around the water, looking for signs of the creatures. A few feet away, at the edge of the beam, there was movement near a sunken root. I sloshed closer. It was another salamander, swimming right toward me. I reached into the frigid water, but the slow-moving beast somehow eluded my grasp. Now my sleeve was soaked, and one of my boots seemed to have sprung a leak, but I didn't care. I was going to catch one, and they were all around.

The three of us split up for a time, never straying far from the glow of the others' lights, and I finally managed to bring to the surface a small, inert amphibian. It lay in my hand like a lump of cold purple Jell-O, barely moving, until I placed it back underwater and it casually swam off.

Then Lee cried softly, "Come over here and see this!"

Quickly reaching his side, I gazed into the ring of water illuminated by the flashlight. A dance was breaking up. A semicircle of salamanders poised head to tail still hovered at a constant distance beyond another group of five or so, but the remainder of the circle was in the process of disintegrating, and salamanders were swimming off in all directions, away from the light. Soon the females in the center began to disperse, and it was as if our coming had signaled the arrival of the vice squad. The party was over.

When we arrived at home after dropping Lee off, I was still strangely exhilarated from seeing the salamanders' dance. It was the kind of thing I used to watch on nature shows, but now it was happening in my backyard.

What wasn't happening in my backyard was greenhouse construction. It was clear that there would be no greenhouse in time for this year's crop. So much for my promise to Kim—the plants would have to share our home once again. But unlike those in our bedroom farm in Albany, all of the seedlings I started a week later were flowers. It had become clear from our experience in the first year of market that flowers were going to be Silverpetals Farm's principal crop. They were easy for us to grow and transport, and they sold well. People seemed genuinely to like the bouquets we made, especially the mixtures of cultivated and wild flowers. They gave us a product that was unique in the market, and a style to match. With twenty or thirty varieties planted in our rows, all blooming at different times, we'd never run out of something to sell, or face disaster if we lost a row or two to some calamity. As things stood, we couldn't compete in growing common vegetables with the big truck farms in New

Jersey or Long Island, who had not only months-longer growing seasons but also big machines and hired help. We could still grow our special cherry tomatoes and Asian cucumbers, but our focus was going to be on the flowers.

This year, I had decided to make a separate bed for perennial plants, the ones that can regrow each year from hardy underground rootstocks. Once they were established, there would be that much less mulch to lay and that many fewer seeds to start every year. These plants would take a full ten weeks to grow sturdy enough to be put out into the field, so they were the ones I was starting early. Some, like yarrow and bee balm, would be established in our perennial beds to substitute for small, potentially unreliable stands of the same wild plants that we had picked for market last year. Others, like salvia—a huge family of plants related to the herb sage, all producing upright spikes with dozens of tiny blossoms in colors ranging from purple and red to silvery white—and butterfly weed, a tall milkweed relative with bright sprays of salmon-colored blossoms, were plants we would be seeing in our field for the first time.

The routine for starting the seeds was now familiar: wetting the soilless mix in a big garbage can, shoveling it into the cell paks, tapping in the tiny seeds, and labeling the flats. Since I still had all the lights and tabletops I had removed from the Albany apartment, it was a simple matter to set them up again in the garage directly beneath our bedroom. With an electric heater underneath the flats for extra warmth and a plastic sheet overtop to hold in moisture until germination, I lowered the banks of fluorescent tubes and turned on the timers, starting the cycle again.

The weather finally did settle down later in the month, and Lee and I began pouring the foundation and putting the frame of the greenhouse together. Although the hole was muddy and the timbers heavy, the work went by with a gratifying speed that was totally unlike my experience with the house. The floor was simply gravel dumped over the dirt. Wall frames were constructed of salvaged boards and wood pallets that fit nicely between the four-foot-apart upright posts. Two two-by-twelve beams were nailed across the tops of each line of posts. Then the big roof trusses were laid atop the post-and-timber framework, swung up into position, and nailed in place. Thirteen cubic yards of rock was unceremoniously dumped behind the north wall and kept from pouring into the growing space of the greenhouse by a crib made of more pallets and some chain-link fence. Finally, a skin of corrugated metal panels (scrounged from the lumberyard when they refurbished their roof) was nailed to the outsides of the walls, and the two-layer plastic sheeting was stretched across the south roof. And presto—in four weeks we had our own solar greenhouse.

Well, almost. It was nearly as funky as any of the ones I'd read about, although it had no chickens yet. It also had no benches, no water, and no electricity. There was no backup heater, and no thermostat to control the temperature. But there would be plenty of time to get those things ready for next year. Because by now it was mid-April, and there were lots of other items on the agenda.

For one, tomatoes. We decided to grow Sungolds and yellow pears, the two varieties we'd had success with last year. Each would get a mulched row and lots of TLC; no weeds would devour our precious crops this year. And that brought up the second item: mulch.

My goal this year was to lay forty rows, and I had high hopes. I was going to train for it like a triathlon, eating, sleeping, and thinking only about the plastic rolls. But that wasn't all; I was determined to eliminate the most medieval aspects of our first farming experience. I had the tractor and tiller, which meant I wouldn't have to rent a walk-behind rototiller that seemed more interested in digging itself to China than in creating seedbeds. And there was another job that absolutely had to go: crawling for a mile with a spade to dig a trench so I could bury the edges of the mulch.

A machine, I reasoned, could do this. To make it work, I rigged up an attachment made of two old metal plow blades on a heavy steel frame, topped by a concrete block for extra weight. This contraption trailed along right behind the tiller (which was attached to the back of the tractor) and could be dropped to the ground from the driver's seat by means of a thick chain. When the tractor was put into gear, moving the whole train forward, the attachment was lowered and the blades dug two parallel furrows into the tilled earth. It performed pretty well—the shallow trenches it dug were spaced just far apart enough to allow a roll of plastic mulch to fit in between, its edges falling right into the furrows. Instead of trying to scoop hard, solid muck with a spade, the human now needed only push the loose earth that the plow blades had hilled up on the outsides of the furrows over the edge of the plastic, burying it. All I needed was an assistant to sprinkle fertilizer as I simultaneously tilled and furrowed, then someone to help me roll out and bury the mulch.

That would be Dan. Kim, who weighed in at about 125 pounds, had never been at her best in the mulch event. In the agricultural Olympics, the mulching contest, like the log roll and the caber toss, would always be dominated by men—it was too bestial to be otherwise. Besides, I knew that Dan already had a deal in mind: he proposed to exchange his time spent helping me on the farm for my time doing some renovations on his house in Rhinebeck. I quickly agreed to his proposal, and we were good to go.

The most amazing thing about the new mulching system was that it worked. In one Ramboesque three-day marathon, Dan and I put down twenty-six rows of plastic. In another week I managed, with some more help, to lay the remaining fourteen rows. Incredibly, the mulching was finished this year by early May.

There still remained the tasks of putting holes in the plastic, seeding, transplanting, and weeding the crops. And I had one more trick up my sleeve. As a substitute for jabbing the mulch twenty thousand times with a dull and brittle bulb planter, an excruciating exercise in tendinitis, I cut a propane torch in half and clamped the business end to the bottom of a long stick. A rubber hose connected the burner to a tank of gas at the top, where I put a handgrip. Now I could walk along the rows and burn holes in the thin plastic with a touch of the flame. I gradually learned how to do it without setting the whole thing on fire, and from then on it was possible to punch and seed about three rows in a day.

But the mulching marathon had taken its toll. And seven-day workweeks, with Kim's help on weekends, barely kept up with the planting schedule. The weather grew hot and dry, and the work was tedious and exhausting. Sure, the field was being planted, but at what cost? I was into Dan for at least a week of my labor, and Kim was barely speaking to me; it seemed she had some problem with working overtime on her Monday-to-Friday job, then putting in ten hours or so to help me in the field on the other days. But if I lacked a sense of what day it was, the only consolation was that it didn't really matter. It was a workday, and the work went on.

The field, though, was looking better than ever. The seeds were germinating well, and the transplants were taking hold nicely. We planted twenty-five rows of annual flowers, including four zinnias, three cosmos, two gomphrenas (commonly called globe amaranth), and a Pygmy Torch; five vegetables, including two tomatoes and two cucumbers; ten perennial flowers; and three rows of sunflowers. In the dry early season, the weeds were not thriving as they had last year. By the second week in June, the last plant—a Sungold tomato—was put into the ground. We would have a farm again this year. If we'd had the energy, we could have celebrated our good fortune. As it was, we went to sleep.

Chapter 12

i'm your pusherman

CHRIS: I noticed her immediately. A small, dark-haired, and wiry woman, she stood a short distance away from our Brooklyn setup, eyeing the tomatoes with an odd mixture of suspicion and lust. She stared fixedly at them for a long moment.

There was some strange dynamic between this waif of indeterminate age and the small, orange globes on display. Although I usually try to let the customer make the first contact, I began to wish that the silence would be broken as soon as possible. Dressed in work-stained jeans and a grubby white T-shirt, she stood in sharp contrast to our usual crowd of office workers, West Indian matrons, and casual-chic young parents from the apartments lining the Promenade by the river. She seemed nervous, anxious to be going yet unable to break away from the magnetic pull of the neatly stacked boxes that covered our tabletop. Finally, she walked up to the stand, keeping her eyes on the quart containers, and spoke. "Are those Sungolds?" she asked in a gravelly and accusing tone.

"Yes," I replied, "yes, they are. You're the first person who's ever known what kind of tomatoes they are . . . they're Sungolds."

"Uhmmhummgrrr," she replied.

Still without looking at me, she plunged a small hand into the nearest quart and extracted a fistful of the ripe, round fruits, thrusting them immediately into her mouth and closing her eyes.

"Mmmhummm. Yeah, they are. Used to grow them at the place

out on the island. Told everyone they're so much better than the Sweet 100's. How much are they anyway?"

Her words came out in a tone so rapid and harsh that I felt for a moment I had lost my breath.

"Well," I said, "they're five dollars a quart." We had raised the price since last year, and so far had heard no complaints.

"Five dollars a *quart*?" she hissed. *"Five dollars! That's a rip-off! You're ripping people off!"*

As her volume increased, I could see that there might be trouble. She seemed to be changing before my eyes into a farm stand version of Travis Bickle, the gun-toting passive-aggressive antihero of the film *Taxi Driver,* and I hoped that she was unarmed. I hoped that, if she was on medication, it would soon start to kick in. I hoped that she would go away before something else happened. But before I could think of anything to say, she quickly spoke again, a little more softly but with no less stridency: "Gimme two. Five dollars a quart! But there's nothing like them. Haven't had them since last year. They're pretty close to peak, right?"

She was right on target. We'd been harvesting them for a couple of weeks, and the juicy orange orbs were still firm but with a strong hint of the winy flavor they would soon develop, before they finally became too squashy to bring to market, or even to pick intact from the bushy vines. It was a good time to eat Sungolds.

"Fill this one up a little more, would ya? I can't believe it, five dollars a quart. Okay, just give me three. I gotta go. I'll take three quarts."

Holding a paper lunch bag in one hand and the square wooden carton in the other, I poured the cherry tomatoes carefully from a corner of the box to avoid spilling. They made a pleasant rustling sound as they slid down the brown paper and plopped to the bottom, and the three bags were soon filled. Then I grabbed an extra pint box and distributed its contents equally, filling the bags to near the top.

Finally, she looked at me.

"Thanks," she said. "I gotta run. I'll see you next week. They ought to be at peak by then."

Three five-dollar bills were thrust at me, and I watched as she vanished into the crowd. I turned to Kim's brother, who was standing beside me with his mouth open.

"David," I began. "Did I . . . see what I just saw?"

It was now early August, about the same time we'd started going to market last season, but this year I already had six markets under my belt and felt like an old pro. Having finished the mulching early, we'd put in the plants and seeds without any unusual problems, and we had begun going to market in mid-July.

Even my dreaded talk with Dan had turned out for the best: he seemed relieved to have summer Saturdays to himself again and showed up unexpectedly at our first markets to shoot the breeze and wish us well, refusing our offers of free flowers and food. David, Kim's two-years-younger sibling, found some free time to do the Brooklyn market with me on Tuesdays and often showed up on Saturdays too, unpaid, to help Kim and me handle the traffic. Also, I had purchased a used cap to cover the bed of the pickup truck. Giving us about four by eight feet of enclosed cargo space in the back, it was perfect for hauling everything to market. There would be no need for Dan's van anymore either. We were finally on our own.

If there was one thing our first market season taught us, it was that there is a lot more to picking flowers than one might think. Though we were often told our bouquets had the feel of being impulsively gathered during a walk down a country road, this couldn't have been further from the truth. By the second season, we knew how to pick the right flowers at the right time in the right way.

Zinnias, for example, grow up in V-like clusters with two long shoots forming the sides of the V and sometimes a shorter shoot coming up through the center. Full, curvy leaves that look like they come from a small head of Boston lettuce fill the blank spaces nicely. It would seem logical to want to cut this plant below the V so you have two or three beautiful flower heads on your stem, along with all their greenery. That is, until you are making a bouquet at market and reach for a flower in your zinnia bucket, only to find the entire contents of the bucket wants to lift out with it. Trying to separate one flower from this mess can drive you crazy as you accidentally decapitate all the flowers you have tended so lovingly for months.

So the rule for cutting zinnias had to be: only one flower per stem and no leaves whatsoever. Each stem was stripped before being placed in the bucket, where it could easily be lifted out when a customer said, "No, I want *that* one." Filler would be added later.

Same with cosmos, the leaves of which resemble widely spaced pine needles. Practically every stem has lovely leafy off-shoots topped by attractive buds. They all had to go. Of course, with both zinnias and cosmos, you wanted to preserve the stronger shoots that would be next week's harvest. So sometimes a mature flower would have to be cut with a shorter stem so as not to take with it buds that might bloom next week.

Another rule we devised came from one of Dan's oft-repeated sayings: "It doesn't do you any good in the field." Chris and I tended to want to "save" flowers for the next market. But we came to realize that there might not be a next time for a particular flower. What looked good today might be shriveled up next week (or even as you were setting up your stand tomorrow if you picked it past its prime). It was okay to have a lot of one thing at a particular market; if it looked good, you could always figure out how to use it. What was not okay was to schlepp in something dead.

The same went for wildflowers. Some, like Chris's "Big Yellow," a.k.a evening primrose, were just not meant to be displayed as cut flowers, drooping after one day or even one hour. Others, like goldenrod and Queen Anne's lace, lasted long and looked great. The weeds had to be picked just as carefully as the cultivated flowers.

Some customers were drawn to those flowers more than any others. One elderly woman told me that goldenrod reminded her of her childhood. A very striking older man with a bald head and flowing, white robes liked to buy big bunches of Queen Anne's lace. Another man said he liked the fact that you would never see these varieties in a flower store. Yet others thought their eyes might be playing tricks on them.

"This looks just like a kind of flower I saw on the roadside upstate!" a youngish man once said to me, as if this were the grandest of all coincidences.

"This *is* that," I assured him.

"Oh!" he said, with a tone of delight mixed with suspicion.

For the skeptics, Chris had a standard speech that he would recite at least five times per market. He would say that goldenrod was grown as a cultivated flower in Europe and was often blamed for allergies it did not cause.

"Goldenrod is insect-pollinated, not wind-pollinated," he would patiently explain. "When people think they're sneezing from goldenrod, it's usually from the ragweed that blooms around the same time." (I was convinced this confusion existed when one woman asked me for "a handful of that ragweed." I assured her I did not sell ragweed nor would I ever.)

But this distinction was not always persuasive. In fact, some visitors to our stand thought it was their duty as good citizens to out us for selling weeds. *"They're selling goldenrod!"* I once heard a man yell in the same righteous yet beseeching tone you might use to shout, "Hey, somebody call a cop!" At times like this I had to remember I was a representative of a larger marketing organization so I could resist the urge to say, "Beat it, Bozo."

But as staunch a defender as I am of one's right to sell weeds in public, there was one wildflower we marketed our second year that gave even me pause. As we were loading the truck one Friday evening to come down to the city, I noticed Chris snipping something right in front of the house.

"What are you doing?" I asked.

"I'm getting a bucket of these," he said, showing me a multi-stemmed plant with dime-size fuzzy purple flowers.

"The driveway weeds?"

"They're not driveway weeds, they're wild bachelor's buttons."

"I drive over them every day!" I protested.

"And they bounce back rather nicely," he replied. "You'll see, people will love 'em."

He was right. The next day I was talking to my mother at our stand in Abingdon Square when a young man came up to me and said, "I'll take a bunch of those purple things."

"These here?" I asked, just to make sure. "These and nothing else?"

"Yes," he said in an annoyed tone that suggested he'd like to know what a guy has to do to buy some weeds around here.

"Chris," I called out. "How much are the drive—— the wild bachelor's buttons?"

"Five bucks a bunch," he answered.

The man paid me.

As I rolled a big pile of the weeds in paper, I kept my eyes down, trying to maintain my composure.

"Thank you," we both said in unison as I handed him the bouquet. As he walked away, I started chuckling. It wasn't that he wanted to buy those particular flowers, it was that he wanted *just* those. He had passed up everything I had literally slaved over, crawled in the dirt for months to produce, and instead chose something that sprang up without any help from me, inches from my front door. If that didn't make me the biggest sucker in the universe, I did not know what did. The more I thought about it, the funnier it became, until I was laughing so hard the tears were running down my face.

"I think Kimi got too much sun," my mother said to Chris to explain my sudden impairment.

As gratified as I was that we were starting to bring home a little money from the markets, I sometimes felt overwhelmed by the fact that the whole operation depended almost entirely on me. If I failed to do some crucial task, if I got sick or just forgot something, the ensuing disaster would be all my fault. If I was too tired to weed, the weeding would not get done. So, although I lived on a flower farm, there was no time to stop and smell the flowers. And if it all failed . . . Well, nothing was irreversible yet. Tractors and land can be sold, and with the house in Brooklyn, we still had a foot in each world. Besides, Kim still had a real job.

But the exhilaration I got from doing the markets balanced the exhaustion of the farmwork. The Manhattan market was our prime spot and chief moneymaker, the place where we had started and remained; the Brooklyn market had a quirky charm all its own.

At Borough Hall, the vendors were set up in a ring around the perimeter of the big plaza: this arrangement formed a kind of amphitheater, bounded by the grand stone steps as the stage on one side, the farmers' stands as balconies on the others, and our customers, the audience, in between. Perhaps the fact that it was clearly public, not private or residential space, encouraged a freedom of expression unmatched at the other markets I had seen.

Beginning early in the morning, as the metal poles that held up the awnings were tossed off the trucks and fell clanking to the pavement with a noise like that of giant out-of-tune wind chimes, a solitary figure could be seen in one corner of the plaza, enacting the slow-motion martial-arts ballet of tai chi. That would be Eric, our market manager, doing his morning exercises.

Throughout the day, others would slowly walk in our midst dressed in outrageous getups, or barely dressed at all. A young blond woman with a heavy Russian accent and a skimpy outfit occasionally came sailing through on roller skates, stopping at various stands and talking to passersby. As I made her a colorful bunch of flowers with an extra bloom for her hair, I wondered if her deportment was a reaction to a previous life in some drab Soviet municipality.

A statuesque West Indian restaurateur, dressed in a sinuous purple-and-yellow silk gown with matching headdress, moved majestically past the crowds, buying armloads of vegetables and chatting with people she knew along the way.

"You must come and visit my restaurant. And I want two big, beautiful bouquets. We grow these flowers back home, you know," she said, pointing at the amaranths, "and we make a food called callaloo from the seeds. I don't care what it costs, but use lots of purple, it's my color. I'm a very flamboyant person."

And she was. But the prize in that category would have to go to Stick Man. We saw him first one morning pushing an old one-speed bicycle slowly through the market. He wore sandals, baggy green pants of a coarsely woven fiber, and a flowing, multicolored African-style robe. On his head was a tight, white, brimless cap with colored trim, and he carried in his hand a wooden staff carved intricately into the figure of a tall, thin, heronlike bird. He stopped at our stand to see what kinds of herbs we were selling.

"I see you are admiring my stick," he stated matter-of-factly. "You may notice that it is made into a representation of the ibis, a bird sacred to the Egyptians. This is a bird of great wisdom. It is the only animal that can give itself an enema, and it does so regularly. It therefore stands for health and self-knowledge. We would all do well to follow its example. Yessss."

❖

It was late August 1997 when I finally had a Tuesday off and could check out the Brooklyn market for myself, after having heard about all the characters Chris and David were encountering. It did not disappoint.

The market couldn't have been more different from the one we did on Saturdays in Manhattan. It was a far bigger group of farmers arrayed in a circle around a large downtown plaza, as opposed to a small string of stands lining a leafy residential street. And, because it was a weekday, everybody was rushing— the people to their offices and the cars and trucks to wherever the busy avenues that crisscrossed this section of Brooklyn would take them. One small woman seemed to be in the biggest hurry of all.

"I need three quarts of tomatoes *now!*" she exclaimed as she scooped up a handful of our Sungolds and popped them into her mouth. "Not as sweet as before," she remarked with disgust. "Give me another quart, I'll take four."

As put off as I was by her surly demeanor, I got out four paper bags into which to pour the tomatoes from the wooden cartons we use for display. *"Can't you move any faster than that?"* she hollered as I struggled with the overflowing bags. "I've got to get back to my car *now. Let's go!"* She practically threw a twenty at me as she grabbed the bags.

"Who in the world was that?" I asked Chris as I watched her angular frame and moppish hair recede into the crowd.

"Oh, that's Tomato Mary," Chris said. "David and I call her that since she's never stuck around long enough for us to introduce ourselves. But she buys from us every week."

"That has got to be the largest and most unpleasant sale I have ever made," I remarked.

"What she lacks in etiquette she makes up for in good taste," Chris said. "She's totally hooked on Sungolds."

She wasn't the only one, and for good reason. The sweet and flavorful punch this tiny tomato packs can almost knock you out. I began to notice that all those who tasted one for the first time made the identical face as their teeth pierced the orange skin and the juice started flowing: all their features would become perfectly motionless except for their eyes, which would travel slowly heavenward. I call this the tomato eye roll. As soon as I see it, I know the person in front of me will be my slave until the end of the summer.

It became a favorite activity of my brother's to hand out free samples, as he quietly hummed the old Curtis Mayfield tune "Pusherman" under his breath. "The first one is free," he would mutter slyly. During one Saturday in the Village, we hooked three people in the space of five minutes.

A thirty-something woman with mousy brown hair was chatting with us about having just moved to the neighborhood from L.A. when she inquired about the bright orange tomatoes.

"Try one," David offered cheerfully as he began to hum. We watched for the eye roll. It took one second.

"Oh . . . my . . . God," she said in a complete state of rapture. "That's all I can say. Oh . . . my . . . God."

A few moments later, a young man with a British accent who said he was a chef picked up a pint container. "I'll take the small one," he said.

"Have you tried one?" David asked casually.

The chef popped one in his mouth. We watched his eyes.

"I'll take the big one," he said.

A young Asian woman with a stylish, blasé air picked up a pint and considered it.

"You can feel free to try one," said Chris, who happened to be delivering bouquets from our nearby staging area to the stand at that moment. As soon as she did, she dug a five-dollar bill out of her purse and raced after Chris as if her life depended on catching him.

Amidst the uncertainty our farm business held, we had at least discovered one thing that is as sure as it gets. We called it tomato euphoria.

❖

And so it went through the rest of the season. We brought as many as twenty buckets to the Manhattan market and eighteen to Brooklyn, and usually returned with little more than a half bucket of excess filler and spent blossoms, along with a couple of buckets of cut-off stem ends and stripped leaves that we swept from the side-walk as we were packing up the stand.

By late August the orange, burgundy, and purple-brown sun-flowers were making their seasonal debut, and they once again attracted a loyal following. I watched in amazement one morning as a line spontaneously formed in front of the stand, the customers patiently waiting for their chance at the pick of the crop. Occasionally, though, there was disagreement about who had the right to choose the next group of the big, colorful blooms, and the warring parties were tactfully separated while we tried to work out an equitable distribution. But that was rare.

Making bouquets to order turned out to be a bigger part of our business than we ever anticipated. Dan had always tried to shy away from this; he felt it was better to give buyers as wide a choice of finished bouquets on view at the stand as possible and let them select from among those. At that market, though, his van was parked far away from the stand, and he was able to assemble the flowers in relative seclusion, then run back with them to stock the display. But here our buckets were arranged in a semicircle next to the table, so anyone could watch as we put together bunch after bunch from the five-gallon pails on hand. In fact, a good number of the bouquets never made it the short distance from the pails to the display.

Often, someone would pause on the sidewalk and watch as the bunch grew from, say, a handful of violet cosmos to a denser mass, as *Ammi majus* filled the spaces between blooms with its white, cloudlike panicles. A circle of droopy monarda, its round, pale purple blossoms stacked one atop another on thick, square stems like Bermuda onions on a rubbery shish-kebab skewer, might grow around the outside. With a sprinkling of small pink zinnias throughout, the pastel palette would be complete. The arranger, aware of being watched, would hold the bouquet at arm's length and rotate it slowly.

At this point, the question most often asked was "Are you making that for someone?"

The answer: "I'm making it for you."

This pattern quickly evolved into the custom-made bunch, or custom for short.

"I like that a lot—but could you add something yellow? How about a dark sunflower in the middle? A few more zinnias—no, just the white ones, please! Some marigolds? Some purple amaranth? Some of everything!"

A lot of people had surprisingly strong preferences for and against certain flowers, and we tried to accommodate them. It was a challenge to keep the regular display stocked, sell what we had on hand, make change, and stay on top of the line of people who wanted special bunches made just for them. Sometimes the ready-made bunches dwindled down to one or two, and people walked past the empty-looking stand while others grew impatient waiting for a bouquet that matched the exact shade of their carpet. But there was really no question that we would do the customs—it was just too hard to say no. And, unless you work in a florist's shop or are

Martha Stewart, it's a rare opportunity to choose and arrange a big variety of garden and wild flowers without having gone to the trouble of growing and picking them.

The made-to-order bouquets also gave us completely new ideas when it seemed our own efforts were growing routine and stale. And sometimes the whole process came full circle. After waiting patiently for a turn, the purchaser might simply say: "Make me something that looks like I've gone out in a field in the country and picked the most beautiful wildflowers."

"It's my birthday—make me something nice!"

"I like what you just made. Can you make one just like that for me?"

"Just make whatever you want—I like everything you're doing."

❖

During our second season, I began to sense that many people wanted something more from us than a bouquet of flowers. And that thing revealed itself in the form of questions—*lots* of questions.

Did we really grow all these flowers ourselves? What did our fields look like? What did we do in the winter? Had we grown up on farms?

The more they talked, the more I realized that our customers wanted to live out a fantasy to which we were the connecting bridge.

"You must have such a great life," I heard more than a few times that year. "It must be so beautiful where you live."

I assured them it *was* beautiful, though perhaps not in the same orderly way as our farm stand. By this time Chris and I had again given up on weeding, so from the road our field looked mostly green with little flecks of vivid color. From a distance, sunflowers were perhaps the only recognizable crop.

Up close, however, it was a different story. Row after row,

those little flecks resolved themselves into the petals and sta-
mens of a thousand perfect blooms. On the other side of the
fence, stately old sycamore trees held court in the thick saw grass
and loosestrife that banked the creek. On a spring day you might
see a giant snapping turtle burying her eggs in the row in which
you were planting, or a blue heron slowly flapping his wings after
a cool dip in the rushing water.

But in the midst of all this beauty, was I living the good life?
I certainly wouldn't call it that. There was way too much work-
related anxiety in it.

I knew by the way my customers sighed and held their faces
up to the sun that they were imagining a stress-free existence in
an Arcadian setting. In other words, the exact opposite of their
harried, urban lives. What would they think if they knew I had a
job that was probably at least as stressful as any of theirs?

I didn't tell many people about that because I didn't want to
spoil the fantasy for them. But little by little I began to see the
irony. Here I was, so concerned about making a fantasy out of my
life for others, yet I hadn't given much thought to making my life
a fantasy for me—the one who was actually living it. What was
my view of the good life, anyway?

Well, the farm was certainly becoming a bigger and bigger
part of that. I did love all the time I spent outdoors in a beautiful setting. Our harvesting routine held so many little jewels of
sight, sound, and smell. There was the creak and then clank of
the truck's tailgate as it was lowered to receive a batch of empty
buckets; the rushing and sloshing of the water as it ran from the
hose into the plastic pails; the crunch of gravel as the truck slowly
snaked its way down the hazardously steep driveway; the click of
the electric fence being turned off with the touch of a button; the
swoosh of the gate as it brushed over the grassy entrance to the
field; the first inhaled breath of sweet cosmos or tart tomatoes;
the crisp snipping of our shears; the way the back window of the

truck framed a Monet-like smear of color as the first load made its way down the packed-dirt edge of the field. Best of all was that Chris and I were building something completely our own. Nobody else's idea of what was important or urgent really mattered.

I also was, to my surprise, beginning to love small-town life. I had thought the local people we encountered would view us with suspicion. After all, what were these two nuts from the city doing coming up here and attempting to start a farm? Our experience was exactly the opposite.

We soon started to hear encouraging honks from car horns as people we had come to know drove past on the road that bordered our field. I couldn't always make out whose car was driving by but always appreciated this sort of "Go, Farmer!" salute as I bent over my labors. I looked forward to calls from the affable town librarian, who never felt she had to leave her name on my answering machine when she cheerily announced, "Kim, that book you wanted is here!" And I was completely tickled that the good-humored cashiers at the local grocery store let me walk out with as much food as I wanted even if I didn't have the funds in my pocket to pay for it right then. It was tempting to give up my double existence and make this my whole world.

But besides the obvious problem of money, I couldn't see leaving the other field in which I had spent so much time. By now I had spent ten years as a journalist, and it was obvious to me that writing would always have to be part of my life. And writing for a big-city paper had a degree of prestige, visibility, and influence that could not be matched.

Still, after having gone to all that trouble securing my job in Albany, I really didn't know if I was going to last. This past year, I had seen the best and worst of what tabloid journalism could be, and found it too often resembled a race to the bottom of the trash heap. I was very hopeful when the *News* hired a terrific editor in chief, who gave a much-needed boost to the paper's content and the staff's morale. But he didn't last the year. Who knew what was coming next?

Besides, even in the best of circumstances, newspapering had its drawbacks. The biggest was that I had too little control over my own life. I could be required to work any number of hours on any day in any location to follow a breaking story. Having worked side by side in Albany with reporters from all over the state, I knew it was the same at any paper worth taking seriously. While it might be more satisfying to work for a broadsheet like the venerable *New York Times* (the paper delivered to my parents' door each day for as long as I could remember), the potential for burnout would be at least as great. None of your time off was truly free.

I started to dread the sound of my beeper because I knew that, when I answered the page, I could find myself on the road to anywhere. On my birthday, for instance, I was sent to Boston to do a rent-control story. I didn't really mind missing out on a celebration for myself. There was nothing special about turning thirty-three. But Chris and I were hoping I would get pregnant someday soon, and I knew that, if we were lucky enough to have children, not missing their birthdays would be far more important to me.

And so would money. It always came back to that. What could I do during the off-season if I didn't work at a newspaper? Was there any way I could do the work I loved, make enough money, and still have a life?

❖

Labor Day came and went, and our fortunes at market were waxing. Now a take of under six hundred dollars in Manhattan was a big disappointment. By eliminating the expenses of Dan's labor and his van, we had reduced our costs to the point where we had to pay for only the market fee and gas, and our profits soared. I still hadn't tallied up the receipts for the year, but it seemed that this would finally be a fair test of whether the whole idea of farming was an enjoyable folly or a viable enterprise. For the time being, I was too busy to care. We had just received our first commission — table arrangements and big centerpieces for a banquet at a small museum in lower Manhattan — and there remained all the usual farm chores to do.

The morning air was chilly in late September, and the Sungolds and sunflowers were both done, killed by a light frost that had struck on the next to last day of the month. But I had one last gambit to try in the strategy of prolonging our market season: along with all of the regular flowers we'd seeded and grown for fresh-cut bouquets, I had planted and harvested a few that were just for drying. Statice and nigella (memorably called love-in-a-mist), artemisia and eucalyptus, along with any interesting seedpods that I found growing on the margins of the field, were cut, rubber-banded together, and hung from the rafters of the shed to dry, against the day when the killing frost would reap everything that grew in the field.

When that day came in early October, we were ready. We brought boxes full of dried bouquets that we'd made from the plants we gathered, put together in a corner of the garage, and stored upstairs. These included the papery, pastel-colored blooms of statice, which look dry even when they are still growing; the aromatic, gray-green, silver-dollar-size leaves of eucalyptus, which are grown just for foliage; and the tiny jester's cap seedpods of nigella. We made wreaths of red rose hips, orange bittersweet, and the silvery artemisia that gave our farm its name, and packed them carefully into the truck. We brought a half dozen buckets of some of the hardier but less showy plants, mostly asters and goldenrod, that had survived the frost. And we went to market.

At the dried markets, it turned out that there was little to do but huddle around a cup of coffee and invent pointless tasks in an effort to keep warm through the blustery mornings. The kinds of fresh bouquets that could be made from this stock were severely limited, and I sorely missed the rush of custom orders. To sit on chairs on the sidewalk, just waiting for someone to buy something, seemed to make the day drag along. But the added effort did let us stay at market for an extra two weeks, and that helped our bottom line. The best thing was that we were able to say good-bye to our customers for the season, instead of just vanishing at the first cold snap. With a now familiar mixture of sadness and relief, we put the farm to bed for the winter in the third week of October.

sex & bugs & rocks &
holes

KIM: As our second market season wound down, I was dispatched to a small town across the Hudson River to investigate a growing governmental crisis: taxpayer-funded S & M instruction for college students.

A branch of the State University of New York had just hosted a conference about female sexuality entitled "Revolting Behavior: The Challenges of Women's Sexual Freedom." According to those who attended, seminars included a sadomasochism workshop and a demonstration on the safe use of sex toys. There were outraged cries for the firing of the college president, and the governor promised an immediate inquiry.

"I need you to go to New Paltz," my editor told me after the news broke.

"Of course you do," I felt like saying.

As luck would have it, the college was planning to host another sex-saturated conference, this one titled "Subject to Desire: Refiguring the Body." It promised a "featured presentation" by a performance artist who called herself Vulva and was best known for reading aloud from a scroll she unfurled from her vagina. I could hardly wait.

On conference day, I put the finishing touches on a long profile of the state education commissioner I had been working on for the next day's paper and then headed out to New Paltz, a lively little college town about an hour west of the farm. The first thing I did upon arriving at the small, modern campus was to check out Vulva's installation at the college gallery. Called "Vulva's Morphia," the exhibition contained photos and illustrations of vaginas, including the artist's own. The thirty-six pictures, each about a foot square, were arranged in a grid of six across and six down.

As I was examining this masterpiece, my pager went off.

"The wire says the president is holding a press conference in an hour," an editor told me when I phoned in. I assured him that I would be there and that I would try to find the photographer the *News* had sent, who was waiting for me in a campus parking lot. I wondered what I would say to him when I found him. "Hi, I'm Kim, and I'd like you to see some sex organs" seemed a bit too forward. In the end, I chose "Nice to meet you, I think we need to get some photos of this art exhibit."

The photographer from the paper (a very straitlaced type) and I went back to the gallery to take pictures of "Vulva's Morphia." I perused an order form for Vulva's latest book, *More Than Meat Joy* ($35 plus shipping), and took notes on the exhibition. I soon ran into a problem. In one of the thirty-six vulva photos, there appeared to be an interloping penis. But because it was all so close up, I wasn't quite sure what I was looking at. I didn't want to say the exhibition was all vaginas if there was indeed a penis amongst them. I had no choice but to ask the photographer.

Adopting my most businesslike tone, I inquired, "Could I describe this as a picture of female *and* male genitalia?"

"*Aroused* male genitalia," he assured me.

I took a few more notes, and then I heard the photographer say, "Did you see that?"

I turned around and found, to my complete amazement, that I had somehow failed to notice the woman in a black leotard hanging from the gallery ceiling by a harness as two men sprayed her with a hose.

"Oh, yeah, I'll get right on that," I said as he snapped some pictures.

I walked over and asked the trio what they were doing. It turned out they were rehearsing for a performance piece to be held later that night. They said the woman was going to hang from the ceiling in a flesh-colored bodysuit and one of the men would put on a G-string and lie beneath her as bronze-colored candles positioned under the woman dripped hot wax on the man's body.

"My work is about endurance," the man said. "I am trying to produce an object, the bronze sculpture of my body."

It was time for the college president's press conference, so the photographer and I headed over to another building, and I phoned the rewrite man who had been assigned to my story. I liked all of the *News'* rewrite people, and the one working with me on this article was a particularly humorous fellow.

"It's Scroll Girl!" I heard him yell out to the entire newsroom as he got on the line.

"No—no scroll yet," I told him, wishing he could take my place here if he was so excited about this. "But I have some other stuff."

I read him my notes from the exhibition as well as some lines from the various brochures I had collected. I could hear him giggling as he typed. He was loving all of it. Well, I thought, it will be an entertaining story if nothing else.

The press conference room was a small classroom overflowing with supporters of the president, who entered to loud cheers.

"This has everything to do with free speech," said the president, who bore some resemblance to the actor Peter Sellers in the movie *Dr. Strangelove.* It was clear he was enjoying his fifteen minutes of fame as he promised the crowd he would not resign in the face of this controversy because to do so would be "to give in to the philistines."

The one critic in the audience, an older man, was not buying it. "What happens if some poor kid has an S & M event in the dorm and it goes too far?" he asked.

"You clearly know a great deal more about sadomasochism than I do," replied Dr. Strangelove, obviously peeved that someone would try to interrupt his moment of meat joy.

After the press conference, I interviewed this detractor, as well as faculty and students who supported Dr. Strangelove's pro-vulvic stance.

After I phoned this all in to rewrite, there was nothing to do but wait for Vulva's performance at 6:00 P.M. I noticed it was scheduled to go on until 7:30. My God, how long was this scroll going to be?

Answer: Not very. In fact, there was no scroll at all. Vulva had apparently given up this part of her act long ago. I knew my rewrite man would be crushed with disappointment. But when I called in my notes, a new shift was on. So I told a different person about Vulva's dipping two animal puppets in ketchup meant to represent menstrual blood, smearing her face with them, and howling at the moon like a werewolf. Then I happily went home. It had been an extremely long day, and I had to get up early the next morning because Chris and I had business in the city.

Though our season had ended, Chris still had to deliver the dried arrangements he made for the museum in lower Manhattan. He had done a beautiful job, and I was very proud of him.

On the way to the city the next day, I asked Chris to stop at the drugstore so I could get the paper and see what they had done with my work.

First I turned to the profile of the education commissioner. Given that the piece was about education, I was not happy to see that it ran under the purposely misspelled headline "No Excuses, Sez Ed Boss."

"Why do they have to do that?" I moaned to Chris.

"Because you work at a tabloid," he answered matter-of-factly.

Then I turned back to the front of the paper, where they had devoted a full page to my stories about Vulva and Dr. Strangelove under the banner headline "New School for Scandal."

"Besieged college prexy sez he won't cave to philistines," read one bold subheading over a picture of Dr. Strangelove making a face like a blowfish expelling hot air. A story that ran alongside it described the goings-on in the art gallery. Or at least it purported to do that. What I read bore little resemblance to what I had seen.

With complete amazement, I saw that my rewrite guy had substituted what the trio of performance artists had told me would take place *later* for the rehearsal I had actually seen. The story, written in the present tense, said the woman was hanging from the ceiling of the gallery in a flesh-tone bodysuit while the man I had spoken to lay beneath her in a G-string.

"Strung between them are burning bronze candles," it reported erroneously. "Hot wax slowly drips from them over [his] naked skin." Maybe it did happen just that way later on in the evening, but my name should not have appeared on a story purporting to bear witness to something I never saw. I was deeply embarrassed by this.

Next came the description of "Vulva's Morphia." "Thirty-six giant photos of vaginas—and an occasional penis—are on display."

Giant? What in the world was he talking about?

"I never said they were giant!" I exclaimed in complete disbelief.

"Well, how big were they?" Chris asked.

"About a foot square," I said.

"That's pretty big," he said in a conciliatory tone.

"Well, it's not giant," I persisted. I was not soothed. In fact, I was disgusted. What was the point in my having spent all day and night working on this story if my observations were going to be so distorted?

Bringing the flowers into the museum was what finally got my mind off my frustration. The clients loved the arrangements and oohed and aahed as we took them out of the boxes. At least somebody in this family was engaged in something productive.

As Chris and I drove home, buoyed by our success, I realized how infrequently I felt this kind of satisfaction at the end of my working day at the *News*. Maybe I was taking everything too much to heart, but I didn't know any other way to do the job. Perhaps it was time to find another one.

After the last dried bouquet was sold and the buckets and clippers packed away for the winter, I tallied up what we had earned this time around. The '97 season seemed like a pretty good indicator of how we could expect to do at market in the near future. But instead of showing us whether we were making it or not, the results left us solidly in limbo.

We grossed about $9,000 in twenty-two market days, an average of $410 per market. Our expenses had been cut to the bone: some seeds, mulch, gas, and market fees were about it, along with a small hourly wage to Kim's brother David, who helped every Tuesday in Brooklyn. That brought the net in at roughly $7,000 before figuring the costs of maintenance and depreciation on the buildings and equipment, which would, for tax purposes, pretty much wipe it out.

There was really no denying that you couldn't live on that kind of money for a year. It was barely adequate as a quarterly income.

Essentially, though, that was what it was: the market season consisted of the months of July, August, and September, with a little slack on either end. If Kim decided to quit her job now, which she appeared more ready to do with each passing day, we would soon be digging wild tubers for dinner and walking—everywhere—unless we could find something else to do for the other three-quarters of the year. Running the farm was what I wanted to do more than anything else, and I was still hopeful that I could build it into the kind of business that would provide us with a decent living. But, in the short term, I had to face the possibility that the farm alone could not support us.

I began to think about some of the same questions I'd pondered when we first moved to this place, the questions our customers at market sometimes asked: What do people do to make money out in the sticks? How do they live?

I remembered the way a real estate agent had once answered that one: "People here do everything that they do anywhere else. We have doctors and lawyers and stockbrokers, people who fix cars and houses and who work in fast-food restaurants. They do everything you can think of."

And that might be true, but it seemed to me that the region's economic well-being didn't depend on any of those things. While there had always been a concentration of old-money families in the grand houses by the river, it was widely supposed that the engine driving our local economy had a name that was made up of just three letters: IBM. Big Blue employed thousands at its offices and assembly plants located just south of us and pumped cash into local coffers by the barrelful. But the same recession that had paralyzed my small construction business had hobbled this giant. The plant shutdowns and massive layoffs in the late eighties had crippled the area's growth. Ironically, it was probably just this fact that had allowed us to move here. If property values had continued to rise instead of fall, we probably would not have been able to afford to buy our land.

But here we were, and so were all our neighbors. What were all these people doing to make ends meet?

The county cooperative extension agent told me that agriculture was still the number-one industry in our county in terms of generation of tax revenue. I'm still not sure exactly how he calculated that, but I knew that they weren't going to get much tax out of me. Presumably, others were making a lot more money at farming than I was. Since I didn't know any of them, there was no one to ask.

Who did I know? In this area, only a few people. None of Kim's colleagues lived anywhere nearby, and my farmwork was mostly solitary. In fact, I'd been so busy concentrating on making the farm happen that I hadn't paid much attention to what else was going on in the community. From somewhere in the back of my mind, some words floated up from a book I'd once read about navigating the shallow coastal inlets of New Jersey: when flowing tides shift the sandbars in ever-changing channels, the prudent mariner will seek local knowledge before attempting to make a passage. Now was the time to solicit some local knowledge on what other ways there might be for someone like me to make headway.

Most of the people I knew around here either had been involved with building the house or lived and worked right in town. I turned to them with a renewed curiosity, no longer just because they were more colorful than or different from the people I had known before but because it seemed that we now shared more than just a common geography. We were all trying to get by in a place where the opportunities were fewer than they might be elsewhere—a big city, for example. Listening to their stories, I tried to grasp how they were making a living here and wondered if I could find a way to fit in.

It turned out that some were making it and some weren't. Ed, for example, had started off with a used truck and some ancient, barely running equipment. Getting contracts through people he'd grown up with, keeping his rates low, and never turning down a job, he had grown his business over the course of a dozen years. Now he drove a new vehicle and worked out of a big, heated shop with up-to-date equipment. He bought snowmobiles for himself and his kids, and took his family on vacation to a camp in the Adirondacks every year. He employed half a dozen workers and was looking to expand into other businesses. There was no question that he worked long and hard, but he seemed satisfied with what he had accomplished.

Lee, by contrast, didn't have as much luck. Although he was bright and well-spoken, he didn't seem to want to fit into any of the molds that might lead to better opportunities. He had traveled around the oceans in the merchant marine and lived in the mountains of Colorado for a time, but he always returned to the homeplace eventually. To make ends meet he worked at night and on weekends at whatever jobs he could find: building decks, running mechanical sweepers in parking lots, doing handyman jobs, shoveling snow. He was laid off for several weeks each year when the construction season slowed in the winter.

One cold season, tired of making regular reports at the unemployment office, Lee got a job in a factory nearby, building modular homes. He performed the same task on house after house, in assembly-line fashion, and he grew to hate it. Working in the huge, noisy, hangarlike building was a bad experience for someone who liked being outdoors most of all and who prized a certain independence in the way he did his work. After that winter he did not return to the factory but simply tried to get whatever temporary work was available in the lean months. Although he didn't enjoy hunting for sport, Lee occasionally fed his family on deer meat he brought home from the woods. He had never been able to save enough money to put a down payment on a home of his own; for all his effort, Lee was barely paying the rent.

One farmer I knew from the Brooklyn market was on his way to creating an agricultural dynasty. He was not much older than myself and had a big spread across the river. His stand was a series of long tables piled high with all kinds of fruits, vegetables, and flowers, under four white canopies at a prominent corner by the entrance to the plaza. He never missed an opportunity to expand his marketing; he knew people at the New York State Department of Agriculture and Markets and the USDA, the Farm Bureau, and the co-op extension. When a pilot program offered farmers the chance to sell at thruway rest areas on weekends, he was one of the first to set up a stand. If they allowed farm stands on New York City subway platforms, he'd be there too. His pretty teenage daughters helped on the farm and at market, and it seemed to me that farming offered him and his family about all it could offer anyone, which was a lot.

However, more than one farmer didn't make it past a season or two at Greenmarket. A neighbor of ours at the Manhattan market came from a place well north of Albany. He and his wife tended the farm and drove more than four hours each way to sell their greens and root vegetables in the city. They were a friendly, attractive, and hardworking couple, and we often compared notes on our farm season and the pace of the market. Around noon one September Saturday, he asked how our sales were doing.

"Pretty good so far, just over six," I remarked. "About the same as last week, nice and busy. How about you?"

He looked dejected.

"Almost two," he said flatly. "I don't know what it is. Our stuff is good, but we can't grow anything that needs a long season, and we can't get into the big markets near us because they're restricted, and we're in the wrong county. The local stores and restaurants won't buy from us unless we can beat the prices they get from their wholesalers, and we can't make any money that way. I really don't know what we're going to do."

His wife told Kim that they lived "off the grid," with no electricity or central heat, and no running water in the house. Like us, they had moved out of the city a few seasons ago and bought some cheap land upstate. They were pursuing the goal of self-sufficiency and seeking a better lifestyle than the city offered them. They were determined to make a go of it where they were. But they did not return to market the following year.

And somewhere in between all of these people, there was us. Fortunately, we were not facing imminent disconnection from the grid, because living without most of the amenities of the late twentieth century really never was my ideal. Although I couldn't seriously consider living off the land, I hoped to make my living by working on the land. If that didn't work, I supposed I could get a job up here. But that wasn't the point either—it was just trading one set of scenery for another. The point was that we were trying to come up with a life centered on doing something we truly enjoyed, something we felt had value, building something with our own hands where no one else could tell us what we had to do. That was my aim in trying to start up the farm.

I was not ready to concede that starting an actual, working farm business in the here and now was a mistake. The question seemed to be, What was it possible for me to do with what I had, not with all of the things that might be? Where were we really going with all of this? True, our sales were up 20 percent this year, and that was encouraging, but perhaps the reality was that they would never grow to the point where we would feel secure enough to cut our ties to the familiar working world. And that might require us to make some choices that we would rather not have to make. But exactly what we were going to choose wasn't at all clear to me yet.

❖

By the time the new year had begun, I was busy covering a defamation trial in the city of Poughkeepsie, two hours south of Albany. When the proceeding began in mid-November, the trial judge predicted it would last three to five weeks. Because of his indescribable ineptitude, it went on for eight months. During this time I watched the judge present a gavel to his stenographer so she could take over his job of keeping order in the court, flee the bench when things got too rowdy, and issue an unforgettable one-word ruling on an attorney's objection: "Whatever."

I also saw a lawyer get dragged off to jail for contempt, a juror get run over by a car, and one defendant cross-examine another about the smell of excrement (don't ask). Because I had to drive to a location other than my office and often arrive hours early to ensure a ringside seat at this circus, I was racking up quite a tidy sum in overtime and mileage reimbursement. But by this time I felt no amount of money could keep me in this job much longer.

When I made occasional appearances at home, Chris and I talked about how we could manage if I left the *Daily News*. After a year in which we had made seven thousand dollars farming, quitting my job didn't strike me as particularly feasible. But the idea of Chris and me becoming farmers hadn't either. And, lucrative or not, I could not dispute the fact that we had indeed created a functioning farm. So what was next?

Chris, as usual, had worked it all out on paper.

"It's not just about how much money you can make," he told me one winter Sunday as we filled out our seed order for the coming season. "It's also about cutting expenses, and there's one thing we could do that would wipe most of ours out."

Sell the house in Brooklyn.

It was obvious but, at the same time, almost unthinkable. If we did this, a huge mortgage would be history, along with the equally outsize gas bills for heating the place, other utilities, and general maintenance. We could use some of the money from the sale to buy the farm outright, eliminating our other mortgage, plus have some left over, perhaps to invest in another property in the country just to rent out.

"Then, if you and I each earned another ten thousand dollars apiece outside the farm," Chris said, "we could live pretty large up here."

Ten thousand dollars a year. There had to be some way I could manage that. But if we did sell our house in Brooklyn, there would be no turning back. I was sure we could never again afford to buy property in the city if we embarked on the life we were now contemplating. Could I, a lifelong New Yorker, handle that? If I let my last claim to the city go, could growing out my armpit hair and playing the lute be far behind?

My love of country life had continued to grow, but I wondered if that was mostly because it provided such a pleasant counterpoint to my big-city stresses. In truth, there were certain ways in which living in the country was more difficult than urban habitation. One April snowstorm, for example, had left us without power and running water for days. Chris and I took baths in melted snow heated on our woodstove and created a makeshift outdoor refrigerator, which was raided by some kind of animal with a very healthy posthibernation appetite. The novelty of this experience wore off very quickly.

And, for sheer convenience, the city could not be beat. In Brooklyn, I had my garbage picked up at the curb; here I had to drive it to a dump miles away. There, I could have a whole roasted chicken delivered to my door at midnight if I so desired. Where I lived now, I could get a chicken late at night only if I went out and killed it.

I still very much considered myself a city person living in the country. Could I ever really become a full-fledged local? Was that what I wanted?

❖

When the weather warmed up and the hard earth turned to mud, I was still mired in the defamation trial. There seemed to be no hope of an end to this before summer. And there seemed to be even less hope for something far more important to me: having a baby. Chris and I had been trying for more than a year, and nothing was happening. It seemed likely there was some sort of medical problem, and we decided we would seek the advice of a specialist. Whatever it was, the stress and long hours of my job could not possibly be helping. I began to feel as if I were literally giving up my firstborn for a vocation that was becoming less and less fulfilling. This was what finally convinced me it was time to leave.

So it was decided: I would stick around to vest in my company retirement plan, which would coincide with the end of the coming 1998 market season. And then I would go.

But meanwhile there was work to do. Chris and Lee had finished the greenhouse, and it was spectacular. Chris took me on a tour of the completed building as we prepared for our yearly seed-starting ritual, which would finally take place somewhere I did not personally reside.

The twenty-by-fifty-foot structure gleamed on a hill in our upper field, its giant roof catching the southern sun as it slanted from a sixteen-foot peak down to the ground. Its skeleton of trusses, which showed through the clear plastic that formed the southern side of the building, were painted the brightest white. The front of the building was made of a textured metal sheeting that was painted forest green. One entered through a white-trimmed double door flanked by two white-trimmed windows.

Inside, the gravel floor was lined with long wooden benches constructed out of old pallets. These would hold the flats—110 in all this year. The north wall was bermed into the earth and lined with egg-shaped rocks held back by a chain-link fence. And then there was the space laid out for the other possible heat source.

"The chickens," Chris said, as we came to the end of the tour, "will live here."

The two of us climbed a small flight of stairs at the back of the greenhouse and entered the loveliest little room I had ever been in. One wall was all glass and looked into the greenhouse. The other three were white-painted drywall. One of those had a large window that offered a panoramic view of the rest of our field and the trees and hills above it, but from an intriguing groundhog's-eye perspective. Because the building was set into the hill, the bottom of this window was only a foot above the ground, allowing the viewer to peer through the dense meadow grass. On another wall, a window and a door opened out onto the southern side of the hill, next to the greenhouse roof. The floor was the same unglazed red quarry tile that Chris had used in our kitchen. The ceiling sloped sharply in the back of the room, giving it the snug feel of an attic. It was an inspiring space—the perfect home office for a prematurely retiring journalist. I could not believe Chris was contemplating giving it to a bunch of birds. In fact, I didn't think we should be getting involved with animals at all, and I fully intended to talk him out of it.

"You cannot, absolutely *cannot,* put chickens here," I sputtered in amazement.

"Why not?" Chris asked, a bit perplexed.

"Because it's just a complete waste!" I exclaimed. "Do chickens need fancy tile floors and a nice paint job? Do they need breathtaking views? No they do not," I declared. "When I quit my job, this room is mine."

"We'll see" was all Chris would say.

The sun rose and the sun went down. In spadefuls of dusty brown earth and droplets of sweat, mounds of green plant clippings on the hot, gray pavement and endless rides in the sweltering truck, the growing season of 1998 had come and gone. It seemed to evaporate like the ring of dampness left behind on the ground after a bucket full of water has been picked up: a darker, circular trace, visible for a few moments and just as quickly gone. It was now fully autumn, but the trees were not making an especially good showing this year. Their brown leaves rattled in the chilly October breezes as I watched the flocks of Canada geese wheeling overhead toward some vanishing point in the southern sky. The summer season had been a disaster, and it wasn't even anyone's fault.

It was our first experience of drought.

Planting had started promisingly enough: More than a hundred flats of seedlings were happily sprouting in the greenhouse by mid-April, awaiting the consistently warm weather of late May to be put in the ground. In their corner of the field, the perennials were already showing new growth from under the dead brown stalks that marked where they'd been last year. Their hardy rootstocks had survived the winter's chill, and although the nights were still cold, the new green sprouts would continue to thrive in the changeable weather of early spring. They would be the first flowers to bloom in the new season. The weather had been mostly dry until early May, when almost two weeks of unending rain left the field under a couple inches of standing water.

This didn't hurt the perennials either, since they'd been planted on a slope above the bottomland basin that formed most of the growing area, but it did make it impossible to do any work in the field. Even if the tractor didn't bog down, the muddy soil would not be amenable to tilling, and the weight of the big machine would crush the spongy earth into a compact hardpan. This dense, crusty layer forms a barrier to the passage of moisture and nutrients that even the patient, inexorable roots would have a hard time penetrating. And I remembered my first experience with bottomland mud, the excavation of Lee's truck, all too well. There was nothing to do but wait.

By the middle of May the field was drying out, but now it was past time to start laying the plastic mulch, and because of the uncertainty about when the field would be ready, I had no help lined up at all. But I remembered an intriguing idea I had heard, although I couldn't remember where: someone had told me that he was able to reuse mulch that had been put down in the previous year. It was just what I wanted to hear.

When I looked at the rows, which were still covered with plastic I hadn't removed from last season, I found that some of them had been ripped to shreds in the process of harvesting, or by the hooves of last winter's herds of deer, searching for food in the sere fields while the electric fence was turned off. But others seemed more or less intact— the plastic had grown brittle with constant exposure to the sun, but with a few patches here and there, and lots of duct tape, I figured I could repair about half of them pretty well. That would save me the trouble of laying eighteen rows of mulch! I could lay the rest in a week or so, and if it worked, this plan would put us right back on schedule. It would cut the mulching labor in half, and there would be that much less plastic to take up and haul to the dump, and that much more time to get the seedlings into the ground early. It sounded so good I had to try it. In the next few weeks I laid the new mulch, fixed what I could of the old, transplanted all of the flats in the greenhouse, and began the direct seeding. And, at first, it seemed to be working.

But what I hadn't counted on was the bugs. Up to now, insect damage had been a pretty minor annoyance; the loss of a few plants here and there was worth the benefit of not having to do much of anything in the way of control. It seemed the pests hadn't yet figured out that my field was essentially a free buffet for them, or at least hadn't called my bluff on pesticide. That was all changing now: I discovered to my regret that the same thin plastic that made such nice beds for my summer flowers offered the insects a virtual Holiday Inn for their winter vacations. And, unlike the Roach Motel, my accommodations included room service: thousands of tender seedlings of every variety brought right to their doors. For the lucky bugs, it was breakfast—in my beds.

In the rows with new mulch, seedling growth followed the same pattern as always: 5 to 10 percent losses in the most susceptible rows and minimal effects in the others. But the damage in the recycled rows showed up dramatically as soon as the seeds began to sprout, or the transplants to take root: it was decimation.

One day you could see, in nine out of ten holes in the row, the light green stalks of tiny zinnias poking up from the earth and spreading their fat, round seed leaves to the sun. The next day, more than half of those plants would be gone—just gone. Or, in a row of transplanted marigolds, yesterday's miniature forest of four-week-old plants with two sets of frilly true leaves on thick stalks would be transformed into an environmentalist's nightmare: a forest of diminutive marigold stumps, each a quarter of an inch above the ground. It looked as if a small army of profiteering elves had clear-cut the row with minute chain saws, dragging away every plant to who knew where. They were sloppy, too—next to the stumps they occasionally left piles of leaves and fronds that they had missed in their rush to exploit the seedlings. And nobody saw them do it.

By the time I figured out what was happening, it was too late to do very much about it. I could never be sure if it was cutworms, Japanese beetle larvae, slugs, or any of a dozen other garden pests, but right now it didn't make much difference even if it were truly elves with bad attitudes—the dead transplants couldn't be replaced. In the direct-seeded rows with the old, bug-infested mulch, I tried some organic pest controls and seeded the plants again. The results were decidedly mixed: sometimes the controls seemed to help, other times it was just free refills at the buffet. In all, maybe half of the plants I'd put into the old rows were now gone. But I still had the survivors of that debacle, plus most all of the plants that had been put into the newly mulched rows. That would have been enough flowers to get through the season.

And then it stopped raining.

Everyone complains about the weather, because it's something that even the most fiercely independent rural folks can generally agree on; furthermore, no one expects anything to be done about it. So, when I heard the first talk about the lack of rain, I passed it off as just chatter—the fields were still green, weren't they? After a while, though, people began bringing up the exact date of the last rainfall in conversation, and it couldn't be ignored: it had indeed been a long time ago, and it wasn't even very much rain at that. Now clouds of dust began to rise behind cars driving on the dirt roads, and some people's wells were reduced to a trickle. By the standards of the village hardware store, we were officially having a drought.

In our field, the plants virtually stopped growing. The ones that were healthy to begin with seemed to assume a darker green color and a more compact form. The ones that had already been weakened by insect damage, temperature, or transplant stress didn't have a chance. They simply gave up the ghost in dismaying numbers. Some hung on for a short time as clumps of spindly leaves around a stunted stalk with premature buds that would never bloom. Others just wilted to crispy brown husks. By mid-July, when the market season was about to get under way, the extent of the damage became obvious: only seventeen of the thirty-six rows I'd planted would be productive of flowers or vegetables. The rest were a total loss.

We couldn't do two markets with half of the normal harvest, and there wasn't much debate about which one we would keep: clearly, Borough Hall would have to go. Brooklyn may have been a sentimental favorite because we had lived there until just recently, but that market would never match Abingdon Square—not in volume, not in regular customers, not in profit. I called Greenmarket with the news in late July, and they weren't surprised. The drought had affected almost every farmer in the program, and there was little any of them could do.

We finally began markets on the last Saturday in July and ended in mid-September, when a light frost finished off the plants that had been weakened in the merciless season. We were able to bring fresh flowers to only nine markets for the year. We stretched out the season with two markets consisting of just dried flowers and wreaths, but it was really too soon in the year to sell many of them. It was still summer in the city, and the drought we experienced upstate was mainly an abstraction or a news tidbit to most city dwellers. When the totals were added up, the result was a big disappointment: our gross income this, our third market season, was a hundred dollars less than it had been the first year we had the farm.

Chapter 14

unlucky break

KIM: I suppose the timing couldn't have been worse. Here I was, about to resign from my job after the least lucrative farming season ever. But things got even more muddled when, after the defamation trial finally ended in July, the *News* asked me to become Albany Bureau chief. The promotion would no doubt come with a substantial raise.

"Maybe you should take it, just for a little while," Chris suggested when I gave him the news.

"No way," I told him. We had talked about my leaving for so long it was a fact. In my heart, I was already gone. And, in my mind, there were thoughts about only one thing: my inability to get pregnant. Concentrating on anything else, particularly my work, was becoming more and more difficult.

In May we had gone to see a doctor who specialized in helping infertile couples. Diagnosing infertility in men is fairly straightforward: you just need a semen analysis. Chris's test came out fine, so it was almost certain the problem was with me. But nothing obvious showed up on any of the tests I had either.

My doctor decided to try me on a mild fertility drug along with artificial inseminations to see if I would get pregnant that way. Not the most pleasant way to conceive a child, this procedure involves using a catheter to deposit sperm exactly where they need to go. In the past, when I had thought about my husband and me making a baby, I had never envisioned lying on an examination table with a doctor and nurse also present. But, as weird as it was, I would have been grateful if the four of us could have produced what just two of us could not.

By the end of the summer, two inseminations hadn't worked. My doctor said he would do four more of these at most before moving on to more aggressive treatments. Should that happen, as now was likely, the stress of a new job would be the last thing I needed.

Besides, as uncertain as our finances were, we were no longer in dire straits. In June we had sold our house in Brooklyn for a very nice profit and paid off all of our debts. I attended the closing with Chris and watched the nice young couple who were buying our place sign papers to take on not one but *two* mortgages to pay for it. Better you than me, I thought.

So the only thing left to decide was, When would I go? I had vested in my retirement plan in September, as the state was moving toward the peak of a very competitive election season. All the major offices—governor, U.S. senator, and attorney general, among others—were up for grabs. As a government reporter, I was right in the middle of all of it and wanted to see it through to the end. I decided I would leave after the general election in mid-November.

Covering the campaigns got me back into the issues-oriented reporting I liked best, so it was a great assignment on which to end my newspaper career. It was also a very fast-paced one. Political candidates really do *run* for office.

One October Sunday I found myself in a pack of reporters jogging down a Long Island beach behind the man who would become New York's next senator, Chuck Schumer. (In a bizarre coincidence, Schumer had recently campaigned right next to our Manhattan farm stand. I hid behind the goldenrod, lest he ask me to go into matters far too complicated to explain.) The next day I was racing through crowds of spectators on Fifth Avenue in pursuit of his opponent, the incumbent senator, Al D'Amato. The senator had arrived late to take his place in the Columbus Day Parade and was performing a remarkably speedy, high-stepping trot to keep from getting left behind. I was running around New York so fast that by my last day on the job, I had shrunk to a size four.

That day turned out to be Friday the thirteenth of November. In the morning, I went for another insemination (the date alone should have told me it wouldn't work), drove to Albany, wrote a couple of brief stories for the next day's paper, and locked up my little cubbyhole for the last time. Tomorrow would be the first day in eleven years I couldn't say I had a full-time job at a major daily newspaper. And, in spite of what happened next, I've never been sorry.

❖

At the time I left the *News,* in November 1998, being a work-ing member of the press was a huge part of my self-image. From the moment I first climbed the narrow staircase of my college paper's ramshackle newsroom to my last walk down the New York State capitol steps, I had done everything I could to fur-ther my career in journalism. Cumulatively, it had taken up more of my mental and physical energy than anything else. So I expected to go through at least some emotional turmoil— maybe even panic—about being unemployed. What would I tell people I was now?

Well, I discovered something interesting. That question is relevant only if there's anyone around to ask it. And there was no one out here in the woods but me. I realized something else, too, that now seems pretty obvious. I was still the same person I had been on my last day on the job. It wasn't as if everything I had done over the past decade was wiped out the instant I stopped working or that I wouldn't be able to perform the job just as well tomorrow if I wanted to. To paraphrase Frank Sinatra, they couldn't take that away from me. It was simply time to find a new way of working. But maybe not right away. For the first time in my adult life I had the chance to enjoy an extended vacation. I decided I would take the rest of the year off. I spent a good part of the next six weeks sitting in front of the woodstove, reading novels and writing holiday cards.

But when January rolled around, I figured I had better get a job because Chris was making me look bad. He was already well on his way to achieving our 1999 off-the-farm income goal of ten thousand dollars apiece. In November and December he had put his construction skills to work renovating several rooms of a Brooklyn town house. And mid-January through April 15 he was scheduled to work as an income-tax preparer for a nationally franchised tax service. Chris was the one who always did our taxes, which had lately become very complicated given our agricultural pursuits and all. The manager of the office where Chris had taken our taxes to be filed electronically noticed his knack for number crunching and offered him a job. It was something he knew how to do, and it fit into our plan nicely. So the question was, What did I know how to do?

I could write news stories and editorials on deadline. But there was no way to do that and not get sucked into the crazy hours and even crazier demands that had made me quit in the first place. However, newspapers were where all my connections were, and that was still the work environment in which I felt most comfortable. So was there any way I could use my journalistic skills and my contacts to make money—any way that would not take up all my time and drive me nuts?

Actually, there was.

When I had been on the editorial board of the *Daily News,* each writer had the responsibility, one day a week, of putting out the Letters to the Editor page. Although we all complained about it, I actually got a kick out of discovering what our readers had to say about what we—and those we wrote about—were doing, and compiling a page of their rantings and musings. Editing letters also had the advantage of a certain amount of predictability normally lacking in the news business. You knew exactly what you needed to do each day and roughly how long it would take. It was also a skill that I figured not many people off the street happened to have. Maybe there was something I could do with this.

Through a friend at *The New York Times* I got an interview with the letters editor there, who told me he could use me as a fill-in editor for vacationing staffers. I was thrilled. I could always stay at my parents' apartment if I did some work at the *Times.* I decided also to tell my old friends at the *Daily News* editorial page I was available for filling in, and they too said they would call me. So it looked like I was happily on my way to a part-time career as a freelance editor.

Unfortunately, it also looked like I was on my way to a full-time career as a fertility patient. In January, after months of taking a mild oral fertility drug and enduring several unsuccessful inseminations, I tried some pretty hard-core injectable fertility drugs (the kind that land you on the news for giving birth to septuplets). But after looking via ultrasound at what this medication was doing to my reproductive system, my doctor took me off of it before we could try to get pregnant. He said it was overstimulating my ovaries and could prove dangerous to me if I *did* get pregnant. However, this reaction did provide some clue as to why I was not able to conceive. It appeared I had an ovulation disorder that caused a hormonal imbalance, which in turn prevented my eggs from maturing properly. There was only one practical treatment: in vitro fertilization.

After a long conversation with my doctor, in which he told me I had a decent chance of becoming pregnant with this procedure, I decided to go ahead. I would have to go back on the very strong fertility drugs and some other hormones, and have eggs removed from my ovaries with a needle. These eggs would then be mixed with Chris's sperm in a petri dish, given some time to fertilize, and put back in my uterus, where, we hoped, at least one would take up residence for nine months.

At this point I would have done absolutely anything to become pregnant and was convinced that the ends would justify the means. But it was with some sadness that I made my plans to go ahead with this very high-tech method of conception. I had wanted a more simplified existence. Now I was about to embark on the most complicated and arduous route to pregnancy there is—and the least natural. In vitro made inseminations seem quaint. When I had gone through the latter procedure, it seemed the room was too crowded to conceive a child. Now, I thought, it would be too empty: my husband and I wouldn't even get to be there. But I didn't feel we had any other choice.

Since my doctor himself did not perform in vitro fertilization, he recommended a med-school friend who did only this. I called and found, though it was January, that his next available appointment was in July. The only positive news was that my own doctor was able to get me on a cancellation list, in case an earlier appointment should come up. Then there was nothing to do but wait—for an editor to call about work or a doctor to call about getting pregnant.

It was hard not to get depressed and frustrated. After all, I had resigned from my job to get more control over my life, and here I was waiting for others to decide my future—even about something as basic as reproduction. What kind of defective creature couldn't manage that, anyway? On my worst days I felt subhuman; on my best, subfemale.

I tried to get my mind focused on other things. Chris kindly gave me the would-be chicken room at the end of the greenhouse, and every day I went there to write. I sat at an old oak desk and wore black knit gloves so my fingers wouldn't freeze before the electric radiator could generate enough warmth to make my breath invisible. But even before that happened, my own little room always felt cozy to me. It had been a long time since I had written anything just for the fun of it. I started writing stories to make myself laugh, mostly about Albany. Some of these grew out of notes I had made on the side of the road, after having pulled over during my long drive from work, in an effort to record what would never end up in the paper but struck me as important nonetheless.

After a few hours I would take a break, put on my puffy goose-down coat, and walk up and down the driveway to try to replace the exercise I used to get each day running up and down the capitol steps in Albany. What were my fellow reporters doing there right now? I often wondered as I listened to my sneakers crunch on the icy gravel. Maybe they were all at a governor's press conference, raising their hands and calling out questions. Some might be waylaying legislators in the carpeted lobby outside the State Senate's gilded chamber, or maybe following the city schools chancellor around on a lobbying mission. I couldn't say. I knew only that I had no wish to rejoin them.

On days that were not too brutally cold, I crossed the road at the bottom of the driveway and jogged around the field. The hard, frozen ground dipped and rose like the craters of the moon.

Then, in mid-February, everybody called at once. The *Daily News* wanted me, in early March, to substitute for an op-ed editor who would be out three weeks on medical leave. I said yes. Then *The New York Times* called me for the exact same time period, so I had to say no. Then the fertility clinic called with a cancellation. The doctor said that, as soon as my gig at the *News* ended, I would have blood work done in preparation for an attempt at in vitro fertilization. The limbo that had seemed interminable had not lasted very long at all.

It was great fun returning to the *News'* New York City office as a specially invited guest rather than a wholly owned serf. I was greeted with lots of hugs and cheers from those who were happy to see me back so soon and perhaps also pleased to know that you can go home again. I spent most of that first day learning the very complicated computer system I would be using to see exactly what the op-ed page looked like and to measure precisely how much space I had for text, headlines, art, et cetera. The next day was to be my first doing any actual editing.

On that morning, I woke up at my parents' house in great spirits. After this first real day on the job, I would be having din-ner with an old friend I hadn't seen in a very long time. He was a columnist who specialized in investigative reporting, and I had worked for him as a researcher at my first newspaper, *New York Newsday.* I was looking forward to hearing about whatever muck he was raking these days. Wanting to look my best, I put on a navy blue suit and some new blue suede shoes. Then I said good-bye to my parents and headed to the subway a few blocks away.

Crossing the street at a busy midtown intersection after my train ride, I found my good mood marred by the dark question that always lurked not too deeply within my consciousness: Would I ever get pregnant? The upcoming in vitro fertilization was the last hope of producing a child biologically related to both Chris and me. Was that something that was meant to be or not?

What I should have been asking myself instead was, Are my feet firmly planted on the ground or not? Because suddenly, instead of walking, I found myself flying through the air and then stumbling on the sidewalk. I landed on one leg, and somehow it twisted around underneath me. I was unable to catch my balance and went crashing to the ground. I was vaguely aware that this might be a bad fall.

At that moment I seemed to become split into two people. One was lying on the ground, bewildered and in unbearable pain. She put her head on her pocketbook, closed her eyes, and quietly said no every time someone in the crowd forming around her asked if she was okay. The other person was hovering slightly above, watching the one lying in shock on the ground. This one was completely clearheaded. She had heard the loud crack made by the breaking bone, a noise that sounded like the snap of a dry tree branch, and knew exactly what was going on. This was serious trouble.

There must have been an ambulance staked out nearby, because it seemed like less than two minutes before a pair of paramedics from the city's fire department arrived. When these two clean-cut, uniformed men began speaking to me, the two halves of myself came back together.

They looked me over briefly, noticing the strange angle of my leg and my obviously swollen ankle. "Your ankle looks broken," one of the paramedics said. "We're going to splint you up and take you to the hospital."

I looked up. Things were becoming clearer now. I was lying on the sidewalk in front of Madison Square Garden. There was a large crowd of people around me wearing worried expressions. The *Daily News* was just down the street. I looked down. My foot looked like it had been put on wrong. I moved ever so slightly and felt a horrific stab of pain. What had I gone and done?

The paramedic who had been speaking to me took out a pair of scissors and began to cut my navy blue stocking off the wounded leg. Please, *do not* tell me they are about to strip off my clothing in front of Madison Square Garden, I thought. But that one piece of nylon was all they needed to remove to make way for the splint. Whew.

"Okay, I'm not going to lie to you," he said when they were done with the splint. "It's going to hurt when we move you."

I gritted my teeth, but they slid me onto the gurney so expertly that the pain wasn't nearly as bad as I was expecting. Then they rolled me toward the ambulance waiting at the nearby curb. Every last one of the onlookers individually filed past to wish me well. I was very touched.

"We'll try not to shake you up too much, but it's probably going to hurt on the way to the hospital, especially the way *he* drives," my paramedic told me, motioning toward his not-as-talkative partner. We all smiled. I liked these guys.

"What's going to happen?" I asked.

"Oh, they'll probably just put a cast on you and give you some crutches. You'll be back at work tomorrow."

I was about as relieved as anyone could be in this kind of situation. But it turned out the remedy was a bit more serious than that.

For nine hours in the emergency room, I waited: first, for X rays, then for a CAT scan, and finally for a room for the night. Through a succession of needles, the pain medication flowed liberally into my veins.

The next day there were several hours of surgery, in which eleven screws and a plate were implanted in my shattered ankle and lower leg. I remember only certain moments from my four days in the hospital. They are blurred shapes in a mist of morphine: the constant jab of needles; the indignity of bedpans; the cold metal of the operating table and the brightness of the OR lights; wondering what all those people looked like under their surgical masks; trying to fight sleep as the anesthesia worked its way into my brain; the uncontrollable shivering after the operation; the kind nurse in the recovery room who said I wouldn't remember her once I left because no one ever did; begging for water on the way back to my room but being told I couldn't have any because I had just thrown up; nodding my head yes when my parents asked if they should stay at my bedside as I drifted off to sleep, even though the nurses were telling them visiting hours were over; counting the minutes before a doctor answered Chris's call to saw the too-tight cast off my agonizingly swollen foot; trying to stand up for the first time and finding that my head was spinning so badly, I needed to be put back in bed; watching Chris and my brother walk to the hospital elevator after a visit and wondering when (or if) I would ever be able to do such a simple series of movements again.

Right then, nothing on this earth seemed quite so impossible.

It was a Tuesday afternoon in early March, and so far everything was shaping up pretty well for the coming season. I'd been working in the greenhouse all day, a welcome break from my Monday-to-Saturday workweek as a tax preparer at a small office in the next town. I was pleased enough to have the job, which brought in a fair amount of much-needed income, but at the height of tax season the best thing that could be said about it was that it made me truly relish the hours I could spend doing farmwork. And, on this cloudy spring day, I was ticking off the chores one by one.

A technician came by in the morning to fix the balky oil burner I'd recently bought from a junk dealer and installed as a backup heater in the greenhouse. Although the dealer said he could personally vouch for the fact that the furnace had never given any problems heating the trailer that was its first home, the repairman was skeptical.

"It don't look like they cleaned it much since it was new—and that was in the nineteen seventies," he remarked. And, since replacement parts were going to be hard to find at best, he decided he would have to modify the burner a little bit.

"Don't worry, we'll get her working just fine," he drawled. "Just have to make things fit in a little different from how they were. But I like jobs like this—just when you think you seen it all, there's something comes along you ain't never seen before."

Since he was a man in his sixties, I took it as a hopeful sign that my heater could still teach him something. And, true to his word, a little before noon I heard the flame kick in and the blower come on with a roar, and we were back in business.

"That ought to keep you going pretty good," he said, "but if you have any trouble you know where to reach me, and if I'm still around I'll come back and fix it again."

He refused to charge me the full rate for his "education time," and by the time he left the temperature was hovering around seventy-five degrees—too warm to keep the greenhouse regularly but just right for a spring afternoon's work.

I was starting seeds, and I had about twenty flats to go—mostly snapdragons and statice, since I'd gotten the salvia done in the morning. I had all the materials on hand: three-cubic-foot bags of crumbly brown peat moss, shiny gray vermiculite, and puffy white perlite to mix with a dash of organic fertilizer into my own blend of seed-starting medium. Then there was a stack of the traylike flats, already lined with empty plastic cell paks with spaces for about fifty seedlings apiece, ready to receive their allotment of soilless mix and seed. And, of course, there were the seed packets and watering can. I cranked up the volume on the radio and got to work.

Starting seeds is probably my favorite farming activity. It's not physically tiring, except when you have to stir about fifty pounds of dry medium with a shovel and swirl it around with water, as if you were mixing a garbage pail full of oatmeal with a giant spoon. But spreading it into the cell paks, leveling it off, and scraping the surface in preparation for receiving the tiny seeds is somehow deeply satisfying. And sprinkling the seeds on the moistened mix seems to me the true beginning of the year's farm season.

This afternoon, however, something kept interrupting my reverie: a noise like a very ill cricket, one that would chirp intermittently for thirty seconds, then go silent for minutes at a time. Perhaps the newly fixed heater had awakened it too early from its winter nap. In any case, I knew from the quavering tone that it must be in some extremity of suffering and it couldn't have long to live. After the fifth series of plaintive chirps I'd had enough, and I decided to end the cricket's misery if I could find it. As soon as I turned the radio down, it started again, chirping even louder. I realized that it knew my intentions and was signaling its approval, telling me exactly where it was. It was right under the telephone.

The telephone. *Was* it the telephone? It never seemed to ring when I was in the greenhouse, and I used it only rarely to call out. I picked up the one-piece receiver and flipped a switch.

"Hello?" I asked tentatively.

"Oh, Chris, hello, it's Michele, and (garble) Kimi is just fine, but I (garble garble) hospital, and (garble garble garble) pay phone, so . . ."

It was Kim's mother trying to tell me something, but I couldn't hear more that 20 percent of what she was saying.

"Michele . . . Michele . . . ," I said, "I think we have a bad connection. Hello? Hello? Can you hear me? I can't hear you at all. I'm going to hang up because I can't hear you, okay? Can I call you right back?"

"(Garble garble) pay phone, and (garble) long line, but (garble garble) . . ."

"Okay, Michele, I'm going to hang up now, because I can't hear you. Call me right back and I'll stay by the phone, okay? Bye."

I put down the phone and waited. Something was up, and I had no idea what it might be. Soon the dying cricket chirped again.

"Hello . . . Michele . . . is this better?"

"Chris, Kimi wanted (garble) call you (garble) an accident, but (garble garble garble), and where are you (garble) . . ."

"I'm in the greenhouse, Michele. I'm working in the greenhouse. I still can't hear you. Are you sure I can't call you back? Michele . . ."

"No! You (garble garble) only pay phone (garble) hospital (garble) no change for (garble garble garble) . . ."

"Michele," I said, "I still can't hear you. I can't hear you at all. Let's try it again, okay? Bye."

The cricket sang one more time.

"Michele," I began, but was interrupted.

"Collect call to anyone from Michele," said the operator. "Will you accept charges?"

"Michele who?" I asked for absolutely no reason.

*"Get . . . out . . . of . . . the . . . greenhouse!"* she yelled. It was the first string of five words in a row that came through audibly, and it was spoken with authority verging on rage. Now there was no choice.

"Okay, going to the house now, bye!" I said, and hung up.

As I made the short walk from the greenhouse, I realized that something serious was going on. Whatever it was, it sounded likely to disrupt the schedule I'd worked out, which left little room for improvisation. I was vaguely annoyed and completely unprepared for what came next.

The following morning I was in my car on the way to the city. Michele had told me (over a much better phone connection in the house) that there was no point in my coming down that night, because Kim was heavily sedated and would have to be prepped for surgery, scheduled for early in the morning. I had spoken to her briefly that night: she was obviously woozy from the painkillers but insistent on my waiting until today to come to see her. She said the doctors told her she had a bad fracture, but she would be fine. In the abstract, it sounded like an unfortunate mishap. But when I got to the hospital, I was shocked at what I saw.

Most hospitals are cheerless and run-down places to begin with, but Kim's floor seemed particularly decrepit. She looked pale, weak, and uncomfortable—like someone who had been in a terrible accident and had major surgery. The facts were beginning to sink in. Although she was happy at our reunion, there was no hiding the pain and exhaustion in her face. This was worse than I thought.

I spent the next two days at her hospital bedside, and when she was released we moved her in a cab to her parents' apartment for the first few days of recovery. She would need help getting to the bathroom and the shower (with a plastic bag on her leg), and would have to be served food, drinks, and medicine. And I would have to go back to work doing taxes.

On the return trip to the country, I began to see the consequences of her accident more clearly, and the doctors' words, in their clinical vagueness, came back to me in an ominous light: "a horrendous break . . . prone to arthritis . . . probably able to do most of the things she always did . . . a period of recuperation . . . physical therapy will be essential." It seemed certain that our attempt to have a baby would be put on hold for a while. But nobody could answer the question that was most on my mind now: Was this the end of our try at farming?

Because, after being with Kim for a few days, I knew what nobody was willing to put into words: that we were in for a long, painful process of recovery, that more operations might be needed, and that no one could say at what point she would be able to do the routine things we did on the farm—planting, seeding, weeding, and harvesting. Without these things there would be no farm, and there was no way I was going to take them on alone.

Kim had been with me through every adventure. Sometimes, just her presence and encouragement were enough to help me through a tough stretch, or to keep a dream alive. Other times she was right beside me in the dirt, sweating and swearing as we tried so hard to make our hoped-for farm a reality. She never gave up, and she helped more than she knew. To think that this accident might mean the end of what we had worked so hard to build just didn't seem fair. Right now, there was nothing to do but wait and see when — or if — she could return to farming.

Chapter 15

one small step

KIM: The accident didn't just take away the use of my leg; it robbed me of all motivation whatsoever. Moving was simply too much trouble. The cast was made of fiberglass, but it may as well have been cement. And crutches? All I can say is, humans were not meant to walk on three legs, two of them being aluminum sticks.

Being newly disabled, I had to learn alternate ways of doing everything. One of the hardest things to learn was to let others do things for me graciously. I needed everyone's help desperately, but I also resented needing it. I remember sitting in my hospital bed watching my mother pack my bag to leave and absolutely seething with frustration. She wasn't folding my clothes the way I did it or putting them in the bag in the same order I would have chosen. I felt rotten resenting the very people who were doing so much for me, but I couldn't help it.

That wasn't a problem when I returned home because Chris simply wasn't around. He couldn't be. Mid-March was the height of tax season, and since the job would be over in a month, it made sense for him to put in as many hours as he could and make as much money as possible; obviously I wasn't going to be making anything.

Not that he wanted to be away so much. The job was tedious and the office dismal. It was a tiny, dingy storefront in the back of an auto parts store. The only natural light came in through a two-foot-square window in the front door. For someone who had just spent half a year working outdoors, this was not living. But at least he got to see the outdoors on the way to and from work.

I was free to go out if I wanted to. The weather was warming up. And I had been trained in the hospital to handle a flight of stairs—tucking both crutches under one arm to brace myself while leaning on the banister with the other arm. But this maneuver was just too exhausting, and I never felt totally secure doing it on the steep, narrow staircase to our second-floor living space. What if I fell or, more likely, dropped a crutch? There was no one anywhere nearby to help me.

So I mostly just took painkillers that knocked me out and stayed in bed. If I got hungry, I would reach over the side of the bed, fish around for the crutches, position them on either side of me, and hoist myself up. Then I would hobble out of the bedroom to the dining room table, where Chris had left some food and drinks for me. If I wanted to consume these things while reclining instead of sitting up straight in a chair, I would have to load them into a plastic shopping bag, loop it over my arm, and then crutch or hop on my one good leg over to the couch.

My main event of the day was showering. I would sit on the toilet and put a rubber-rimmed plastic bag over the cast, swivel myself over to sit on the edge of our claw-foot tub, and then gingerly transfer myself to the waiting plastic-topped metal stool. I used a handheld shower nozzle on a hose to wet myself down. There was no way to keep the water on me while I soaped up, so I always ended up getting unpleasantly cold. Then I would put on my invalid's uniform: wide-legged black sweatpants and a loose-fitting cotton turtleneck shirt.

One Saturday, the New York City couple who own the house nearest to ours came over to visit and offered to take me to lunch in town. Lunch out—what an amazing concept! But, as I was getting ready, the pill I had taken shortly before they arrived started to kick in and I felt my head spin. "You guys go ahead," I said. "I'm just not feeling up to it right now."

❖

For the first few days after Kim came home, there was no time to think about anything except how to get her through the hours as comfortably as possible. She needed a breakfast and lunch that were easy to prepare, and ready access to lots of drinks while I was at the office from eight to five. But the drinks couldn't be in big bottles because they were too hard to carry while she moved around on the crutches or hopped on one leg from place to place. Glasses of juice were out for the same reason. Ditto for cans of soup—they were easy enough for her to prepare on the stove but impossible to bring to the table without spilling. A small plate with a tightly packed sandwich was good, because it could be easily moved.

At my day job, all the novelty I'd felt at returning to work in an office after about five years' absence had long since worn off. I had a desk and a computer, a phone and someone to answer it, and in between appointments I had time to think about the future. In the near term, it wasn't too encouraging. Kim, who normally avoided aspirin until her headache became head-splitting, was gobbling narcotics like bonbons. Taking them made her spacey and irritable. Not taking them made her withdrawn and miserable. There was nothing to do but wait until she felt better, but it was impossible to discern any change in her condition from day to day.

Meanwhile, the bitter winds of early March were yielding to the cool, sunny calms of spring, and the question we had avoided for so long was now staring me in the face: Would we have a farm this year?

No one ventured to give us a date when it would be possible for Kim to do any physical labor. But the season would not wait, and the dismal routine of office work and inactivity forced me to the only possible resolution I could see: however difficult, we would have to try to get her going. I would simply act as if the farm would continue as usual, and if we were forced to stop because of her physical limitations, then at least we would know we'd tried everything that could be done. We would not go down without a struggle.

One sunny Sunday afternoon, I walked her slowly out to the greenhouse. It was the longest distance she had traveled on foot since leaving the hospital weeks ago. She stopped to rest several times along the way, leaning forward on her crutches. She was breathing hard but did not seem to mind gulping in the fresh outdoor air.

I set up a folding chair in the shade of the metal roof, sat her down, and set a wooden plank across the armrests.

"There," I said. "This is your workstation. I'll set up some flats full of wet medium on this side, and you can seed them. When you get finished, put them over on that side and I'll pick them up and give you some more."

"What if I want to get up?" she asked, looking down at the board that was penning her in.

"When you're finished seeding, we can discuss that," I said with a smile. She smirked back at me, and I saw a glimmer of her old self.

I set the first four flats in front of her, and she started to work, scraping the medium with a Popsicle stick to loosen it and then tapping out seeds from the packet. Seeding the hundred or so flats that would be needed in order to plant the crops we'd planned for that year was going to be a slow and painstaking process, but after a short while she began to attack the flats with gusto.

"I think I can handle this," she said.

It was music to my ears.

❖

You knew it wouldn't be long before Chris had me in the field again. Fortunately, he allowed me to get my cast removed first. This occurred in mid-April, three days after my thirty-fifth birthday. My joy at this event lasted until I saw what my leg had turned into after six weeks in captivity: a scaly, hairy stick with scars like those of Frankenstein's monster and half a dozen screwheads making visible lumps beneath a light covering of skin. And I now had no calf muscle whatsoever.

"Can I put weight on it?" I asked my surgeon as I sat on his exam table and looked down at this shriveled thing that was purported to be a part of my anatomy.

"You can," he said, "but you won't feel like you want to."

I got off the table and tried it, but almost fell down. The ankle was completely unmovable and the leg weak as spaghetti.

"I think I'll hold on to these crutches," I said as I hobbled out.

A few days later Chris told me it was time to pull up the forty-odd rows of old mulch that were still lying on the field from last season.

"I have a great job for you—something you can easily handle in your condition," he said.

"I can't wait to hear this," I answered.

"I'll pull up the mulch," he said. "All you have to do is drive the lawn mower behind me with the cart attached so I can put the plastic in, and then you can drive it to the edge of the field, where we'll pile it up. Just try it," he added when he saw the look on my face.

"Oh, all right," I said.

When we got down to the field, I found that driving the riding mower was actually no problem. I could rest my now-sneakered bad foot comfortably next to its working counterpart as I rode around the field to help Chris collect the ripped and shredded sheets of plastic. In some places the sticky mud held the mulch down like glue; in others, it had come loose and was flapping in the breeze. Chris started pulling it free, and soon there were small piles of it all over the field. I would drive to one of the small piles and wait for Chris to stop pulling and load it into my cart. Then I would drive it to the big pile.

On one of my trips back, I pulled up next to a waiting load and watched Chris struggle with a particularly difficult stretch of tightly stuck plastic. This is going to take him a while, I thought. I looked down at the muddy clump of old mulch waiting to be put in my cart. I leaned over and tried to grasp it, but it was just past my reach. Chris was still struggling with his recalcitrant row. He would be at this for some time, and I was already bored with waiting. So I hopped off the cart on my good foot and tried to touch the pile of mulch. It was still out of reach, but only by two steps. What the hell.

I lifted my bad leg and put it down on the ground a little ways in front of me. Then very, very gradually I transferred my weight to it. When I thought I was steady, I picked up my good foot and quickly put it in front of the bad one, landing with a lurch. I had taken a step. I reached over, grabbed the mulch, and started reeling it in toward myself, hand over hand. When I had gathered the dirty plastic to my chest, I pivoted around on my good foot so I was facing the cart. I transferred my weight to the bad leg again and almost toppled into the cart as I unloaded my mulch. But I had done it. I was walking.

"Chris," I screamed, "look at me!"

Two weeks later, still using one crutch as a support, I limped into the fertility clinic, lay down on an operating table once again, and went to sleep. When I woke up, twenty-eight eggs had been removed from my body to be fertilized with Chris's sperm. The next day a nurse from the clinic called and told us some good news: it looked like we had thirteen viable embryos. This could give us a good three tries at in vitro fertilization without the need to retrieve any more eggs, something I could well do without. The actual procedure wasn't so bad, since it was done while I was unconscious. But the part leading up to it was awful. I took half a dozen drugs, most of which Chris had to inject into me nightly. One gave me hot flashes, another made me feel light-headed, and the rest left my ovaries so full of eggs, I became uncomfortable getting up or sitting down. I was truly glad that part of the process was behind me.

In a few more days, we returned to the doctor, and he put three of the embryos back into my body. I lay on a table for an hour to give them a chance to implant. Then we went home to wait for what I expected would be an excruciating two weeks until I could take a pregnancy test.

Fortunately there was a lot to do to take my mind off the question of whether the procedure had worked. It was planting time, and the field had been fully laid with mulch, in large part thanks to me. I had done none of the physical work—there was still no way I could, even though physical therapy was bringing improvements every day. But I had done something even better. I had found a machine that Chris could pull behind his tractor that would lay the mulch with minimal human effort. And I had gotten it for free.

I had always suspected that there must be a less feudal way of mulching, and Chris challenged me to find it. So I called an agricultural extension agent we had met at a farmers' conference that winter. Not only did he know what kind of machine we could use but he knew of a farm that had one and wasn't using it this season. When I called the manager of the farm, she said if we were willing to pick it up and bring it back, we could borrow it at no charge.

"You are awesome," Chris said when he heard the news.

❖

The machine resembled a cross between an enormous plastic-wrap dispenser and a four-foot-wide, five-hundred-pound trowel made of three-sixteenths steel plate. Six big farmworkers lifted it onto the bed of my pickup, and I watched the springs in back settle down under the load. I figured gravity, and possibly some lengths of pipe to use as rollers, would help me get it off the truck. But once I had it on the ground and figured out how to hook it to the back of the tractor and set the blades and discs properly, it worked like a dream. When it was all set up, the process of mulching went like this: Bury the end of the roll of mulch on one side of the field. Put the tractor in gear and drive to the other side, preferably in a straight line. When you get there, cut the roll of mulch and bury the loose end in the dirt. Now get ready to start the next row. For the first time in the four-year history of Silverpetals Farm, the mulching was done in a matter of days, not weeks. Never again would we lay mulch by hand.

❖

But even though the mulching had been handled by mechanical means, transplanting and seeding still had to be done the old-fashioned way, so we got to work. My first job was transplanting the celosia, which were now thin, brightly colored sprouts of pink, orange, and green. As I put them into the ground one by one, I thought about the transplants I was hoping would take root in my own body. And I finally realized something I should have known all along. It just wasn't up to me. I could do everything I could think of to make sure both my seedlings and my embryos reached their full potential. But, in the end, it would be forces much larger than myself that would decide. Having absolved myself of such an enormous responsibility, I felt all the tension in my muscles slip away. I had never experienced such a relaxed state in the midst of this ordeal before and probably wouldn't again. But, for that one moment, I was completely at peace with whatever the outcome might be.

❖

When the two weeks were up, I went for a blood test at my local hospital. They would phone the results in to my fertility doctor, and his office would then call me. I could hardly stand the waiting.

We were still planting, and Chris decided to keep working while I went back to the house in our station wagon and checked the answering machine. It said I had one message. My heart started to pound. I played the recording and heard the voice of a nurse who had assisted the fertility doctor in transferring our embryos.

"Hi, Kim, this is Cathy. Are you there? Hello? I *hate* leaving this kind of message on an answering machine . . ."

I knew right then the news wasn't good.

"Kim, you're not pregnant. But we can go right into a new cycle if you want to. Call and make an appointment to speak to the doctor about it. Let us know what you want to do."

I knew immediately what I wanted to do—try again. What I didn't want to do was drive down to that field and tell Chris it hadn't worked. He had always remained more optimistic than I had. Would this finally cause him to lose all his hope?

I got into the car and drove down the hill. As soon as I could see him standing in the field watching me, I started to shake my head in the negative. No, I mouthed silently, my hair brushing one cheek and then the other. No, no, no, no.

❖

Although I couldn't help being a little discouraged by the news, it wasn't completely unexpected. I had pored over the statistics for starting a pregnancy via this procedure, and I realized that success on the first shot was unlikely. But, after a few tries, the odds started to look pretty good. Plus, the doctor was very reassuring, in a charming mad-scientist sort of way.

"These are the figures we *publish*," he said with a twinkle in his eye, "but I can tell you that your actual chances are a bit higher. Don't worry, we will do everything we can for you, and there's no reason in your case to give up yet."

We had been busy with a multitude of projects since the ending of tax season, and with it my office job, on April 15. Not only was Kim healing her ankle and enduring a butt-full of needles containing the doctor's special pregnancy cocktail, but we were getting ready to set up an irrigation system, preparing for three markets, and looking for hired help.

The first point on the agenda had been dictated by our disastrous season last year. After asking around, I had decided to invest in some simple watering equipment: a huge plastic tank capable of holding five hundred gallons of water, a used shallow-well pump scrounged from a junk seller's front yard, and fifteen hundred yards of drip tape. This last item was nothing more than a flattened tube fabricated from spun-bonded polyethylene fibers, the same tough material that express-shipping envelopes are made of, with one difference: under as little as two pounds of water pressure, the tape inflates into a round tube that leaks moisture prodigiously, sweating like a sumo wrestler in a sauna. Since it's designed to be placed underneath the plastic mulch, very little water is lost to evaporation; most trickles right down to the plant roots where it's needed.

Running the well pump from the generator for half an hour would fill up the big tank with cool, clear water from the stream. After that the tank, placed on a mound of dirt about six feet higher than the field, would develop enough pressure to inflate the drip lines and irrigate the field for a whole day. The following day, if necessary, the generator could be turned on, the tank refilled and allowed to trickle out again. It was a low-tech solution I liked a lot.

As to the other points, I had, in addition to our regular Abingdon Square gig, signed us up last winter for a second Saturday market at a new location in Brooklyn, as well as a Sunday market at Tompkins

Square Park in the East Village. It seemed that the only way we were ever going to make money on the farm was by doing multiple markets, and if we could pull it off successfully, the extra labor would be well worth the expense. By now I felt that we knew well enough how to grow flowers and how to do markets, so it was really just a matter of doing as many as we comfortably could, and getting some good help. Of course this was well before Kim's accident. But I was still determined to try it.

Now, it turned out that Kim's brother had a friend whose youngest brother was just back from California and living in the city, and he was looking for some extra cash. When we talked to him, it sounded like a perfect fit. Johnny had worked at a florist's shop in Santa Cruz and seemed eager to try the farmers' markets. We agreed to hire him as soon as we were ready to supply the second Saturday market. And, in another fortunate coincidence, we were introduced to a neighbor who had spent her whole life in the area we now called home and was willing to help us in the field.

June was a somewhat petite, broad-shouldered, and pretty woman of about my age, with white-blond hair and a more or less permanent tan. She raised horses and made beautiful traditional crafts including quilts and dried floral wreaths, and as an avid gardener, she was very interested in what we were trying to do on the farm.

She had four children, three of whom were still at home. She also had a tremendous advantage when it came to fieldwork—she was impervious to the sun. While Kim and I took cover under large hats and long-sleeved shirts and pants, June, hatless and shoeless, quickly picked her way through the rows with the sun shining directly on her bare arms, legs, and even feet. Her favorite picking outfit had a level of attitude we could never hope to match: a leopard-print bathing suit and faded cutoffs, accented by a rhinestone necklace and bright red lacquered fingernails. Like her childhood friend Lee, she was slight but extremely strong, with the same oversize, work-toughened hands. She and Lee also shared a love of animals:

besides her horses, June kept several breeds of dogs, a cat, birds, and an occasional ferret. She also loved the outdoors, and she especially loved hunting. Kim would later report back than she had passed June on the road one day and was amazed by what she told her when the two pulled over to talk.

"You should have seen her face," Kim said. "Her eyes were shining and she had this huge grin. I asked her what was going on, and she said she couldn't wait for her vacation because she was going to the Adirondacks to do some bear hunting on horseback."

June was our kind of picker. With her help, we were all set to go back to market. The weather was cooperating, too. It had been a warm spring, wet enough but with plenty of balmy days that were as good as you could get for planting seeds in the field, weeding, and all the other chores that needed doing. By the eleventh of June, when we went back to the fertility clinic for a second attempt, the plants were maturing rapidly.

Our first market was scheduled for Saturday, June 26, a month earlier than last year. The results of the pregnancy test would be available the day before.

Kim went to our local hospital early Friday morning for the blood work. She was instructed to call the clinic late that afternoon to hear the verdict. It was going to be a tense day in the field. It was a warm day, too. The narrow valley steamed up like a tropical savanna, and we sweated over the first harvest of the season. Before the appointed hour we had picked a dozen buckets. Now it was time to go back to the house and call the doctor's office. When Kim reached them, she spoke to a different nurse, while I listened anxiously.

"We're looking for hCG levels of over a hundred," the nurse explained to her. "Yours are over a thousand. Your levels are huge."

"Does that mean I'm pregnant?" I heard Kim ask.

"You're very pregnant. Your due date is March fourth. Congratulations."

We brought lots of coreopsis, yarrow, and wild daisies to market the next day, along with some mixed salad greens to sell by the half pound. Almost all of our regular customers returned that day, and we swapped abbreviated stories of what we'd done over the winter. But that season already seemed part of the remote past. David showed up midway through the hot early-summer morning to help with the cash and the heavy lifting, because Kim had been told not to pick up anything over thirty-five pounds. Trading silly smiles, we drank iced teas under the umbrellas during the lulls in sales, and he gave us cigars, on the condition that we wait to smoke them with him outside the maternity ward. Of course, we agreed.

no turning back

KIM: "You're pregnant."

It was as if someone had touched a magic wand to my head. I felt like the most special and blessed human being on earth, notwithstanding the few hundred million other people who must have been walking around the planet at that moment in the same condition.

The nurse said I should take a nightly injection of the hormone progesterone as an added insurance against miscarriage in the first trimester. Other than that, I could just live life as normal. Finally.

And what was "normal" by this time? Certainly a way of life I could not have imagined when I first saw Dan's bouquet on my dining room table in Brooklyn. I was using both my mind and my body in ways completely different than I had as a journalist; and I was loving it.

My favorite thing was selling our produce at market, especially making custom bouquets. The people who asked for these were doing something particularly self-indulgent, and I liked helping them get the maximum amount of pleasure from it. After all, it wasn't that long since I had been a harried New Yorker myself and needed a little spoiling once in a while. And, by the summer of 1999, I had gotten pretty good at this.

First the customers would give me my assignment:

"Make me something very summery."

"Make me something mostly red and purple."

"Make me something tall."

I would look at them, look at the flowers around me, and try to envision a match. And then I would get to work.

Often the person stayed to watch, offering encouragement or suggestions. Sometimes he or she would wander off to visit some of the other farm stands while I worked. This was always fun because I could have waiting a happy surprise that usually elicited one of the following responses:

"Is that *mine*?"

"Oh, wow!"

"That's great!"

My favorite response came from a gentleman at Abingdon Square, who ended up with a colorful bunch of zinnias poking out of a fringe of goldenrod.

"This makes me so happy, I just can't explain it," he said.

"Believe me," I replied as I rolled his bouquet in a piece of newspaper, "I know exactly what you mean."

I still got a lot of people who speculated aloud on the great life I must be living. And, while things had improved dramatically since I had first heard this presumption, by the fourth market season I knew enough about farm life to understand it's not for everyone. In fact, I had developed a handy quiz to identify people who should think twice before they start looking for land. These are the people who would say any of the following:

"I like money and feel that I need a lot of it."

This disqualifies you instantly.

"I hate bugs, and when one lands on me I tend to scream like I'm being brutally murdered until someone flicks it off. I'm not much fonder of dirt."

Get used to both. As a farmer, you will be covered with them most of the time. But you will get to learn which bugs are truly your friends and which you should kill with wild abandon.

"I feel I might want to work for someone other than myself again someday."

Forget it. You will be completely ruined for this. And should you ever find yourself back in a corporate workplace environment, you will immediately wonder why everyone is dressed so uncomfortably and how they can take themselves so seriously.

If you decide to go ahead and become a farmer, here are some issues you might be faced with:

"What do I do with all this panty hose?"

It's good for straining leftover shellac.

"How do I tell my friends about my workday and make it sound like I did something?"

What, you mean you don't think "I kneeled in the dirt for eight hours and pulled tiny weeds out of a hole in the ground" sounds like anything?

"Will I ever be able to ride the subways or an elevator again without feeling extremely claustrophobic and revolted by all the people breathing on me?"

No. Perhaps a gas mask would be helpful on these occasions.

I figured I could hand this out on a flyer to those who openly mused about changing their lives. But then I thought better of it. There's nothing wrong with having a dream.

Our new market at Tompkins Square in the East Village was just beginning. Since the market happened on Sunday, it saved us from making two round trips to the city every week. Instead, we'd stay over at my parents' house Saturday night and have June drive down in the evening, ferrying in the flowers she'd picked that day and returning to the country with the empty buckets from the two Saturday markets.

June's younger children, Jimmy and Betsy, usually accompanied her on the ride down the parkway and into the busy suburbs of New York City, an unfamiliar terrain for these country kids. Arriving in lower Westchester around eight on Saturday evening, they seemed to find the sounds of sirens, bustling traffic, and loud music coming from passing cars enough excitement to offset the monotony of the two-hour round-trip ride. In fact, I learned that going anyplace south of mid–Westchester County, especially on a busy weekend evening, more especially if it involved a stop at a fast-food restaurant or other establishment, constituted a trip to "the city," and thus was an adventure to be enjoyed, envied, and discussed for days when back at home. And this, I found, applied to adults as well as children.

In truth, they were simply noticing something that I had forgotten: our two worlds were vastly different, though separated by only a few miles. Just as our suburban family might have driven upstate on a Saturday afternoon to eat hot dogs on a picnic table by a lake, they were making the reverse commute. The difference was, June was getting paid to do it. And, as the summer market season wore on, we began seeing much more of her.

With Kim's pregnancy in its full-blown first-trimester discomfort, the heat and exertion of fieldwork proved more than she could handle. The picking itself was especially arduous this year because we had to pick enough flowers to supply two Saturday markets: our regular gig at Abingdon Square, plus the new market that Johnny was doing in Brooklyn. The extra dozen buckets we'd picked for this market would be deposited at a Brooklyn park a few blocks from where Johnny lived at 6:45 A.M. As the last one was coming off the truck we could count on seeing Johnny's mop of curly hair flying past the parked cars and iron fences as he raced toward the market site on his skateboard. Leaving him the flowers, along with a kit of tables, display buckets, and sundry wrapping materials, we sped toward Abingdon Square, where it was already time for us to begin our regular market day. After the Manhattan market was finished and the gear and remnants packed into the truck, we would return to the Brooklyn park to find Johnny sitting beside a stack of empty buckets; these, along with the setup, had to be loaded back into the truck and our accounts tallied up before we could head for home. It was a long market day.

Fortunately, June was ready to come to the field and pick flowers and tomatoes with me on Friday too, after she finished her route as a rural mail carrier for the post office. The rural P.O.'s, instead of maintaining a fleet of mail trucks and drivers, simply hire part-time workers with their own wheels, assign them routes, and give them magnetic U.S. Mail signs to stick on their vehicles. June was responsible for a route near our farm.

Sometime after noon on Friday, I usually saw her black pickup emblazoned with its rural mail carrier insignia come bouncing down the dirt track into our field. When the truck pulled to a stop, June hopped out, hoisting a gallon cooler of lemonade, a pack of Marlboros, and a plant clipper from the backseat. If the day was especially hot—and every day was that summer—and if she had come prepared with a bathing suit, she peeled off her T-shirt, grabbed her clippers, and got right to work.

Picking cherry tomatoes was a job nobody relished, but June could pick them faster than anyone else. She didn't seem dismayed by the seemingly endless rows of waist-high plants that forced the picker to stoop down to each one, or the sticky tomato pollen that eventually covered the arms and legs with a bright green powder that was an allergy sufferer's nightmare. As she began picking, reaching far into the bushy plants to grab the ripe fruits, the staccato drumbeats the small tomatoes made as they bounced off the bottoms of the empty plastic pails were soon muffled to silence as the buckets filled. Eight or ten gallons of juicy, orange Sungolds were gathered in an hour or so, one tomato at a time. Then June would help me finish picking whatever flowers we needed to supply the two Saturday markets. And she would be back in the field the next day, picking for Sunday.

One particularly oppressive Friday, as the temperature soared and the humidity reached saturation, dark clouds began rolling across the sky from the west. Although there was no breeze to relieve the torpid, buzzing heat in the field, it was clear that a storm would soon break the stillness of the muggy afternoon. It would be a blessing. The only question was, Would we get everything picked before it hit? Soon lightning flashed inside the lowering clouds, and the distant grumbling of thunder we'd been hearing for some time grew louder. Bolts were striking the ground just beyond our valley, and the air seemed charged with electricity as the sky darkened.

"What do you think?" I asked June, looking at the sky.

"Think it's gonna *rain*," she replied with a smile. "Here it comes now!"

The first raindrops were small and slow, a baptism of cool relief from the heavens. They ran down our necks and tickled our hands, making a pleasant tapping sound when they hit the plastic mulch all around us. I opened my mouth and tasted the pure drops that fell from the sky, and the salty ones that flowed down my face. We looked at each other, and she shrugged.

"Feels pretty good," she said.

"Yeah," I replied. "It sure does."

We both bent back down to the rows of plants and resumed picking. As long as we didn't get hit by lightning, I thought, it would be one of the more agreeable picking days of the whole summer.

In a few minutes, the raindrops turned bigger, colder, and steadier, and thunder seemed to rumble right overhead. I didn't mind getting wet—since I was soaked with sweat anyhow in a long-sleeved shirt and jeans—but the thought of being quick-fried by a stray bolt of white electricity from the sky made me nervous. I turned to June, who was picking in the next row.

"I don't know," I began. "Maybe we should wait in the truck until it passes."

"Yeah," she said. "I guess we ought to. It won't last long."

But neither of us moved to go. There were still flowers to be picked, and the novelty of being cool was too good a sensation to give up just yet. We bent down again, casually, and picked a few more stems, each of us looking to see what the other would do. Neither wanted to be the one to call it quits.

The rain fell harder still, and the air turned cold. It was a real soaker now, and the plants were shedding so much water that it was like picking them from under a waterfall. My feet were squelching in my shoes, and the shirt and jeans stuck to me like flypaper, hindering my movement.

"Okay, I guess I'll go in now," I said, turning in June's direction.

"Sure," she replied. "We know enough to come in out of the rain."

We began moving slowly toward my truck, which was parked at the far end of the field, still picking more flowers as we ambled along the rows. Suddenly I felt a sting on my neck, and simultaneously, as if someone had just cranked the volume on a radio, the soft patter of raindrops on the mulch became a noise like a loose piece of automobile being scraped along a concrete road.

"Hail," June said, catching a tiny chunk of ice in her hand. "Hope it doesn't get too heavy; the plants won't like it."

We picked up the pace. The black plastic mulch seemed to be turning gray from the accumulation of bouncing hailstones, which were now about the size of chocolate chips, and we were getting pelted. The hail was mixed with rain, and it was coming down so hard that there appeared to be a continuous sheet of water falling everywhere I looked. Finally we made a run for it, and we piled into the cab of the truck, soaking wet but not unhappy to be cool at last. We were just in time to witness a huge lightning bolt strike a tree on a hill nearby, followed by a terrific crack of thunder, when suddenly a blast of cold air blew through the fractionally opened window of the truck, and the entire vista turned white.

The rain had turned completely to hail, and the hail was coming down faster than anything I had ever seen. The noise it made hitting the roof of the truck was too loud to talk over, so we watched the fury of the storm in silence. We could see just a few feet into the field, but the plants we observed were being lashed mercilessly. I hoped that there would be a few left when the storm was over. Right now I could only watch the spectacle.

When the hail finally stopped, the rain continued, and we decided to call it a day. We would have enough flowers for both markets, and although it had seemed impossible an hour ago, my wet clothes felt chilly against my skin and the air was cold. I started the engine and dropped June by her truck, and the two of us drove out of the soggy field, closing the gate behind us. After their pummeling, the plants didn't look much worse for the wear, and I still had a long drive and some dry clothes to look forward to. I continued up to the house, wondering if Kim would think I'd been hit by lightning or just mesmerized by the power of the storm.

The Tompkins market was unlike any of the others we had done before. In some ways, the customers seemed very different from us. For one thing, they woke up late—many looked as if they'd just rolled out of bed when they sauntered by the stand at noon. Their clothing ran the gamut from fetishistic leather and vinyl gear to retro takeoffs on sixties and seventies hipster styles, from the uniform of distressed jeans and T-shirts to outré garments of every description. A few ornamented their bodies like canvases, with spiked and dyed hair, tattoos in profusion, and piercings of all descriptions on every visible part of their anatomy. It would be hard to picture them walking down Main Street in our town.

Yet in other ways we were hardly different at all. Unlike most of the customers in our other markets, many Tompkins Square people seemed to have no secure place in the larger world of mainstream American society: a job that paid regularly, a permanent place to live, a comforting routine. But they were trying to make a place for themselves anyway, homesteading in the urban environment, not the rural. If they spent five bucks for a bunch of flowers, you knew they really wanted them. And they did.

The sellers were a different crew, too; many lived in the city and worked the farm stands as a weekend job. Others came in from the country to test the waters at an uncrowded, undemanding market. Some found it agreeable and came back year after year. Since the market got off to a slow start, with little activity before lunchtime, there was plenty of time for chatting with neighboring vendors. Most seemed to have known one another for a long time; it was a little like walking onto the set of an edgy soap opera.

"What is it about Americans, anyway?" said the baker at the table next to ours in a thick middle European accent, as he sliced up some fresh loaves for samples. "That they're sooo interested in . . . baseball." He had overheard Kim's brother David talking about last night's game and was looking for a little argument to get him going.

"In the whole rest of the world it's football—you know, soccer, as you call it—that's the game to watch. Baseball: a bunch of fat guys standing around in a field waiting for someone to throw a ball at them. Ever seen them try to run? They waddle! They're too busy thinking about their big fat salaries to even attempt to look like athletes."

With a half smile, David took up the challenge. "Soccer—you've got to be kidding. You want to talk about waiting for something to happen? Soccer is the most boring sport on the planet—next to cricket, if you can call that a sport. Here's a soccer announcer: 'Oh look, down on the field, something might be about to happen, it looks like maybe something's going to happen . . . well, no . . . but now maybe somebody will do something, it looks like somebody might do something . . . well, no, but . . .' It's no wonder that they practically have a heart attack every time some player scores a goal. *'Goal!!! Gooooooal!!!!!! GO . . . uggghhhhrrrrllll.'* "

By 11:00 A.M., Kim was ready for lunch.

"Aren't you hungry?" she asked me.

"Well, actually, no," I replied.

"Well, I am. C'mon, give me ten bucks, I need to get a spinach burrito."

"But that's practically all we've made so far."

"I need a spinach burrito *right now!*" she bellowed.

There was no arguing with a pregnant farmworker, even if she was about to eat most of our profits from the morning. She disappeared down the street, leaving David and me alone to mind the flowers.

The baker had gone to sleep in the midday heat, in a nook in the back of his truck, leaving his helper, Ace, to handle the leisurely sidewalk traffic.

"Hey, how are you doing today?" Ace asked every conceivably eligible woman who passed in front of his stand.

Those who answered him said, "Fine."

To more than a few, he replied, "I can *see* that you're fine, but I wondered how you were doing."

He managed to sell some bread anyway.

Later that afternoon, the traffic increased. A young, well-dressed woman stood in front of our display, staring silently at the bouquets. She seemed lost in some sad, private reverie. After a few moments, I asked if I could help her with anything. The young woman shook her head slowly from side to side, and silently she began to cry. The tears flowed down her cheeks as she stood before the flowers biting her lower lip; there was nothing anyone could say. Soon she lifted a bunch of dark red and purple blooms from the galvanized bucket and held it up toward me.

"That's five dollars. Would you like me to wrap it for you?" I asked softly.

She shook her head no, placed a bill on the table, and walked slowly away from the stand, staring at the bouquet she held before her. We never saw her again.

A man came up to our stand and started talking to Kim about the flowers; he was seeking advice. He was going to brunch at a restaurant nearby, where there was a waitress he very much admired. He said he wanted to tell her that he had picked the wildflowers from a field especially for her. It was important that they give just the right impression, and he wanted a woman's opinion.

"Well, you can pick them yourself from out of the buckets. That counts," she said. "Just pick out whatever you like, and I'll help you arrange them if you want me to."

He stepped behind the stand and gathered a handful of black-eyed Susans, yellow coreopsis, and white and purple yarrow, and held them tightly in his hand. They needed no arranging at all. They looked like an impulsively collected bunch of posies, which was just what they were.

"Would you like it if you were her and I gave these flowers to you?" he asked.

"I would *love* it," she answered.

Who wouldn't?

# Epilogue

KIM: I bring the last of the flower buckets up from the field around 5:00 P.M. Chris is waiting for me by the house and comes over to help me unload the electric blue ageratum and strongly fragrant marigolds. As we transfer the laden pails to the garage, we hear, out of a small speaker perched on a folding chair, what sounds like a loud sheep's bleat.

"I'll get her," Chris says, and we both smile.

He runs upstairs and returns a few moments later carrying our four-month-old daughter, Samantha. She has dark hair, big, rosy cheeks, and blue-gray eyes framed by the longest, thickest lashes you've ever seen. Chris places her in a bouncy chair in the shade just inside the open garage door, and she immediately begins rocking and making loud raspberry noises—not a comment, I hope, on the quality of the produce that surrounds her.

It's a good haul, considering how early it is in the season. Twenty-six buckets altogether, with lots of variety. I'm already imagining what I might be able to do with the silver artemisia, indigo salvia, and powder blue veronica, with perhaps a few Queen Anne's lace thrown in.

Planting was especially tough this year, given that our newborn required round-the-clock breast feedings, many of which I did in the field. But one thing's for sure—there is no better way to whip off the extra pounds accrued during months of prenatal spinach burrito bingeing than to plant seedlings and haul buckets. I'm actually five pounds lighter than I was before I got pregnant.

Still, I do wonder how long Chris and I will be able to carry out all the physical chores that must be done to keep this farm going. Maybe the answer will be to hire more field help as we get older, assuming that makes sense financially. Or maybe we'll find some other way to make a living from our farm. I'm really not worried about it anymore. We've been through far too much in the five years we've been here for me to doubt that we'll figure something out.

I know Chris is counting on Samantha and any future siblings she may have to help out with the farming tasks, but who knows if farming will even interest her? Maybe, as an act of rebellion, she'll decide to become a lawyer (or even a tabloid reporter). That won't really matter to me. What's important is that she make her own choices and follow her heart wherever it takes her. Of course, if that happens to be down into the dirt, Silverpetals Farm will be waiting.

# Postscript

When Samantha was seven months old, Kim and Chris were astounded to find that they had conceived another child quite by accident. No sooner had they recovered from the shock of this happy news than it was time to prepare for their seventh farming season. Because Kim was in her eighth month when it came time to ready the field, she got out of all mulching, planting, and weeding chores—but was not as happy about this as might have been expected and plucked a few weeds here and there when no one was looking. Chris had Samantha working in the field at the age of fifteen months. She helped plant gladiolus bulbs. In July 2001, her sister, Juliana, was born.